The Spirituality of Men

The Spirituality of Men

Sixteen Christians Write about Their Faith

Edited by Philip L. Culbertson

Fortress Press
Minneapolis

Contents

Contributors

Mike Bathum holds a Bachelor of Arts degree in design from the University of Washington, a Master of Fine Arts in painting from Fort Wright College, and two Master's degrees in theology from the School of Theology and Ministry at Seattle University. Mike has been a public school and community college educator for twenty-five years and was the marketing coordinator for the School of Theology and Ministry at Seattle University for five years. He is the author of eight art resource books published by Simon and Schuster. Currently he is the owner/designer of Artigiano, a studio specializing in liturgical art. His fine-art work has been represented in galleries in the Pacific Northwest.

Michael Battle, a priest in the Episcopal Church, is Assistant Professor of Spirituality and Black Church Studies at Duke Divinity School in North Carolina. He also taught spirituality and moral theology at the University of the South in Sewanee, Tennessee, for five years. He is the author of *Reconciliation: The Ubuntu Theology of Desmond Tutu* (1997) and is currently at work on *A Christian Spirituality of Nonviolence: A Ghandian Critique,* a book in consultation with Arun Ghandi. He has worked as an inner-city chaplain with Tony Campolo Ministries, in Kenya and Uganda with the Plowshares Institute, and as a research-fellow-in-residence with Archbishop Desmond Tutu (who ordained him). He holds degrees from Duke, Princeton, and Yale, and certification in spiritual direction from the Shalem Institute.

Stephen Boyd is the J. Allen Easley Professor of Religion at Wake Forest University, where he teaches historical theology and the history of Christianity. Currently the President of the American Men's Studies Association, his previous publications include *The Men We Long To Be: Beyond Desperate Lovers and Lonely Warriors* (Pilgrim Press, 1997), and *Redeeming Men: Religion and Masculinities* (Westminster John Knox, 1996).

Lee H. Butler Jr., an ordained Baptist minister, is a member of the faculty at the Chicago Theological Seminary, where he serves as the Director of the M.Div. program, and a professor of theology and psychology teaching in the areas of pastoral theology and the practice of ministry. His professional development includes experience in pastoral ministry, chaplaincy, pastoral counseling, ecumenics, denominational and seminary administration. He has research interests in African American religion, theology, spirituality, and sexuality, with two books forthcoming: *A Loving Home: Caring for African American Marriage and Families* (Pilgrim Press), and *Liberating Our Dignity, Saving Our Souls* (Chalice Press).

Donald Capps, psychologist of religion, is William Harte Felmeth Professor of Pastoral Theology at Princeton Theological Seminary. In 1989 he was awarded an honorary doctorate from the University of Uppsala, Sweden, in recognition of the importance of his publications. He also served as president of the Society for the Scientific Study of Religion from 1990 to 1992. Among his many significant books are *Men, Religion, and Melancholia: James, Otto, Jung, and Erikson* and *Freud and the Freudians on Religion: A Reader* (both from Yale University Press); *Social Phobia: Alleviating Anxiety in an Age of Self-Promotion* and *Jesus: A Psychological Biography* (both from Chalice); and *The Child's Song: The Religious Abuse of Children* (Westminster John Knox).

Philip L. Culbertson, an Episcopal priest, is Director of Pastoral Studies at St. John the Evangelist Theological College, an affiliate school of Auckland University in New Zealand. He is also a psychotherapist in private practice. His previous publications include *New Adam: The Future of Male Spirituality* (1992), *Counseling Men* (1994), and *Caring for God's People: Counseling and Christian Wholeness* (1999), all from Fortress Press.

Marvin Ellison teaches Christian social ethics at Bangor Theological College in Maine. He is also co-chair of Maine's Religious Coalition against Discrimination. His previous publications include *Erotic Justice: A Liberating Ethic of Sexuality* (Westminster John Knox, 1996) and a cross-disciplinary curriculum for clergy on domestic abuse.

Robert E. Goss is Chair of the Department of Religious Studies at Webster University in St. Louis. He is author of *Jesus ACTED UP: A Gay and Lesbian Manifesto* (1993), coeditor of *A Rainbow of Religious Diversity* (1996), *Our Families, Our Values: Snapshots of Queer Kinship* (1997), and

Take Back the Word (2000). The Center for Theology and Natural Sciences has named Goss a Templeton Foundation winner in the international course competition in Science and Religion. In addition, he is a transfer clergy from the Catholic Church into the Universal Fellowship of Metropolitan Community Churches.

David J. Livingston is Assistant Professor in the Religious Studies Department at Mercyhurst College in Erie, Pennsylvania. He has worked with violent men in a batterers' treatment program for several years. His first book, *Healing Violent Men: A Model for Christian Communities* (Fortress Press, 2001), addresses violence and reconciliation.

Merle Longwood is Professor of Religious Studies at Siena College, Loudonville, New York, where he teaches religious thought and ethics. He has written widely and provided consultation on issues related to masculinity, masculine spirituality, and male sexuality. A member of the Board of Directors of the American Men's Studies Association, his previous publications include *Redeeming Men: Religion and Masculinities* (Westminster John Knox, 1996).

Mark Muesse is Associate Professor of Religious Studies at Rhodes College in Memphis, Tennessee. A native of Waco, Texas, he completed his graduate work at Harvard, where he received an M.T.S. from the divinity school and a Ph.D. in the Study of Religion from the graduate school of arts and sciences. His research focuses on Asian religious traditions and gender studies. He is coeditor (along with Merle Longwood and Stephen Boyd) of *Redeeming Men: Religion and Masculinities* (Westminster John Knox, 1996) and currently serves as vice president of the American Men's Studies Association.

James Newton Poling is an ordained minister in the Presbyterian Church (USA), a pastoral psychotherapist, and Professor of Pastoral Theology, Care, and Counseling at Garrett-Evangelical Theological Seminary in Evanston, Illinois. In recent years he has been doing pastoral research in sexual and domestic violence. He is the author of many articles and books, including *The Abuse of Power: A Theological Problem* (Abingdon, 1991), and *Deliver Us from Evil: Resisting Racial and Gender Oppression* (Fortress Press, 1996), in which he challenges the church to make male violence against women and children a priority for theological reflection and action.

Edward Thompson Jr. is Professor of Sociology and Director of the Gerontology Studies Program at Holy Cross College in Worcester, Massachusetts. Over the past twenty years, he has taught a number of gerontology-related courses and published on men and aging, caregiving, and masculinities and family life in journals such as *Family Relations, Sex Roles, Journal of Gerontology: Social Sciences,* and *Journal for the Scientific Study of Religion.* He edited *Older Men's Lives* (Sage, 1994), the first collection of original articles examining elderly men as men, and serves as one of the organizers of the men's issues interest group for the Gerontological Society of America. Current projects include a book on men as caregivers (Springer).

Jerrald Townsend and **Robert Bennett** have been a clergy couple for many years. Robert, with a Ph.D. in ancient history from Yale University, is Professor of Classics at Kenyon College in Gambier, Ohio, occasionally teaching in its Women's and Gender Studies program. He has earned a Master's degree in theology as well. Jerry is an Episcopal priest in the Diocese of Ohio, who has served as Assistant Rector, Associate Rector, and Interim Rector in seven parishes. He has also taught European history and now works as a professional counselor, working in an alcohol and drug treatment agency and a psychologist's practice.

Brett Webb-Mitchell is a pastor in the Presbyterian Church (USA) and is Assistant Professor of Christian Nurture at Duke Divinity School, Duke University. His previous publications include *God Plays Piano, Too: The Spiritual Lives of Disabled Children* (Crossroad, 1993), *Unexpected Guests at God's Banquet: Welcoming People with Disabilities into the Church* (Crossroad, 1994), *Dancing with Disabilities: Opening the Church to All God's Children* (United Church Press, 1997), as well as *Christly Gestures: The End of Christian Education* (Eerdmans, forthcoming).

Preface

Philip L. Culbertson

Being a man in the church these days can be unsettling, if not downright scary. As Stephen Boyd points out in his essay herein, sometimes it feels like we just can't do anything right. There are men who don't like us, and women who don't either. There are bishops, superintendents, presbyters, priests, and ministers who don't like us. There are people in our congregation (if we have hung in there with the church) who don't like us, and there are the memories of those who didn't like us when we were still in the church (if we have thrown in the towel and left). For many men in the church today, no place seems predictably safe. Sometimes it feels like the only place left for us is in the margins.

This volume is written for men smack in the midst of parish life, as well as for men in the margins of the church who still believe that men have a place in the church, but are not sure what kind of men they are supposed to be. The essays are written by sixteen American men who call themselves Christian, are active in the church, and are struggling to find a new personal voice in a rapidly changing church. Many of these men realize that, for now, their voices are best heard in the margins of the Christian community rather than at its center. For now, the margins are a safer place to be, and interestingly, they are a place where we meet again our Christian sisters who are also struggling. In the margins, we struggle together to find God's vision for men and women in the Christian community. bell hooks writes:

> I am located at the margin. I make a definite distinction between
> that marginality which is imposed by oppressive structures and
> that marginality one chooses as site of resistance—as location of

radical openness and possibility. . . . We come to this space through suffering and pain, through struggle. We know struggle to be that which pleasures, delights, and fulfills desire. We are transformed, individually, collectively, as we make radical creative space which affirms and sustains our subjectivity, which gives us a new location from which to articulate our sense of the world. (hooks 1990, 153)

When chosen rather than imposed, the margins can be a good location. When I was a kid we played "Drop the Handkerchief." The place of safety was on the edge, the margin; the most dangerous place to be was either outside the encircling boundary or smack in its middle. Fifty years later, I understand, with bell hooks, that the most radical creative space is often found just there: on the edge, in the margins.

But as hooks points out, the margins are also a place of struggle. For men in the church today, this struggle includes some very hard questions about who and how we are supposed to be as male Christians. However confused we feel, we know two things: that something's got to change, and that change usually hurts. Fifty years ago, German theologian Dietrich Bonhoeffer wrote of the painful cost of Christian discipleship. He wrote in an age before inclusive language had become the norm—when "man" meant "men and women." But when we read him today, we can read "man" as meaning "males," and his words become even more poignant:

> When Christ calls a man, he bids him come and die. It may be a death like that of the first disciples who had to leave home and work to follow him, or it may be a death like Luther's, who had to leave the monastery and go out into the world. But it is the same death every time—death in Jesus Christ, the death of the old man at his call. (Bonhoeffer 1965, 99)

These essays are very much about dying to old masculine gender roles and rising again into new ways of being men. To die to the old and rise to the new is to respond to the call of Christ.

There are, of course, many ways of "being a man." That is why we speak of masculinities rather than masculinity. Men in the church are in very different places today, and we cannot even assume that our sense of gender unites us. Some men have actively engaged feminist thought and theology, while others grit their teeth and wish it would go away. Some have become obsessed with the flaws in the traditions of the church and the unexamined assumptions of our theological heritage; others can't see much wrong with the status quo, nor what all the fuss is about. The single thing that seems to unite most of us, however, is that we feel unsettled as men. Our masculine identities in the church, as Christian men, just don't seem as secure and stable as we remember they once were.

The sixteen authors of these essays represent a cross-section of men, mostly standing at the margins and unafraid to talk about their struggle, who are addressing the cutting edge of men's gender issues in the church-to-come. The authors themselves are white and black, straight and gay, old and young, lay and ordained, and come from a variety of mainline denominations. All are literate and articulate, and all are dedicated to helping men carve out new ways of being masculine in the church.

Because men in the church are presently at such different places in their gender awareness, I recognize that not every essay in this collection will have the same individual appeal. Some readers may prefer the simplicity of Mike Bathum's, Jerrald Townsend's, or Robert Bennett's essays. Other readers, who are in a different place in their sensitivity to gender, race, sexuality, or social justice issues, may prefer the essays of Michael Battle and Lee Butler, or Robert E. Goss and Marvin Ellison. The goal is not that every essay will appeal to every reader, but that every reader will find at least one essay that speaks to his or her passion, need, and life experience.

The original idea for this collection came from a Canadian minister named Jim Love. In an exchange of e-mail among colleagues already working to address men's issues, Jim commented that his wife had been reading two highly successful collections of essays in the pastoral care of women—*Women in Travail and Transition* and *Through the Eyes of Women*. She had asked him whether there was a similar collection dealing with men's issues. After another flurry of e-mail, some of us decided that a companion volume would indeed be useful, and I agreed to solicit and edit essays. Though not everyone I approached to write for the book was free to do so, in general the response was quick and generous. With the help of Stephen Boyd, a list serve was established through Wake Forest University, by means of which all sixteen of us were able to share ideas, swap essay drafts, and establish a cyber community of Christian men in conversation about need, change, and creative new directions. We called that list serve "ParishMen," and now that the book is done, I think all of us will miss the conversations that went on there.

We all had hoped that the list of authors would be even more representative than it turned out to be. There are no Asian, Hispanic, or Native American/First Nations' writers in this collection. Some were approached but were too overcommitted to participate. As this book goes to press, I am newly and painfully aware of how few indigenous writers on men's issues we have in the church. Theirs are important voices to be heard, but we have not yet found the right medium or venue. I am also aware of topics that are not addressed in this book, such as the identity struggles of adolescent males, the gendered experiences of male immigrants or recovering addicts, the pain of angry men and depressed men, the journey toward recovery of men who have been beaten, raped, or sexually, emotionally, or mentally abused, the confusing struggle to know how to define "family" in the twenty-first century, or how to parent well our daughters and sons in a changing church. These essays need to be written; these voices need to be heard. I fear for how many men dwell silenced and wounded within our congregations, cut off from a potential community of support. As we struggle through the articulation of changing Christian masculinities, the community of male authors is as yet too small, and many of the subjects missing here are not yet the topic of safe uncovering or open discourse. I long for these men and their voices and what their experience has to teach us all.

I will seize one last opportunity to say thank you. First, to Michael West of Fortress Press for encouraging this project. Second, to the essayists here. I gave these "ParishMen" one simple assignment: talk to "the man in the pew" about masculine identity in a rapidly changing church. Each author worked hard to find a topic he was passionate about, to avoid "academic glossolalia," and to meet deadlines. As the completed draft of each new essay arrived on my computer screen, I found myself excited all over again. I believe this collection is a valuable next step for men in the church, as we seek together to find masculinities that are not abusive, do not create victims, and that hold out the promise of a new and more inclusive, welcoming, caring community of Christian men and women witnessing to the future church. Someday, the church will again be a safe place for us all.

Bibliography

Bonhoeffer, Dietrich. 1949, 1965. *The Cost of Discipleship.* Unabridged edition. New York: Macmillan.

Glaz, Maxine and Jeanne Stevenson Moessner, eds. 1991. *Women in Travail and Transition: A New Pastoral Care.* Minneapolis: Fortress Press.

hooks, bell. 1990. *Yearning: Race, Gender, and Cultural Politics.* Boston: South End Press.

Moessner, Jeanne Stevenson, ed. 1996. *Through the Eyes of Women: Insights for Pastoral Care.* Minneapolis: Fortress Press.

Part One

Spirituality

1

Don't Just Do Something, Sit There: Spiritual Practice and Men's Wholeness

Mark Muesse

Although it was a personal tragedy, my divorce fifteen years ago freed my spirit. Finding myself without the familiar moorings that had defined my marital life, I was suddenly open to try new things and critically question the old. Searching to understand the forces that brought about the painful dissolution of my marriage led me to men's studies. Seeking to be made whole again brought me to the practice of Buddhist insight meditation. As I have continued on the paths of men's studies and meditation practice, I have grown aware of how my meditation has deepened my understanding of myself as a man and how it has helped restore the fundamental goodness that socialization into masculinity took away. Today, I remain a dedicated practitioner of Buddhist spirituality and am more convinced than ever of its value for men in the West, including—or perhaps especially—men in the Christian churches.

Men's Studies and the Analysis of Masculinity

Divorce entered my life in spite of great resistance. Up until the end, I had not even allowed myself to think of ending my marriage, even during its darkest hours. As a devoted Christian nurtured by Lutheran and Southern Baptist traditions, I considered divorce a moral and spiritual failure. My ex-wife and I worked hard—harder than any other couple I have ever observed—to keep our marriage together. When divorce came despite our white-knuckled efforts to stay together, I needed to reevaluate my theology of marriage and the ethics of divorce. But most importantly, I was challenged to reexamine how my life had been shaped as a man and to recognize the ways my masculine conditioning actually contributed to the end of my marriage.

At the time, I was completing my graduate work in theology and the study of religion. I had devoted a good share of my studies to feminist theory and the many theologies based on that body of work. While I had studied the social dynamics that shaped the lives of women in our culture, I had not even considered that studying the life of men might be worthwhile, much less essential. I had fairly well accepted the dictum that virtually the entire corpus of knowledge was "men's studies." When my divorce mediator suggested that I might find some of the literature on the lives of men personally helpful, a radically new idea entered my mind. He led me to some early material from what was to become the mythopoetic movement, the version of the men's movement usually associated with Robert Bly. Although today I am more distant from the mythopoetic perspective, at the time I found it liberating and enlivening. Writers such as Bly, Robert Moore, and Sam Keen helped me to recognize the problematic features of the lives of many men in the late twentieth-century West, and they inspired me to imagine solutions. They also spurred me to explore the burgeoning work on critical male gender studies, which was still in its nascent stage.

Men's studies acquainted me with my own masculinity. Men's studies named a reality that was so much a part of who I was and am that I both knew it intimately and yet did not know it at all. The concept of masculinity is often problematic, even for those who study men's lives, so it is important to be clear about its usage. By masculinity, I mean the expectations and ideals of behavior and modes of being societies believe to be appropriate to men. In this sense, masculinity varies from culture to culture and from time to time. There is also variation within cultures according to race, class, and other factors. The masculinity shown to me by men's studies to be my own was the dominant, contemporary Western construction of masculinity, called hegemonic masculinity by some theorists. Hegemonic masculine ideals are relatively easy to characterize: a preference for linear rationality and a suspicion of affective and arational modes of being; a tendency to be emotionally inexpressive; identification with the mind and separation from the body; a perceived need for control; competitiveness, risk-taking, and a goal-orientation; the perception of the self as an individual entity separated from other individuals; homophobia. The list could be continued indefinitely, but the picture is clear.[1]

Few men are so utterly socialized as to embody these traits fully. More commonly, these qualities describe who most Western men *think* they should be and how they would like others to regard them. These characteristics represent the criteria by which most men judge themselves. In the modern West, conformity to these ideals brings reward for men; nonconformity brings ostracism, ridicule, and sometimes physical violence. To resist these qualities, to seek to live by other virtues and values, thus requires tremendous courage and inner strength.

There is nothing necessarily problematic about these masculine qualities in themselves. There are moments in the lives of all people—men and women—when it is desirable to think rationally and dispassionately, to set goals and work hard to achieve them, to manifest independence. The difficulties arise when men are expected—and expect themselves—always to embody these traits (and, conversely, when women are expected never to express them). Such a distortion of our natures leads to much of the malaise of men in our culture. Stephen Boyd sums up this constellation of masculine characteristics when he describes many men as "lonely warriors" and "desperate lovers" (Boyd 1995, 2). With these images, Boyd echoes what James Nelson sees as the fundamental affliction of masculine men: disconnection (Nelson 1988, 38–43). According to Boyd, Nelson, and many others, men today are often separated from women, children, and other men, from their own bodies and affective natures, from the earth itself, and, we might say, from God. Consequently, men who embody masculine qualities sometimes find themselves lonely and isolated, yet desperate to enjoy a deeper connectedness. But the very qualities that empower a man in the public sphere disable him in the arena of relationships and spirituality. What helped me to be successful as a student and teacher of theology, I now believe, crippled me as a husband and friend.

One of the particular cruelties of this masculine affliction is that not only does it lead to loneliness and desperation, it also militates against seeking relief from its agonies. The man who is supposed to be strong and dispassionate finds it difficult to become vulnerable enough to acknowledge his suffering to another—and often, even to himself. He is usually not even aware of the depth of his pain, much less aware of how to address it. Frequently, such masculinized men require a personal tragedy to awaken them to their own destructive habits. Thus, it is often the loss of a job or the loss of youth—or, in my case, the loss of a marriage—that forces a man to become self-critical and self-reflective. But even this moment of disillusion is not sufficient to generate self-transformation. It is one thing to become aware of one's suffering and destructive traits; it is quite another to change.

The Practice of Buddhist Spirituality

I wish I could say that when the pain of divorce touched my life I found solace in the churches and the resources of the Christian traditions. I wish

I could say church helped me understand how the culture had shaped me as a masculine man and showed me ways to heal the distortions wrought by male socialization. But that is not true. If anything, the churches appeared to me to be coconspirators in masculine conditioning. By making the salvation of my soul dependent on holding correct beliefs, for instance, they seemed to reinforce my propensities to hyperindividualism and rationality. By insisting that only men hold positions of power in the institution, they strengthened the notion that control is appropriate for men. At the time, I understood this situation as a failing of Christianity. Today, I see that the Christian traditions do in fact contain resources that could have benefited me, but these are not the features of the faith that most churches in North America accent. I had to look beyond the traditions of my upbringing to discover sources of understanding and transformation. I had to become estranged from Christianity to find relief from my suffering.

In men's studies, I came to greater clarity about the problems of masculinity. I saw that the suffering I brought to myself and to others stemmed not from my inability to live up to the prevailing ideals of masculinity but from the fact that I manifested them so well. But the academic study of men told me precious little about how to remove and recover from the traces of masculine conditioning. The emergent men's movements that I sampled offered some help but not a lot. Profeminist men encouraged me to seek personal healing through the pursuit of social justice, especially for women and disenfranchised men. But the profeminist men's movement seemed to me to be one of the most dispirited groups I ever encountered; it lacked any appreciation of the spiritual dimension of life and seemed to have little "good news" for European-American, heterosexual, middle-class men like me. The mythopoetic men's movement, on the other hand, seemed very much aware of men's need for personal renewal and transformation but lacked an understanding of the social dynamics that wounded men in the first place. Mythopoetic men also seemed to grasp the importance for men to recover their intuitive and affective natures and to integrate body and spirit, but their stress on initiation ritual and weekend retreats smacked too much of the Baptist emphasis on momentary conversion experiences. If men could simply have an intense breakthrough, mythopoetic men and Baptists seemed to say, transformation could be accomplished. In theological terms, both groups seemed naïvely to stress justification to the exclusion of sanctification. Men's studies and the men's movements all offered insights and clues to what I needed, but all were lacking in some fashion.

What I needed was a method, a technique, a discipline for change. I needed a conversion of practice more than a conversion of belief.

I discovered that discipline in Buddhist insight meditation. I had learned the rudiments of this practice earlier as a way of coming to a deeper understanding of the Buddhist traditions, which I was studying in graduate school. As was characteristic for me at the time, I learned meditation for academic purposes; only later did it occur to me that this practice might have some personal, existential relevance to my life. It took even longer to recognize that this practice also provided much of what I sought but did not find in the men's movements and the churches.

For many persons, the term "meditation" may be so laden with negative associations that they find it difficult to muster the courage to learn about it, let alone actually practice it. This was true for me. My Southern Baptist roots ingrained in me a deep xenophobia about nonchristian—or more precisely, non-Southern Baptist—traditions. As an undergraduate at Baylor, I heard preachers routinely warn against the practices of pagan religions, especially things like Transcendental Meditation (TM), which was gaining popularity at the time. According to these preachers, emptying the mind (as they believed meditation did) made one susceptible to the onslaught of demons, which were presumably lurking above, poised to possess any unguarded soul. By the time I entered graduate school, I fancied myself too sophisticated to accept such premodern superstitions. Yet my xenophobia persisted, now buttressed by my growing desire to be regarded as an intellectual. I was more completely associating with the life of the linear mind and had little interest in anything that was not rational. In my dualistic thinking, I had even divided the graduate school faculty into types, the "softies" and the "crusties" (today I might say "feminine" and "masculine"), based on how I judged their conformity to the canons of hard, critical thought. Needless to say, I scrupulously avoided the softies, and meditation and spirituality belonged to their world. I was only interested in truth that could be formulated, not touchy-feely stuff. But as I said, getting slapped in the face by life often does wonders for awakening one from a dogmatic slumber. I began to set aside some of the prejudices of my past, including my religious and spiritual xenophobia.

Just Sitting There

Pascal once quipped that all the problems of humanity were caused by the fact that people just could not sit still in their rooms.[2] Buddhist insight meditation, I have come to conclude after fifteen years of practice, is little more than learning to sit still in your room. But this simple exercise, practiced with regularity and commitment, can bring transformation and tranquility to troubled lives.

First practiced and taught by the Buddha 2,500 years ago, insight meditation, or *vipassana* (Pali for "clear gazing"), is a technique that strengthens attention, promotes self-understanding, and deepens one's experience of the world. The fundamental procedures of insight meditation can be learned rather quickly but take years of dedicated exercise to master.[3] Unlike spiritualities and therapies that invest everything in a moment of conversion or experiences of extraordinary significance, *vipassana* emphasizes development, training, and the richness of the ordinary. For forty-five minutes every morning and evening, I seat myself on a cushion in a quiet place and try to observe without judgment, commentary, or analysis whatever happens in my mind and body. I sit upright but comfortably, gently endeavoring not to move. There is nothing exotic or mysterious about it. I find it helpful to focus awareness on my breath. When my mind wanders or when I experience a sensation, I silently note "thinking" or "feeling," and return to my breath. The mind, of course, is so subtle—and we identify with it so completely—that it is often a long time before we even become aware that we *are* thinking or having a sensation. It is ironic that although we spend so much time living in our minds, absorbed by our thoughts, we do not know our own minds (nor our bodies) very well at all.

Insight meditation does not seek to induce certain kinds of experiences; it merely accepts what is. One does not try to create ecstasy or establish mystical union with the divine, though these experiences may occur. One does not attempt to "empty" the mind or to stifle thoughts. I have personally never had any success at creating such a tabula rasa, and I am skeptical that anyone who has not attained *arhantship*, or complete enlightenment, ever could. At any rate, *vipassana* meditation is not about the elimination of thoughts or the quest of specific experiences. The practice is not an escape from reality but a headfirst plunge into it. There are days I emerge from my meditation feeling refreshed and happy, and there are days it feels like a colossal waste of forty-five minutes. But I know the fruits of meditation practice are gained over time, not in particular momentary fragments. And, paradoxically, the great benefits of meditation cannot by attained by striving for them. Even to make enlightenment or ecstasy the goal of meditation projects us forward into the future, but the temporal locus of meditation is now, this moment, the only reality there is.

Meditation and Masculinity

On the face of it, insight meditation seems quite at odds with the virtues of masculinity. Masculine ideals encourage planning and action, accomplishment and control, but *vipassana* teaches being still and acceptance of the way things are. Masculinity would have us focused outward, whereas meditation draws us inward. The masculine encourages us to divert attention from our bodies, yet meditation makes our bodies a subject of awareness. Masculinity conditions us to identify with rational thought and makes the mind the seat of personality; insight meditation, however, trains us merely to observe thoughts and to regard the mind as a sense organ.

Meditation, nevertheless, cannot be characterized as feminine. "Feminine" traits unbalanced by the "masculine" also distort our natures, albeit in different ways. The Buddha taught what he called the "Middle Way," the path between extremes. Femininity and masculinity are extremes, and if anything, the practice of meditation encourages us to dwell in neither. Even though meditation provides an effective treatment for the negative consequences of masculine conditioning, it also draws upon some of the qualities with which masculine men are already familiar and comfortable. Sitting meditation is not easy. It requires hard work and discipline to learn to relax, surrender, let go, and be still. When I teach meditation to my students, they are initially excited by the prospect of experiencing a state of relaxation and bliss. It only takes a few moments of sitting practice to realize that meditation does not immediately confer such a state. "Meditation," advises an old saw, "is not what you think." There is, however, one aspect of meditation that most men will find easy: silence!

Although one does not practice meditation with particular goals, except perhaps the intention to pay attention to what is, the practice confers clear benefits on its practitioners. As I have indicated, I think these benefits are especially relevant to the lives of men who seek to understand and recover from the destructive effects of masculinity.

I begin with a benefit derived not from what meditation does but from what it keeps us from doing. In the half hour or forty-five minutes while one meditates, one does not climb the corporate ladder, one does not enhance a résumé, one does not earn someone else's approval, and one does not harm another being. The first benefit of sitting, then, is that it absents us from traditional masculine pursuits, and this, I contend, is profound and itself a transformative act. As men, we often experience drivenness in our lives. We feel compelled to work, to achieve, to prove our worth. Usually, we are not even aware of the conditions that urge us on so ruthlessly. Many of us unconsciously fear that were we to stop the frantic pursuits, we might be overwhelmed by an inner loneliness, or by a rage built up over decades, or by the sadnesses of many losses. If we have the courage to sit and not just do something, we can, at least for a brief while, stop the maddening activity that often runs us ragged. For those of us who have been socialized into masculinity, it takes more guts to sit and listen to ourselves than it does to make that sale or impress our coworkers.

But sitting meditation does expose us to our inner rumblings, and this interior space is not a place most of us men have had much experience navigating. We do not do a very good job equipping our boys to care for their souls. Is it any wonder then that when they become men, they flee their souls? Sitting meditation can acquaint men with themselves. Before we can know how to respond to those powerful feelings and thoughts, we first must become aware of what goes on in the dark recesses within our flesh. *Vipassana* meditation teaches how to do this, how to experience thoughts and feelings calmly and dispassionately, as an observer. To observe dispassionately does not mean a cold indifference to thoughts and feelings. It merely means we recognize our inner movements for what they are and try not to judge them as good or bad. Such non-judging awareness, of course, takes time to develop. As masculine men, we learn early in our lives to assign value to our feelings: grief and fear, for example, are bad and are better not expressed—even better, not felt at all. So thorough was my own masculine socialization that I struggled for years simply to recognize and name the emotions that ebbed and flowed within me. Learning how to respond to those emotions once I had recognized them was still another thing entirely.

If the thrust of masculinization is to teach men how to repress their affective natures, then the emphasis of conventional psychotherapy is to encourage us to do the opposite: to express our emotions. Venting feelings, I was told, was healthier than repression. Bottling up feelings causes stress and illness and pain and suffering for ourselves and those around us. Following this psychotherapeutic wisdom, I spent much of my life in those early post-divorce days releasing pent-up anger and grief by word and deed. Gradually, I came to realize that the wholesale expression of painful feelings only provided temporary relief, a palliative, but over the long-term it tended to reinforce my propensity to indulge in painful feelings. The free expression of anger, in other words, predisposes us to respond in anger. There are times, to be sure, when the expression of anger, grief, and other emotions is appropriate and, indeed, essential. Yet there are times when the expression of emotion is not wise and wholesome. I had simply allowed the pendulum to swing from near total repression to cavalier expression.

In meditation, I discovered a third way. Both repression and automatic expression are predicated on the dynamics of stimulus and reaction. A sensation arises that we identify as a particular feeling and we react, generally unconsciously, like a knee-jerk, with a smothering denial or an instantaneous display. As one learns merely to observe feelings and sensations in meditation practice, a gap opens between stimulus and reaction. We neither deny the appearance of feeling nor spontaneously express it. Within that small fissure, we come to exercise greater conscious management of our inner workings. Our rage, our grief, our joy can now be creatively channeled, wholesomely expressed, if appropriate, or simply befriended and acknowledged as one of the countless sensations that parade through our bodyselves during the course of a day. We can learn to respond rather than react.

The corollary of traditional masculinity's suppression of emotion is its encouragement to overidentify with the mind. In Buddhist spirituality, the mind is merely an organ, not the center of the self, as it is often taken to be in Western psychology and theology. Indeed, there is no such center, since, in the Buddha's view, the human being comprises interrelated and constantly fluctuating energies. There is no everlasting agent or subject who thinks; as the Buddhist adage puts it, "there is thought but no thinker." Granted, such a notion is tough for the Westerner to grasp, but it is no less easy, I suspect, for Asian Buddhists. Yet I want to argue that such a perspective has real, practical benefits for those who conceive the mind in this way. It is especially valuable for men who seek ways to break their identification with linear rationality.

The mind, I have come to see, loves to rule. It loves to rule my life, my body, my friends and family; indeed, it would love to rule the world. The problem is that my mind is unruly. It is not fit to rule me, much less those around me. Buddhists compare the mind to a monkey that scurries from place to place, first fascinated by this object, then attracted to that one, with no sense of attention, no discipline. Our minds are like this most of the time, though rarely do we train our attention on them long enough to become aware of it. Even when we think we are being attentive to the task at hand, our mind rushes into the future to ponder what's for lunch, what has come in the morning mail, or a thousand other matters both important and trivial. Or perhaps the mind is slogging around in the past, recalling some ancient memory, nursing the anger caused by a colleague's slight, fantasizing about revenge. The mind is usually anywhere else but here. That is the nature of the undisciplined mind. Although we usually submit to its demand to rule, it is more suited to serve.

The unruly mind needs discipline. This is precisely what meditation can furnish. In *vipassana*, we learn to watch the mind, simply to observe how it works. Early in the practice, it becomes evident that the mind has a mind of its own and that any efforts to disrupt its hegemony must be gentle and evolutionary. The mind tolerates no coups. The practice teaches how to notice the arising of thoughts in the mind and to allow them to pass through, like clouds pass through a clear blue sky. We can discipline ourselves simply to let our thoughts come and go. It is not necessary to chase or develop them, although that is what we usually do. Before we know it, a single stray thought has caught our attention, and we become absorbed in the interior drama we produce based on it. In meditation, one endeavors to be alert to the rising of thoughts and to return attention to the breath. Of course, vast stretches of time may pass before one even becomes aware of being lost in thought; that is how subtle the mind is and how weak is our attention. The mind wants to take us somewhere else, out of the present moment, and we gently but firmly return it to the breath. In this manner, one is able gradually to see how the mind works and train it to serve.

Attending to thoughts as they pass through the mind wonderfully relativizes them. Thoughts, we can see, are like so many other elements of our experience. In the course of a day, we have innumerable thoughts, feelings, sensations, and perceptions. Yet we are conditioned to attend to some and ignore others. Those to which we attend condition further thoughts and experiences. The first verse of *The Dhammapada* (1986, 78), a classic of Buddhist wisdom, avers that the mind shapes our experience. All the more reason to keep a watchful eye over the kinds of information we feed the mind and the thoughts we allow it to pursue. In meditation, it becomes possible to learn how to regard thoughts merely as thoughts, not as formulations of any great ontological significance. By this I mean there is no thought—or anything else—worth becoming slavishly attached to. Beliefs, opinions, metaphysical speculation, ideas—these are just so many "views," as the Buddha called them, and like everything else in our experience, they are subject to change. If we cling to thoughts, no matter how beautiful or sublime they may seem, the Buddha advises that we are liable to suffer. If we must hold beliefs, we ought to hold them lightly.

Buddhism and Male Identity

The Buddha's understanding of views has profound implications for the way we construct our identities. Few of us we really know much about ourselves. What we know are the labels we and others attach to us. Our identities as men are especially constructed this way. We usually take these markers as clues to who we are, and then we behave and think accordingly. In meditation, these labels mean nothing. They are only thoughts that appear and pass from view. As they recede, we are left facing who we are apart from the signifiers. Meditation then becomes a discipline for stripping away the layers of who we think we are, who we have been told we are, and who we think we should be. Meditation deconstructs masculinity.

Everything changes. The Buddha made this fact the cornerstone of his teaching. Few sages have taken this fact so seriously and pondered its ramifications as thoroughly as the Buddha. In the practice of sitting meditation, impermanence is brought to awareness with stunning clarity and undeniable reality. To see the forces of change at work in ourselves is at first terrifying, but the dispassionate gaze grants us the opportunity to accept and finally embrace change. As masculinized men, we find it difficult to accept change, particularly the impermanence of the body. Most women, we are told, have less difficulty with bodily change, since they routinely face the vagaries of menstruation, pregnancy, lactation, and menopause. Because many young men are rarely aware of their bodies enough to recognize the subtle ways in which they do change, they often convince themselves of their own indestructibility. We might give intellectual assent to the notion of our eventual decay and demise, but we do not really believe it—or we do not act as if we do. Surely much of masculine men's risky behavior is predicated on the delusion of their immortality.

Eventually, it is no longer possible to deny changes in our bodies. When we are no longer able to persuade ourselves that we are not losing our hair, when we realize that we simply can no longer eat whatever we want with impunity, when the legs slow and the body takes longer to recover from illness, when Viagra begins to seem like an option, then we begin to take notice of the reality that has been proceeding apace since we were conceived (and, say Buddhists, even before that). For most men, the acknowledgment of our passing youth is a crisis, plunging us into depression or the frantic effort to resist the inevitable.

Meditation, Death, and Compassion

Resisting the body's impermanence, like resistance to all change, causes suffering, for ourselves and frequently for others. In the film *Moonstruck*, one female character asks another, "Why is it that men have affairs?" The other answers, "Because they must die." To be more precise, it is not death that drives our self-destructive behavior, but our fear of and resistance to death. In meditation practice, one grasps how the body, as well as the mind, transforms from moment to moment. With each passing instant, we die and are born anew. By seeing both the futility of resistance to our impermanence and the suffering it engenders, we relax our opposition to the natural rhythm of life. We accept and embrace our death and the changes in the body that precede it.

One of the chief reasons we so often deny death is the sense of separation and loneliness it suggests. Entering death may be the only thing that we absolutely must do by ourselves. Many of us masculinized men are terrified by loneliness even as we dwell there much of the time. On the face of it, it might seem that meditation practice would only exacerbate that terror; yet meditation has the capacity to alleviate our fears of aloneness. In this sense, it is practicing for death. In one of his many brilliant sermons, Paul Tillich distinguishes between loneliness and solitude and recommends that we learn how to transmute the negative state of loneliness into the more positive and wholesome state of solitude (Tillich 1963, 15–25). Although Tillich does not mention it, meditation is certainly one crucible in which that alchemy can occur. Paradoxically perhaps, it is when one enjoys solitude that one may feel the greatest sense of connection to the rest of life. Solitude dispels loneliness.

In the silence of my meditation, I gaze upon the insubstantiality of my being, I recognize the ways in which my body and mind have been formed and are being formed by forces outside myself, outside my control. I am not a self-made man. The food I eat that becomes my bodyself is produced and prepared by countless others. It embodies the sun, the rain, the wind, and the earth. My very life depends, therefore, on these elements and these other human persons. I understand myself and the world with words that were given to me, words not of my making. I look within and see my parents and grandparents; I see Stalin and Jesus. I cannot deny my kinship with all other people, with the whole of the cosmos. Buddhism calls this experience *shunyata*, "emptiness." Although a negative-sounding term in translation, emptiness is not negative. It means, in this context, empty of separate selfhood (Hanh 1988, 7–10). All reality, therefore, is intimately and profoundly interrelated. Meditation practice delivers this insight in a way that merely stating it cannot.

The ineluctable response to emptiness is compassion for all there is. When I realize that "I" am not a separate self, that my life indwells in the lives of others and others' lives in mine, I cannot help but be concerned for them. Knowing what causes me to suffer, and knowing that other sentient beings are like me, I am loath to inflict pain on them and eager to ease it if I can. I see the folly of mindless competition and the endless comparisons of myself to others. Meditation practice, however, does not provide answers to the hard questions of social justice. It does not tell me whether to vote Democrat or Republican or support equal rights for gays. But neither does it promote my isolation or indifference to the world around me. The practice does not terminate with me seated on my cushion, blissfully enjoying feeling one with the universe. The awareness of emptiness elicits my love for the world and propels me out into it. Meditation develops my desire for a just and safe world, even if it does not specifically articulate how to create such a place.

Leaving the cushion is as important as sitting down in the first place. Meditation is *practice*, practice for the rest of our lives, practice for living in the world, and practice for dying. It creates in us mindfulness, the meditative attitude in our everyday lives. Mindfulness is alertness and awareness. It sharpens all our senses and confers a deeper experience of everyday reality. The world in its plainness seems richer, more vivid, more real. It breaks our masculine attachment to abstractions and returns us to the realm of the concrete.

Can You Be a Christian and a Buddhist?

I have argued that Buddhist meditation practice provides an ideal discipline for men seeking relief from the stresses and distortions caused by masculinity. But is it an appropriate discipline for *Christian* men? Understandably, Christians will want to know about the compatibility of their faith with practices not original to their tradition. There are several ways to respond to this concern.

First, as is now clear, Buddhist meditation puts little stock in labels. While words help us to engage reality, they can equally distort it and draw us away from it. Hence, it may even be misleading to speak of "Buddhist" meditation, as if one had to be a Buddhist to practice this discipline or as if there were some substantial, unchanging thing called Buddhism to which meditation belongs. It would be unbuddhist to regard *vipassana* as somehow "belonging" to Buddhism. From the perspective of Buddhism, then, one need not be a Buddhist to practice *vipassana*—or to realize the truth. In his own life, the Buddha affirmed the precepts and practices of many traditions as long as they were wholesome and conducive to human happiness.

From the Christian perspective, it is important to remember that *vipassana* meditation is a practice, not a belief system. In principle, it is compatible with a wide range of beliefs. *Vipassana* only cautions against becoming attached to beliefs—any belief—because attachments of any sort lead to misery. As far as I can tell, there is nothing about meditation per se that would make it difficult for even the most committed Christian to practice. It is still possible to have faith in Jesus as the Christ and in God the creator even as one takes up this discipline. Indeed, there are a number of similar practices in the lesser-known traditions of Christianity.[4]

When I began my search for some practical assistance in coping with my suffering and masculine socialization, I was unaware of these meditative and contemplative disciplines in Christianity. Because of this lack of awareness, I had to distance myself from the church. But that, too, was a good thing. It challenged me to face my spiritual xenophobia and to overcome the prejudices I carried against nonchristian traditions and dimensions of life that did not fit my narrowly-conceived rationalism. And facing my spiritual xenophobia gave me courage for dealing with the xenophobias bred into me as a masculine man, particularly my fear of the feminine and my fear of other men. What I discovered in this great adventure of estrangement was not only something new. I was also given new eyes for the old things. I was able now to see myself as a man in a different, fuller way and to see the religious traditions that shaped me in a wholly different light.

Bibliography

Boyd, Stephen. 1995. *The Men We Long to Be: Beyond Domination to a New Christian Understanding of Manhood.* San Francisco: HarperSanFrancisco.

Culligan, Kevin, Mary Jo Meadow, Daniel Chowning. 1994. *Purifying the Heart: Buddhist Meditation for Christians.* New York: Crossroad.

The Dhammapada. 1986. Trans. Eknath Easwaran. Petaluma, Calif.: Nilgiri Press.

Goldstein, Joseph. 1994. *Insight Meditation: The Practice of Freedom.* Boston: Shambhala.

Gunaratana, Henepola. 1991. *Mindfulness in Plain English.* Boston: Wisdom Books.

Hanh, Thich Nhat. 1988. "Commentary." *The Heart of Understanding.* Ed. Peter Levitt. Berkeley: Parallax.

Hart, William. 1987. *The Art of Living: Vipassana Meditation as Taught by S. N. Goenka.* San Francisco: HarperSanFrancisco.

Mirsky, Seth. 1996. "Three Arguments for the Elimination of Masculinity." *Men's Bodies, Men's Gods: Male Identities in a (Post-)Christian Culture.* Ed. Björn Krondorfer. New York: New York Univ. Press. 27–39.

Moore, Robert, and Douglas Gillette. 1990. *King, Warrior, Magician, Lover: Rediscovering the Archetypes of the Mature Masculine.* San Francisco: HarperSanFrancisco.

Nelson, James. 1988. *The Intimate Connection: Male Sexuality, Masculine Spirituality.* Philadelphia: Westminster.

Pascal, Blaise. 1958. *Pensées.* Trans. W. F. Trotter. New York: E. P. Dutton.

Rosenberg, Larry. 1994. *Breath by Breath: The Liberating Practice of Insight Meditation.* Boston, Mass.: Shambhala.

Tillich, Paul. 1963. "Loneliness and Solitude." *The Eternal Now.* New York: Charles Scribner's Sons. 15–25.

Notes

1. What I am calling "hegemonic masculinity," or simply "masculinity," is referred to by some writers as "immature" masculinity, with which they contrast "mature" masculinity. See, for example, Moore and Douglas Gillette. I prefer not to use the notions of "immature" and "mature" masculinity because I believe masculinity—as the constellation of cultural ideals of manhood and as distinguished from something called femininity—is always problematic. I agree, therefore, with Mirsky's "Three Arguments for the Elimination of Masculinity."

2. "I have discovered that all the unhappiness of men arises from one single fact, that they cannot stay quietly in their own chamber" (Pascal, 39).

3. The best books I have found on techniques of meditation are Gunaratana, Goldstein, Rosenberg, and Hart. Reading books about meditation is, of course, no substitute for the actual practice of it.

4. Some places include the writings of St. John of the Cross, Thomas Keating, and William Shannon. A work that more fully discusses the practice of Buddhist meditation within a Christian context is Culligan, et al.

2

African Male Spirituality

Michael Battle

Writing about African male spirituality is a hazardous enterprise, because there need to be discrete boundaries by which to judge the extent of the study. This becomes even more difficult considering the subject in hand. Which African male experiences of God are we are talking about? Unlike the patronizing research that goes on in the Western world, in which Africa is perceived more like a country than a continent, to do careful research on what "African" means would require a perspective that ranges from the Mediterranean to the Cape of Good Hope. Included in this expanded perspective is an interreligious context in which there are Muslims from Cape Verde to the Red Sea and throughout the continent, as well as Christians, Hindus, Sikhs, Buddhists, and many others. Most of all, pertaining to what is African, there is African Traditional Religion, in which there are rites of passage in the discovery of what African means. I cannot cover the breadth of the meaning of *African* in this essay, but I, who carry the description of African, can describe African male experience through the context that I am given—being African and Western.[1]

The Problem of African Male Spirituality

In the West, especially from the time of the Enlightenment, spirituality has been understood as a personal endeavor for distinct individuals who have unique values and distinct rights. In Western spirituality, persons have the right to make something of their lives, to take responsibility for their life direction, and to use their talents and gifts to the full. Such an emphasis puts supreme value on the right of individual self-determination, self-achievement, and self-satisfaction. Such personal responsibility for the shaping of one's spirituality is a good, and it flows from the Judeo-Christian understanding of the dignity and worth of each human being. What is weak in Western spirituality is the bonding of the person with the community. A spirituality of community is unintelligible, as personal spirituality becomes the cultural norm.

When Western persons, formed in this worldview of the importance of the personal fulfillment, meet African persons, they meet people whose experience of the self is distinctly different. In contrast to the West, the African individual does not exist apart from the community. The classic phrasing of this intrinsic relationship was started by John Mbiti and carried on by Archbishop Desmond Tutu. I call it an *Ubuntu* sensibility, namely: "I am, because we are; and since we are, therefore I am." The person is part of the whole, and one's identity flows from the corporate experience and never in isolation from it (Battle 1997). The uniqueness of each person is affirmed, but one's own individuality and freedom are balanced by the destiny of community. Such a balance is behind the construction of gender in African societies.

Despite Western influence, various initiation rites that describe being male still remain in some African cultures. More important to the establishment of opposite gender, these rites act as rites of passage to integrate the person into the society so that he can find his identity within it. In other words, it is important for both male and female to journey through communal practice in order to discover self. For many African cultures, the construction of community is the same movement as the construction of gender. This double movement of community and gender continues beyond death, since ancestors, who maintain their gender, are regarded as intrinsically part of the community, able to influence events and guide the community. Instead of masculinity being the opposite of femininity, in African life there is one continuous movement of social experience from birth to death. The emphasis is upon a spirituality that flows from the community to the person and back again. Different from the Westernized conception of self, the African male becomes conscious of himself only through the social interaction of initiation rites. To be male, therefore, in African culture means that one acts in concert with the female and not apart from her.

This presupposition that community is the basis of gender must be stated clearly in order to avoid the stereotypical understanding of the African male. What are usually acknowledged are two stereotypes of the

African male—promiscuity and patriarchalism. For example, regarding the image that African males are naturally promiscuous, one may look at the recent national crisis in the black church regarding Reverend Henry Lyons. This was a controversy in which Lyons, as president of the National Baptist Convention USA, was accused of both mishandling church funds and promiscuity. Lynn Neary, a reporter on National Public Radio News, conducted the following interview with Robert Franklin, President of the Interdenominational Theological Seminary, concerning the impact of Lyons's impropriety on the black church:

> Neary: And there may be another factor that could protect Lyons from strong censure. The black church, says Dr. Robert Franklin, believes in the power of redemption. And, he says, there is a long history of forgiveness for errant leaders.
>
> Franklin: And generally, if leaders have been good for the community—Adam Clayton Powell, Marion Barry, any number of other leaders who, again, have occupied the morally ambiguous sort of gray area—the community's been willing to forgive them if they delivered on behalf of the poor and the oppressed. And so I think that the jury is still out, no pun intended, on the question of whether Dr. Lyons has delivered sufficiently to reap the benefits of a very forgiving black church community.
>
> Neary: As Reverend Lyons meets the members of his church in Denver this week, his wife has her own problems. She still faces charges of burglary and arson in connection with the fire in the home that Lyons still owns with Bernice Williams. (Neary 1997)

Franklin provides the standard descriptive analysis of the black church, namely, that the personal leadership style that empowers the black community far outweighs personal piety. This description of what may occur in the black church need not define the spirituality of black churches. To assume that the black church as a whole forgives the sexual sins of black men only insofar as these black leaders empower community does not accurately describe the African formation of identity. At this point, I would suggest more substantive work be done by theologians to correlate the differences between what is meant by the black church and the African church. If what is meant by the black church is an identity trapped in the double standard between integrity of justice and personal promiscuity, then the black church is a victim of the Western individualism that perpetuates such dualisms. Furthermore, such a black church perpetuates what I name as colonial stereotypes of black sexuality.

Through what I name below as Ubuntu, perhaps the time is ripe to rename the black church as the African church. In an African church that does not yet accept the split identities caused by Western individualism, promiscuity is not typical of black men, as so many people in the colonial world are led to believe. The African church allows me to make this argument against colonial stereotypes of black men, who exist in a taxonomy akin to a natural selection process, ensuring the role of the black man as the natural human worker in society. This taxonomy of the black male carries the connotation that black men *should* be promiscuous in order to ensure strong, servile offspring.

To further my argument against the colonial construction of black male identity, one need only look at black women to see that no such natural selection process is definitive of black male identity. If black men are naturally promiscuous, then there should be no inordinate behavior by black women in response to what is supposedly natural. This is not the case, however. For example, Reverend Henry Lyons's wife, who tried to burn down his house, gives evidence that a black male leader's sexual practices are not simply instances of sexual indiscretions or momentary bouts of uncontrollable lust. A less violent example of an African woman's protest against the construction of black male identity comes from Chikwenye Okonjo Ogunyemi, a female Nigerian scholar. Ogunyemi further illustrates my contention that the stereotype of the African male is due to a colonial perspective in which black men were used to breed the strongest progeny for slavery. Ogunyemi, an African womanist, boldly defends the construction of African masculinity and suggests that Western interpretations of the African male have only been as the "invasive addressee, who should be an eavesdropper/voyeur now turned primary audience" (Ogunyemi 1996, 12). For Ogunyemi, the Western person who tries to deconstruct black male identity only further maligns black identity, because the agency of forming identity should come from the marginalized identity itself. With this rationale of a contextual defining process of identity, Ogunyemi goes on to critique feminism and womanism in light of Western assumptions of individualism given to both.

In Ogunyemi's worldview there is no place for "firebrand feminists," a political orientation in which "all the women are white or passing" (Ogunyemi 1996, 108). Ogunyemi sees feminism as a "monologue haranguing men" rather than the dialogue between women or between women and men, which Ogunyemi states as her agenda (139). Despite what one may think of Ogunyemi's critique of Western feminism, the invaluable contribution that she makes helps Western persons see the empty and meaningless stereotypes of what it means to be an African male. Instead of participation in the meaningless speech between white colonizers and Africans, which Ogunyemi defines as *palaver*, she advocates conciliation of gender through her womanist discourse, the *palava*, which provides her title.

The problem of the second stereotype, of being patriarchal, remains, however. Throughout Ogunyemi's own analysis of Nigerian history and culture, women struggle against "eruptions of masculinism." Ogunyemi provides the harsh criticism that such masculinism is characterized by a "continued collaboration between inept black leaders and white men" that has effectively restricted African women to "a woman's space" (11). Patriarchal practices, instead of leading to interdependence of gender, can create segregation. She goes so far as to say that patriarchal practices keep the African continent underdeveloped and result in power clashes "that eternally plague gender relationships" (6). More specifically, she refers to how the patriarchy creates female oppression that includes polygamy, clitoridectomy, and poverty so great that "women have little energy left to pursue things political or pleasurable" (58).

While Ogunyemi does not condone cultural practices like polygamy, she argues that, at least historically, it "enhanced female bonding" (86). She argues more strongly against clitoridectomy, that which Nwapa euphemistically refers to as "a bath," as a custom that is "patently senseless" (138). Physical abuse of women, which she sees as part of a general misogyny in Nigerian culture, was traditionally avenged by male relatives, unlike what she describes as the less satisfactory modern method of calling disinterested police. For Ogunyemi, the foundation of black male misogyny is, then, historic white male domination and African male impotence "in failing to respond effectively to aggressive colonialism" (11).

The problem with Ogunyemi's analysis is her dependence on yet another stereotype of the African male, that of being violent. Instead of codependent reliance on colonial history to both justify history and react against it, a better analysis of African male spirituality can be seen through the African conception of community. Ogunyemi's analysis of male and female construction in African culture is more constructive through *friendly fire*, a discourse with men while remaining true to womanhood. All involved are better served through Ogunyemi's keen point of complementarity rather than the disruptive notion of equality (Ogunyemi 1996,

52). Recovery, in Ogunyemi's terms, might best be attained through a more detailed study of communal space that becomes a site of power. As she indicates, before colonial influence so corrupted and eroded traditional roles of male and female in communal space, there was a complementarity of power.

Division of labor by gender is not a central concern for Nigerian women; she states: "female power is and should always be different from male power" (Ogunyemi 1996, 61). She does not, for example, invite men to share parenting, interpreted as a traditional source of female power, particularly in Nigeria, for that would be "eroding the space that gives her authority" (78), nor does she agree with the view she attributes to American feminists that "motherhood is a cornerstone of patriarchy" (75).

Ogunyemi stresses repeatedly that her text, like the novels she reads, is an example of the "Afro-centric discourse," the palava that will heal the divisions between genders that do not recognize opposition or dualities. But oppositions and contradictions do occur throughout Ogunyemi's work. Her hostility toward her Western audience contradicts her stated intention "to establish healthy relationships among people, despite ethnic, geographical, educational, gender, ethical, class, religious, military, and political differences" (Ogunyemi 1996, 123). For her, "Western women are as much of a problem to us as black men"; however, she adds, "it might be worthwhile to work or walk with them, at least some of the way" (107). Ogunyemi discourages Western and African synthesis.

The key benefit to Ogunyemi's critique of Western perspectives is that African research very often happens outside of Africa. For example, in large parts of sub-Saharan Africa that lack the facilities for Westernized research, very little research is being done by Africans on Africa. To be a scholar entails flight out of Africa to learn about Africa. The reason for this is that there is a lack of technology by which one may accumulate information on the continent. On average, there is only one telephone per one hundred people in sub-Saharan Africa. Now it seems as though the exponential growth and spread of the Internet will leave the African continent almost untouched, again heightening the fear that the gap between the "information rich" and the "information poor" countries, especially the African ones, will get even deeper (World Telecommunication Development Report 1995). Nelson Mandela states, "Eliminating the distinction between information rich and poor countries is also critical to eliminating economic and other inequalities between North and South, and to improving the quality of life of all humanity. . . . For in the 21st century, the capacity to communicate will almost certainly be a key human right" (Mandela 1995). It is to these "other inequalities" that this essay turns to address the problem of the articulation of African male spirituality. In short, I define this problem as the invisibility of African male spirituality.

More than fifty years ago, it was Ralph Ellison's (1947) novel that detailed the notion of "invisibility" for African Americans. Through the presentation of the book's main character, Ellison was able to capture the essence of the quest for self-affirmation that African American people struggle with so desperately. Now, at the threshold of a new millennium, there is renewed interest in providing important insights into African male spirituality, because no segment of the population has been more misunderstood and mischaracterized than black men. Consequently, it is easy to imagine how African men encounter beleaguered spirituality when they receive services and treatments from people who have little or no knowledge of their personhood (Parham 1999).

It is also important to recognize that the invisibility syndrome must be understood both within and outside of a historical or contemporary American context. Invisibility is a global phenomenon for African people, particularly in places where remnants of European colonization exist or continue to exert influence over people of African descent. Describing who one is and deciding who one wants to be sound like similar questions. However, although related, they are not the same. Who one is constitutes a question of identity; who one wants to be is more a question of congruent actualization.

Spiritual Recovery

This decision to maintain congruence with one's identity is at the heart of the meaning of spirituality. The most fundamental question for African masculinity is: How do I maintain a sense of integrity in a world that does not support and affirm my humanity? I answer this question through seeing African male identity as an interdependent identity instead of what has usually been afforded African masculinity, what I call the invisibility construct. More specifically, this invisibility construct of the African male is perhaps best seen through the critical incidents African men endure. The African male, then, is believed to be made invisible by a series of sociocultural challenges that erase his ability to successfully navigate the pathways of life.

The invisibility construct is not new and certainly did not begin in contemporary America. It is similar to the analysis advanced by W. E. B. Du Bois in his classic work entitled *The Souls of Black Folks*. There, Du Bois highlights the psychic dissonance most people of African descent feel in struggling to live in two societies: one being white America and the other being the African American reality in the context of a racist and oppressive society. What makes this struggle so pronounced for African men is the degree to which they are socialized to seek approval and validation from competitive identities. For example, to be a black man in the United States means that one must be athletic, violent, and rebellious. All such identities are based on competitive schemes that imply there is no innate character; hence, the African male identity is invisible by nature.

To solve the problem of invisibility for African masculinity, one must recover a sense of African cosmology. In the African cosmology, all of creation is charged with the presence of the invisible—God and the spirit world, both good and evil—and so it is said that "African peoples 'see' that invisible universe when they look at, hear or feel the visible and tangible world" (Mbiti 1997, 57). A universe alive with power generates both fear and awe, and therefore also characteristic of the African approach to the world is the desire to live in harmony with it, not apart from it, together with fear of the spirits that dwell in the forest, bush, and rivers. John Mbiti states that "people report that they see the spirits in ponds, caves, groves, mountains or outside their villages, dancing, singing, herding cattle, working in their fields or nursing their children" (Mbiti 1997, 81).

The spirits can communicate with persons through dreams, visions, and mediums. The relationships vary with each African society, but the sense of the presence of the spirits is pervasive for both Christians and traditional believers. The spirits are linked with the ancestors, and "bad sprits" are often understood to be those who have not been accepted into the "community of ancestors" because of the way they lived on earth. Now they cause problems for their families here. A Gananian priest once prayed in the thanksgiving liturgy "for delivering him from the fear of evil spirits." He was not denying the existence and activity of such spirits, but rather their power over him.

All of these elements of the African view of the world and creation thus are distinctly different in many ways from the Western perspective. The African male brings the experience of harmony with nature, a lack of domineering attitude toward it, a sense of the invisible world alive in the visible, and a strong conviction that various spirits can communicate with the person and the community. These challenge Western perceptions of the secularity of the universe, a sense of control over it, and at least a great skepticism about the existence of any kinds of spirits or similar beings with power to influence human behavior (notwithstanding the contributions of modern psychology, which have shown us that we are far more complex than we had dreamed).

Different also are Western and African understandings of religion and its relation to life. During the past several hundred years, religious belief, practice, and experience have become options for Western persons, not core ways to organize life experience. For those who remain believers, too often religion is a separate compartment of life, with various religious duties to be "done" but with little influence on ordinary life other than the vague desire to do good and respect the rights of others. One attends church on Sunday and then gives little thought to religious commitment the rest of the week. Organized religion in the West has seen its influence decline in many ways as this dichotomy between religious and the secular has become more pronounced. Even the rise of various fundamentalist groups has not challenged this approach, since personal faith is seen as operative in a fairly narrow, restricted sphere with little social or political implication for the wider society.

The Western person brings much of this perspective to spiritual direction when the matter to be discussed is only that which is "religious." Prayer experience is important, but one's involvement with a local political party apparently is not. Any approach or suggestion that reinforces this dichotomy between "religion" and "life" in Western experience widens the gap. African experience is radically different, for religion is seen as inseparable from African culture. In African traditional religions, formal distinctions between the sacred and the secular, the spiritual and the material dimensions of life, do not exist. Life and religious expression are one, since the invisible world of the sacred is so intimately linked with ordinary life. The universe is basically a religious universe. Traditional African religious experience is thus a daily affair, permeating every aspect of life: rising; getting water; cooking food; going to the farm, office, or school; attending a funeral or wedding; drinking beer with friends. Certain religious rituals surround specific life events such as birth and death, but the African religious worldview is broader, since it encompasses all that is human and part of life.

Africans who become Christian look for an experience of religion that also encompasses their whole life: language, thought patterns, social relationships, attitudes, values, desires, and fears. It is not enough to "do religious things" regularly, since their desire is for a religious worldview that will fill the world with meaning and be especially sustaining in times of fear and crisis. The African person brings her or his desire that the experience of God be found in every facet of life, without exception. Western persons, formed in the pattern of religion as one part of life, can be disconcerted by the holistic view presented by their African brothers or sisters, but they have much to gain from it. This worldview is as pervasive as the air one breathes, and it is often only through either direct cross-cultural experience or vicariously through study of other cultures that one begins to realize that the "oxygen content" of one's particular kind of cultural air is a bit different from another culture's.

If the usefulness of research is limited to privatized individual or Western interactions, then we miss a golden opportunity to make an impact on larger segments of society. In the context of the invisibility syndrome, we can use the insights gained from African experiences to intervene in the larger social arena. If our discipline can help society learn to better support and affirm the dignity and humanity of African people and other members of our community, then we decrease the probability that cross-racial interactions will necessarily lead to invisibility. The tendency to restrict the etiology of the invisibility syndrome to socially oppressive phenomena involves factors that instigate feelings of anger, frustration, confusion, and negative social forces (that is, racial slurs, discrimination) that occur in the context of cross-racial interactions (usually African American and white). It is important to remember, however, that experiences that fail to affirm the humanity of a person individually, or people collectively, do occur both within as well as outside of the culture. For example, differential career expectations on the part of African American men and women toward each other could create a scenario in which one partner's "dream" and resulting behavior comes into conflict with the assumptions of the other partner about what he or she should be doing. Consequently, the man or the woman could be subjected to negative attitudes or behaviors that project his or her partner's displeasure at the other's life choices. This could potentially result in perceptions that significant aspects of oneself must be more dormant (invisible) to escape the harsh criticism and unsupportive tones of the other partner.

There are dynamics associated with the energy and life force of African people that demand that the model address the spiritual dimension of being male. The African-centered worldview conceptualizes the world as a spiritual reality, where the manifestation of spiritness is the essence of one's humanity. From this viewpoint, it is therefore reasonable to believe that being a male must include a deliberate focus on the spiritness that permeates the male self. Only then will one be able to understand how the dynamics of invisibility contaminate the energy and life force of a people, both individually and collectively.

Ubuntu is the quality of interaction in which one's own humanness depends upon its recognition in the other. By the African cultural conceptualization of recognizing one's identity in the other, Archbishop Desmond Tutu's theology guards against the Western propensity for racial classifications. In other words, Tutu's Ubuntu seeks to show that persons are more than either black or white. And Ubuntu combined with the metaphor of the *imago dei* becomes a concept that describes the divine life, just as the Son and the Holy Spirit are defined by the Father, so likewise personhood is defined in the other. One would not know the meaning of salvation or intelligence unless such meanings were made intelligible by the reference of someone else. Tutu's Ubuntu is a system in which each person is not only unique and "unrepeatable," but so are the nations of the world. The world is to be inter-national. Tutu explains:

> A self-sufficient human being is subhuman. I have gifts that you do not have, so, consequently, I am unique—you have gifts that I do not have, so you are unique. God has made us so that we will need each other. We are made for a delicate network of interdependence. We see it on a macro level. Not even the most powerful nations in the world can be self-sufficient. They are forever, almost obsessively, concerned about their balance of payments situations, which reflects the relationship of trade between nations. It is not good for a nation to be alone. It is not good for a nation to have a large deficit situation, and it is not good for a nation to have too large a credit balance, because it tends to throw the global trade situation out of kilter. (Tutu 1992a, 37)

Therefore, Ubuntu implies more than a nonracial, nonsexist, and nonexploitative society. Rather, it "is a touchstone by which the quality of a society has to be continually tested, no matter what ideology is reigning. It must be incorporated not only in the society of the future but also in the process of the struggle towards that future" (Wilson and Ramphele 1989, 269). The concept of Ubuntu demonstrates that persons are not defined by natural sets of properties but by the relationships between them and others. Tutu concludes:

> Ubuntu refers to the person who is welcoming, who is hospitable, who is warm and generous, who is affirming of others, who does

not feel threatened that others are able and good for s/he has a proper self-assurance that comes from knowing they belong in a greater whole, and know that they are diminished when another is humiliated, is diminished, is tortured, is oppressed, is treated as if they were less than who they are. What a wonderful world it can be, it will be, when we know that our destinies are locked inextricably into one another's. . . . We are being forced if not by prosperity then by impending disaster to realize that we are one another's brothers and sisters. To share the prosperity of affluent countries with indigent ones is not really altruism. It is ultimately the best kind of self-interest, for if the poor countries become prosperous in their turn, then they provide vigourous markets for the consumer goods produced elsewhere. The debt burden is a bomb that could shatter the economy of the globe to smithereens. And so a new and just economic world order would benefit both rich and poor countries. (Tutu 1992b)

Ubuntu: Interdependent African Male Spirituality

I end this essay with the construction of Ubuntu that I contend ameliorates the problematic of antagonistic, promiscuous black male identity. My construction of Ubuntu comes from a study of Archbishop Tutu, who provides the following three steps in the Ubuntu process: (1) In order to understand Ubuntu, one must first see the difference between African ways of knowing (that is, epistemology) and Western ways of knowing; (2) For Tutu, the church provides the essential character by which he appropriates the African concept of Ubuntu; and (3) Lastly, Tutu shows us how identity need not be individualistically defined. Further elaboration of these three steps will provide a better understanding of Tutu's Ubuntu.

As mentioned above, in order first to understand Ubuntu one must encounter differences between African and Western ways of knowing. According to much of current African scholarship, African epistemology begins with community and moves to individuality, whereas Western epistemology moves from individuality to community. The problem with these generalizations is that they die of a thousand qualifications. For example, Western definitions of "community" connote a "mere collection of self-interested persons, each with private sets of preferences, but all of whom get together nonetheless because they realize that in association they can accomplish things which they are not able to accomplish otherwise" (Menkiti 1971, 166). This definition of community is really an aggregation, a sum of individuals. Not only does this go against onto-logical claims of community, but methodologically, this definition of com-munity becomes a circular argument. Ifeanyi A. Menkiti states that John Mbiti's aphorism "I am because we are" does not include an additive "we," but a "thoroughly fused collective 'we.'" However, Tutu's Ubuntu antici-pates its own problematic, namely, the needs of the many outweighing the few. Therefore Tutu stresses the Christian definition of relationship to define Ubuntu, as opposed to other social forms of communalism.

Following the African epistemology of community, the next step of understanding Ubuntu requires that one see how Tutu assumes the identity of the church to provide the essential character of the concept. Influenced deeply by the spirituality of the Anglican Church, Tutu is able to overcome African philosophy's tendency to go to the extremes of discounting person-ality for the sake of community. For Tutu, trained in the theology of God as trinity, human persons are properly related in a theological Ubuntu that does not denigrate individuality:

> No real human being can be absolutely self-sufficient. Such a per-son would be subhuman. We belong therefore in a network of del-icate relationships of interdependence. It is marvelous to know that one who has been nurtured in a living, affirming, accepting family tends to be loving, affirming and accepting of others in his or her turn. We do need other people and they help to form us in a profound way.
>
> You know just how you blossom in the presence of someone who believes in you and who helps you have faith in yourself, who urges you to great thoughts and yet accepts you as who you are and not for what you have or can achieve, who does not abandon you because you have failed. And you know just how you tend to wilt in the presence of someone who is forever complaining and finding fault with you. You didn't know you could be so clumsy being all thumbs until you got to this lady's house and trust you to break her favorite antique or to drop ashes on her beautiful Persian carpet.
>
> Jesus has had tremendous faith in people and got them having faith in themselves with a proper kind of self assurance, exorcising them from the horrible paralyzing sense of inadequacy that plagues so many of us. After the resurrection He met Peter and did

not berate Him for denying Him because he helped him cancel it out through a three-fold positive assertion: "Yes, I love you." To this man who had denied Him, Jesus gave not less but increased responsibility—Feed my sheep. Become—(you vacillating old so and so)—my chief apostle and pastor. (Tutu 1985)

Ubuntu is not humanism in the Western sense of favoring enlightenment notions that truth claims are located in the rational capacities of individuals. The African conceptualization of being human is antithetical to enlightenment notions because Western humanism tends more toward materialism than toward the African balance between material and spiritual realities.[2] This means that, for Christians and for people who are members of the church, the processes of dehumanization cannot be tolerated. In this light Tutu reasons, "Is it not revealing how when we meet people for the first time we soon ask, 'by the way, what do you do?' meaning what gives you value?" (Tutu 1991, 20).

Lastly, in order to understand Tutu's concept of Ubuntu, one must see how identity need not be individualistically defined. The worst effects of individualism are competitiveness and selfishness. From Tutu's perspective of Ubuntu, the reader learns that the formation of a person need not encourage a high degree of competitiveness and selfishness. Any formative processes of human identity that defines self over against the other demonstrates the greatest discrepancy with God's creation of interdependence (Tutu 1989). Tutu shows this discrepancy as he recounts the creation narrative, in which Adam needs Eve, as a sign of our interdependency:

> Apartheid says people are created for separation, people are created for apartheid, people are created for alienation and division, disharmony and disunity, and we say, the scripture says, people are made for togetherness, people are made for fellowship.
>
> You know that lovely story in the Bible. Adam is placed in the Garden of Eden and everything is hunky-dory in the garden. Everything is very nice, they are all very friendly with each other. Did I say, everybody was happy? No, actually Adam was not entirely happy and God is solicitous for Adam and He looks on and says, "No, it is not good for man to be alone." So God says, "Adam, how about choosing a partner?" So God makes the animals pass one by one in front of Adam. And God says to Adam, "What about this one?" Adam says, "Not on your life." "What

about this one?" "No." God says, "Ah, I got it." So God puts Adam to sleep and out of his rib he produces this delectable creature Eve and when Adam awakes, he says "wow, this is just what the doctor ordered!" But that is to say, you and I are made for interdependency. (Tutu 1988, 3)

Tutu's interpretation of the creation narrative illustrates the profound truth that instead of being made male for disproportionate differences, God's creation continually informs persons that identity and relationship go hand in hand. The obsession with individualism and self-achievement is countered for Tutu in Jesus' claims of disciplining individuals to move outside of competitive cosmologies. Tutu's Ubuntu exhorts us to move from Western definitions of "community," which connote a mere collection of self-interested persons, each with private sets of preferences. In the West, community is not natural, but it is useful, insofar as a collection of self-interested persons gets together because they realize that in association they can accomplish things that they are not able to accomplish otherwise (Menkiti 1971, 166). Tutu's Ubuntu argues against the naturalization of this definition of community because it is really not community, but rather an aggregation, a sum of individuals.

Given this understanding of Ubuntu, and given the West's emphasis on individuality solely constituting the self and how the self forms only through private choices, one now has a language by which to address how Western identity runs counter to African ideals of what constitutes a human person. Tutu's inheritance both of the spirituality of the church and of African thought does not allow him to postulate individualism as an all-determining factor. Community is therefore vital to self-identity. The crucial distinction between African and Western thought is that, in the African view of humanity, it is "the community that defines the person as person, not some isolated static quality of rationality, will, or memory" (Menkiti 1971, 158). The African male identity must be understood through the African conceptualizations of community, not the antagonistic process of how male identity comes into being through the individualism of the Western world.

Bibliography

Battle, Michael. 1997. *Reconciliation: The Ubuntu Theology of Desmond Tutu.* Cleveland: Pilgrim.

Carter, Robert. 1995. *The Influence of Race and Racial Identity in Psychotherapy: Toward a Racially Inclusive Model.* New York: John Wiley.

Cross, William E. 1991. *Shades of Black: Diversity in African American Identity.* Philadelphia: Temple Univ. Press.

———. 1971. "The Negro to Black Conversion Experience: Toward a Psychology of Black Liberation." *Black World* 20, 13–27.

Du Bois, W. E. B. 1903. *The Souls of Black Folks.* Chicago: McClurg.

Ellison, Ralph. 1947. *Invisible Man.* New York: Vintage.

Franklin, A. J. 1999. "Invisibility Syndrome and Racial Identity Development in Psychotherapy and Counseling African American Men." *The Counseling Psychologist* 27, 761–93.

Helms, Janet E. 1990. *Black and White Racial Identity: Theory, Research, and Practice.* Westport, Conn.: Greenwood.

Jones, James M. 1997. *Prejudice and Racism.* 2d ed. New York: McGraw-Hill.

Mandela, Nelson. 1995. "Speech of Nelson Mandela." Presented at Telecom 95 Opening Ceremony, Geneva, October 3, 1995. <http://wn.apc.org/technology/nmteleco.html>.

Mbiti, John. 1997. *African Religions and Philosophy.* New York: Anchor Books.

Meer, Fatima. 1998. *Higher than Hope: The Authorized Biography of Nelson Mandela.* New York: Harper & Row.

Memmi, Albert. 1965. *The Colonizer and the Colonized.* Boston, Mass.: Beacon.

Menkiti, Ifeanyi A. 1971. "Person and Community in African Traditional Thought." *African Philosophy.* Ed. R. A. Wright. New York: Univ. Press of America.

Mosley, D. 1972. "Toward a New Specialty of Black Psychology." *Black Psychology.* Ed. Reginald L. Jones. New York: Harper & Row.

Neary, Lynn. 1997. "Church to Decide Leader's Fate." Morning Edition, National Public Radio (NPR), September 1.

Oduyoye, Mercy Amba. Winter 1997/1998. "The African Experience of God through the Eyes of an Akan Woman." *Cross Currents* 47:4, 493–504.

Ogunyemi, Chikwenye Okonjo. 1996. *Africa Wo/Man Palava: The Nigerian Novel by Women.* Chicago: Chicago Univ. Press.

Parham, Thomas A. November 1999. "Invisibility Syndrome in African Descent People: Understanding the Cultural Manifestations of the Struggle for Self-Affirmation." *Counseling Psychologist* 27:6, 794ff.

———. 1993. *Psychological Storms: The African American Struggle for Identity.* Chicago: African American Images.

———. 1989. "Cycles of Psychological Nigrescence." *The Counseling Psychologist* 17, 187–226.

Parham, Thomas A., and Helms, J. E. 1985. "Relationship of Racial Identity to Self-Actualization and Affective States of Black Students." *Journal of Counseling Psychology* 32:3, 431–40.

———. 1981. "The Influence of Black Students' Racial Identity Attitudes on Preference for Counselor's Race." *Journal of Counseling Psychology* 28:3, 250–56.

Pfister, Roger. 1996. *Internet for Africanists and Others Interested in Africa: An Introduction to the Internet and a Comprehensive Compilation of Relevant Addresses.* Bern: Swiss Society of African Studies.

Setiloane, Gabriel. 1976. *The Image of God among the Sotho-Tswana.* Rotterdam: A. A. Balkema.

Sue, Derald Wing and David Sue. 1990. *Counseling the Culturally Different: Theory and Practice.* 2d ed. New York: John Wiley.

Tutu, Desmond. 1992a. "God's Dream." *Waging Peace II: Vision and Hope for the 21st Century.* Ed. David Krieger and Frank Kelly. Chicago: Noble.

———. July 14–15, 1992b. "The New World Order." Paper in absentia, the International Foundation for Socio-Economic and Political Studies, Moscow.

———. Advent 1991. "Grace Upon Grace." *Journal for Preachers* 15:1.

———. Printed after October 7, 1989. Unpublished Sermon.

———. 1988. "Transcript of Sermon in Birmingham Cathedral Address, April 21, 1988." Published by Committee for Black Affairs, Birmingham, England, Diocesan Office.

———. October 6, 1985. "Genesis Chapter 3." Handwritten sermon. Presented at St. Mary's, Blechingly, Surrey.

White, Joseph L., and T. A. Parham. 1990. *The Psychology of Blacks: An African American Perspective.* Englewood Cliffs, N.J.: Prentice Hall.

Wilson, Francis, and Mamphela Ramphele. 1989. *Uprooting Poverty: The South African Challenge.* Cape Town: David Philip.

Woodson, Carter G. 1933. *The Miseducation of the Negro.* Washington, D.C.: Associated Publishers.

World Telecommunication Development Report 1995. 1995. Geneva: International Telecommunication Union.

Notes

1. I am an African American, male, Christian theologian. For an interesting discussion of African from an African woman, see Oduyoye. In this article she is helpful in her distinctions of what is African, especially doing away with the patriarchal models that substitute the will of the male for the will of God.

2. Some European historians counter this claim by painting a picture of Southern Africa in which missionaries discovered tribal wars and famine. However, African scholars such as Gabriel Setiloane state that such accounts leave out three elements that may have contributed to such war and famine 150 years (in 1652) before missionaries arrived in South Africa, i.e., "White man, the horse and the gun and ammunition." See discussion in Setiloane 1976, 123.

Part Two

Mental Health

3

The Psychosocial Roots of Sin and Possibilities for Healing

Stephen Boyd

Pat Conroy, in his book *The Prince of Tides*, expresses well what it can feel like these days for a guy like me—a white, heterosexual, middle-class, middle-aged, Protestant, Southern, able-bodied, Euro-American man. The protagonist, Tom Wingo, recounts that he grew up in South Carolina, well-schooled and gifted in his hatred of African Americans. The Civil Rights Movement caught him on the wrong side of the racial barricade and proved him both "wicked and wrong." But, being sensitive to injustice, he worked to change himself and got involved in the movement himself. Proud of this transformation, he then found himself in an exclusively male ROTC program and was spit on and vilified by those offended by the uniform. Eventually, he became a part of those demonstrations. Finally, when he thought he had changed as much as he would need to, the women's liberation movement "bushwhacked" him and he found himself on the wrong side of the "barricades" yet again. Wingo laments, "This has not been an easy century to endure.... I seem to embody everything that is wrong with the twentieth century" (Conroy 1987, 9).[1]

Many of us feel like we also have been "bushwhacked," and the bushwhackers are those African Americans, peaceniks, women, and more recently, gay/lesbian/transgendered folk, "tree-huggers," differently abled people, and the elderly (to name a few). And indeed, sometimes we do get labeled, blamed, or mistreated by members of these groups. But for those of us who profess to be followers of Jesus, that's not the end of the story. In fact, Jesus seemed to think that these "strangers" are not the cause of our distress and may well be the source of our healing.

I want to develop and explore this notion with some reflection on "The Good Samaritan" story (Luke 10:29-37) and on insights offered by Howard Thurman in his book *The Luminous Darkness*.

He Was Robbed and Left Half Dead: The Installation of Dominative Masculinity

In Luke 10, a teacher of the law tests Jesus by asking how he might gain eternal life. Jesus responds, "What is written in the law?"[2] The man answers, "You shall love the Lord your God with all your heart, and with all your soul, and with all your strength, and with all your mind; and your neighbor as yourself." Jesus confirms this assessment by saying, "You have given the right answer; do this, and you will live." Then, seeking to justify himself, the man asks, "And who is my neighbor?" Rather than answering directly, Jesus tells a story with a surprising twist—a twist that illuminates our situation in helpful ways.

Jesus says, "A man was going down from Jerusalem to Jericho, and fell into the hands of robbers, who stripped him, beat him, and went away, leaving him half dead." As he lay there, a priest and a Levite each came walking along, saw him on the road, and "passed by on the other side." Then a Samaritan came by, and when he saw him he had compassion, and "went to him and bandaged his wounds." The Samaritan took the wounded man to an inn and said to the innkeeper, "Take care of him; and when I come back, I will repay you whatever more you spend."

Jesus then turns back to the teacher of the law, "Which of the three, do you think, was a neighbor to the man who fell into the hands of the robbers?" The teacher replied, "The one who showed him mercy." Jesus then said, "Go and do likewise."

I was directed to this passage in a recent sermon by George Williamson, who was back in Winston-Salem, North Carolina, to commemorate the fortieth anniversary of the sit-ins, in which he participated as a student, that integrated lunch counters in our city. As a white, male, heterosexual, educated, first-world Christian, Williamson identified himself not with the priest, the Levite, or the Samaritan. Rather, he exclaimed, "I'm the wounded man on the road. I've been mugged by the piercing hurricane of racism; lightning bolts of nationalism; giant demons of militaristic idolatry; suffocating gray clouds of homophobia. I am wounded, writhing in wretchedness."[3]

He is right. Many of us have been stripped and beaten and left half-dead. It may just be growing up male in this society, but it can be brutal.[4] Simply because we are boys, we experience a violent conditioning process that functions to cut us off from significant contact with whole groups of people. If we run like a girl, throw like a girl, do anything like a girl, or get to close to little girls we are called "sissy," "wuss," "pussy," or "wimp." None of these are good things in the minds of the name-callers. And if we don't stop doing whatever we are doing that prompted the verbal violence, it can escalate into physical violence. To protect ourselves, we learn to distance ourselves from those aspects of ourselves that are targeted for abuse, and to avoid closeness to girls and women. We build an attitudinal and behavioral firewall internally between us and "femininity" and externally between us and females. It is also dangerous after a certain age to get too close to other boys and men, lest the epithets "fag," "queer," or "homo" get directed at us. The verbal violence can easily and quickly escalate if we don't build an emotional firewall between ourselves and other males. This firewall is called homophobia. For a white guy like me, raised in the South, getting too close to people of color, particularly African Americans, brought yet more name-calling ("nigger-lover") and censure. Although we had only one Jewish family in my community, Jewish jokes made it clear to me that they were somehow different and not really part of "us." As a middle-class boy, I learned that associations with those beneath us on the socioeconomic ladder threatened to pull us back into the working class from which we had struggled so hard to emerge. And associations with folks above us were out of the question, because "they" were qualitatively different from "us" and were unreliable and morally suspect.

There are a lot of internal (psychic) and external (relational) firewalls that we erect in order to protect ourselves from the verbal, emotional, and potentially physical violence that gets directed at us. I've developed the following diagram to illustrate, graphically, what happens to us (Boyd 1997, 48):

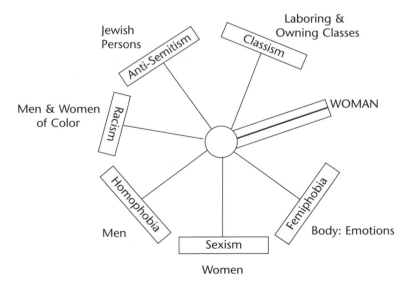

Since we are created to be profoundly relational creatures, with the capacities and needs to relate deeply with many creatures on many different levels—physical, emotional, intellectual, and spiritual—this conditioning is extremely painful. These firewalls systematically cut us off from whole groups of people with whom we have the potential to develop warm, loving, just, and life-giving relationships. Except for perhaps one woman ("WOMAN," as Sam Keen has called her)[5] with whom closeness is acceptable, we are left alone, bleeding on the road.

How do we respond to this woundedness, this pain?

Responses to Violence

I want to outline two possible responses to this woundedness. The first is pretty unproductive, but I'm afraid it is the most common—at least in my life and experience. The second seems to hold the promise of healing and a way out of the pain of isolation.

"Judge not that you be not judged": Projection of the Pain onto Target Groups

Many of us, who find ourselves lacerated and bleeding on the road, may be tempted to blame those on the other side of the firewall between us and them. It is easy to do.

In a recent workshop, I asked about fifty white, middle-class church men, ranging in age from the early 20s to 70, to name groups that they personally, or men they knew, did not like or that irritated them. On their behalf, I must say that they were very reluctant at first. I had to prompt them and encourage them simply to identify groups that cause irritation for some folks they know. Here is a list of the groups they identified:

Native Americans	Poor people	Rich people
Clergy	Hispanics	Gays and Lesbians
Asians	Women	African Americans
Jews	Teenagers	Organized criminals
Pagans	Muslims	People of other generations
Uneducated people		

Next, I asked them to pick three or four of the groups and list what it was about that particular group that irritated them or the people they knew. They picked women, African Americans, and the poor.

Women were:
- too emotional
- hostile
- irrational

African Americans were:
- prejudiced against whites
- lacking understanding of whites
- sexually promiscuous and lacking family values

The poor were:
- lazy
- untrustworthy
- lacking in good judgment

As we worked on this part, several men pointed out that these were stereotypes, and that we shouldn't say that this is the way people in each group really are. I acknowledged that, but encouraged them to continue for the sake of the exercise.

Then, with those lists taped up off to the side, I asked them to name the qualities "real men" were supposed to have and exhibit. Next to that list, we also recorded the characteristics that men were not supposed to exhibit. The lists looked like this:

Manly	Unmanly
strong	weak
aggressive	passive
rational	irrational
breadwinner	dependent
practical	artistic
successful	a loser
goal-oriented	aimless
disciplined	undisciplined
logical	emotional
athletic	lazy
tolerant	snobbish
desire women	desire men
consistent	inconsistent

Unlike the previous exercise, these lists came very quickly and with little prompting from me. It seems clear that many of us know very well what the script is for us and, when given permission to do so, can identify its major features.

Next I asked them to look at the list we made of the characteristics that irritate us about other groups and the list of "unmanly" things we must repress in order to avoid censure from others. After they studied them a while, light bulbs began to go off in the heads of a few men, and then more and more.

One man exclaimed, "They're the same!" Another challenged him, "What do you mean, 'they're the same.'" The first answered him, "Well, we get angry at women for being emotional, but that is what we aren't allowed to do. Maybe we are envious. They can do it, and we can't."

So, then we looked at the groups to test this hypothesis—we are irritated at groups who we believe engage in behavior that we feel is prohibited to us. Let's begin with women as an example.

We must be "logical and rational"; any behavior that does not measure up to "logical and rational" is, we have been taught, not valuable and is to be disdained, even despised. We are rewarded for developing competence in left-brain, linear thinking and end up devaluing right-brain, intuitive thinking as soft and ineffectual. We are conditioned to separate our feelings from our thoughts and to think that the former should have nothing to do with the latter. So we split off our feelings and intuitions, lest we be targeted for abuse for showing or exercising them, and often end up projecting them onto women. These projected qualities become distorted, exaggerated, and viewed negatively. Women become, in our minds, excessively emotional (Freud called it "hysterical") and thus irrational. Our own anger at having to distance essential parts of ourselves can also be directed at women, who are safer objects to project onto than those who required the suppression of these parts. Some of the hostility that we believe women bear toward us is really our own projected onto them. Our anger has multiple levels: we're angry at what has happened to us; we're angry at those who did it to us; we're angry at women who seem freer and contemptuous of our incapacities; and way down deep, we're angry at ourselves for buying all this.

Similar dynamics are involved in the social and psychological transmission of racism and classism. Because of the violent conditioning that punishes the expression of parts of ourselves, we repress or occlude those parts of ourselves and project them onto members of groups targeted for mistreatment.

Due to the residential segregation that results from racism, many white people know little about the cultural values, family traditions, and religious experience of African Americans, and often form opinions on the basis of misinformation and stereotypes. Too much of what we think we know about African Americans is prejudicial. So, our natural curiosity about a group of people is stunted by social segregation, leading to profound ignorance that we project onto African Americans.[6]

As Cornel West observes, white racism has also a deeply embedded sexual component. According to social scientists, interracial sex and marriage constitutes many white people's deepest fear of black people (West 1993, 125). This is not surprising. If mere social intercourse targets us for violence from other white people, well, another kind is really scary. Therefore, we must repress anything, particularly sexual desire, that leads us into close association and, therefore, target status. Though black sexuality is "virtually taboo" for whites in public discussion, "behind closed doors, the dirty, disgusting, and funky sex associated with black people is often perceived to be more intriguing and interesting" to us. This fascination is then projected out onto black women and men in such stereotypes as "Jezebel (the seductive temptress)" and "Bigger Thomas (the mad and mean predatory craver of white women)" or "Jack Johnson, the super [sexual] performer" (West 1993, 119–20). Our own forbidden and repressed sexual interest in black people gets projected onto them and we see them as "sexually promiscuous and lack[ing] family values."

Finally and much more briefly, classism leads many in the middle strata of our economy to repudiate any part of ourselves that threatens our productivity and, therefore, our chance at upward mobility. We then label it "lazy, untrustworthy, and lacking in good judgment." These undesirable qualities then get projected onto the "poor."

The dynamics that encourage us unconsciously to split off parts of ourselves and project distorted images of these parts onto groups targeted for mistreatment—apart from the obvious grief they cause members of those groups—produce significant problems for us.[7]

First, in judging others, we are literally judging ourselves. The more disdain we have for women's "overemotional" responses, the more contempt we pour on the part of ourselves that is longing not only to feel what we feel but to express it. And the more contempt we pour on that part of ourselves, the further underground it goes, making it less likely that we will ever be able to feel what we would like to feel, express what we would like to express, and experience what we would like to experience. The more we project our ignorance onto African American people, the more we reject our own curiosity about them and assure our continued ignorance and the fear it inspires. The more we denounce perceived promiscuity in "them," the more we foster the rejection of sensual/sexual expression in ourselves and the concomitant isolation and deprivation of that rejection. The more we censure the "laziness" and "irresponsibility" in the poor, the more we condemn the impulses toward rest, creativity, and recreation in us, leaving ourselves more vulnerable to exploitative employer demands and exhausting work habits.

Jesus said it this way: "Do not judge, and you will not be judged; do not condemn, and you will not be condemned . . . for the measure you give will be the measure you get back" (Luke 6:37-38). When we judge, we are judged. When we distance ourselves from what we dare not accept about ourselves, distort it in negative ways, and project it onto others, we are condemned to stay blinded to the real source of our difficulties and are locked in a self-alienated prison.

The second problem our projection creates is that we misidentify the source of our woundedness. The projective process leads us to believe that members of the target group are responsible for our discomfort, our anger, or some problem in the social order. In fact, the problem for us, personally, has most likely been caused by people most like us—that is, other men, white people, and middle class folks who have required splits inside of us and the mistreatment of target groups as the condition for belonging. If we manifest attitudes or behaviors that members of these groups of people most like us deem inappropriate, we risk reprimand and, ultimately, excommunication from the fraternity of men, the community of whites, or the socioeconomic group to which we aspire.

Recognizing this dynamic leads to further difficulties. We feel a profound dependency on those communities of folks who have been most responsible for our wounding. Blaming them or resisting them or confronting them is a frightening prospect. It was frightening when we were small, when the installation most significantly took place, and it is still frightening for us now—even in adulthood. To refuse to accept the conditions of belonging most likely means that the sanctions threatened earlier will be imposed now—reprimand, humiliation, ostracism, and possibly violence. It is less threatening to direct our anger toward a non-dominant group (women, African Americans, the poor), rather than at a dominant group that holds in its hands, or so it seems to us, our very lives and their meaning.

But even to identify the groups of people whose attitudes and behaviors helped install our own sexism, racism, and classism does not get to the source of the problem for us. For the sources of the insidious forms of alienation they passed on to us flow from beyond them. Those sources are historically older, institutionally deeper, and culturally broader than anything that could have originated in any particular group to which we belong. In other words, "our struggle is not against enemies of blood and flesh, but against the rulers, against the authorities, against the cosmic powers of this present darkness, against the spiritual forces of evil in the heavenly places" (Ephesians 6:12).

For many post-Enlightenment, twenty-first-century people, the New Testament language of "principalities and powers," demons, and Satan is a little hard to swallow. The whole notion of these personal, evil beings that inhabit a three-story universe make little sense to many who have cut our intellectual teeth on modern physics, astronomy, and psychology. However, the enormity of our species' destructive capacities and the depth and intransigence of these firewalls I have been describing have led some contemporary Christians to reappropriate some of this Biblical language to describe what Marjorie Suchocki calls those sinful "structures of consciousness that bode to our ill-being" (Suchocki 1990, 1994). Walter Wink, in his three-volume study of the "powers," argues that that early Christian language pointed to "the actual spirituality at the center of the political, economic, and cultural institutions of their day." So, according to this reading of the Biblical witness, the internal and external sin that we are up against is enormous, persistent, and at times can feel overwhelming.

To recognize this is not to encourage defeatism and, thus, quiet acceptance. Rather, this kind of reality check can serve as an inoculation against the impatient desire for quick resolutions to the troubles that beset us—an impatience that can easily give way to frustration, despair, and resigned acceptance of the status quo. A sobered wisdom is more conducive to a humility that encourages us to look for obstacles within ourselves rather than primarily in others; to ask for help (divine and human); and to persist when there seems to be no way through, around, or over these firewalls.

Healing and "the Samaritan"

A second, more productive response to our woundedness is suggested by the Good Samaritan story. As the man lay there half-dead, from whom might he expect his help and healing to come? Might he look to the priest, to the Levite? In the story, Jesus says that help came from the despised

Samaritan, not from the priest or Levite. His healing came not from someone most like the injured man, but from someone unlike him, from someone on the other side of a long-standing firewall, from a "stranger." Is this surprising? Maybe not. Who better to recognize our projections, refuse them, and thus hold a mirror up, showing them to us, than someone onto whom we customarily project the parts of ourselves that forms of systemic oppression have sliced off from our souls and bodies? Of his own healing from the "piercing hurricane of racism, lightening bolts of nationalism, giant demons of militaristic idolatry, and suffocating gray clouds of homophobia," George Williamson observed:

> Priests can't help me with empty rituals of forgiveness. God knows a legalist can't. I need a compassionate African American to confront me, guide me beyond racism; an emerging world revolutionary to stand up to me; a lesbian to show me what the closet is like, and being out of the closet.

And, indeed, he and people like him and me all do. There is the potential for healing brought by one on the other side of a firewall, but who is willing to step up to or across that wall and seek out those on the other side and show himself or herself to them?

In my own journey across the firewall of racism, I have found both challenge and healing in the writings of the African American mystic Howard Thurman and in my friendship with an African American colleague, Alton B. Pollard III. In *The Luminous Darkness*, Thurman brilliantly describes and analyzes the ways in which African Americans involved in the Civil Rights Movement held up a mirror for white Americans.[8]

Published in 1965, this book contains Thurman's frank assessment of the roles of the African American and white churches in the Civil Rights Movement. After describing "the churning abyss separating white from black," Thurman articulates ways for people on both sides of the firewall of racism to transcend "the walls that divide" and to "achieve in literal fact what is experienced as literal truth: human life is one and all men [and women] are members of one another" (Thurman 1965, x). As a white person, I found myself asking Thurman as I read, "So, what would you have us do? What do you want from white people in this process?" Or to put it another way, I found myself asking a "Samaritan"—someone on the other side of a firewall—"What must I do to be saved?" or "What can I do to be healed?" And this Samaritan, Howard Thurman, has a clear, concise answer:

A man can send his imagination forth to establish a beachhead in another man's spirit, and from that vantage point so to blend with the other's landscape that what he sees and feels is authentic—that is the great adventure in human relations. But this is not enough. The imagination must report its findings accurately without regard to prejudgments and private or collective fears. But this too is not enough. There must be both a spontaneous and a calculating response to such knowledge which will result in sharing of life and resources at their deepest level (Thurman 1965, 100).

These are things, Thurman says, that everyone can do so that one experiences what we all long for—to be at home in one's own house and not seem to oneself to be an alien. So what does it take to experience healing from the other-destructive and self-alienating effects of our conditioning? Using racism as an example, I summarize here, under three tasks, Thurman's counsel for white people:

Use your imaginations to understand what it is like to be an African American in this society. Once we are willing to see, many African Americans are willing to talk with us about what it is like for them.

Report what you see. That is, break the complicity of silence and name the injustice, discrimination, mistreatment, stereotyping, and rationalizations that you begin to see.

Do something about it. I think the key is to work on issues affecting African American people under their leadership. For example, one might work on issues in education, housing, job training, or police profiling through local organizations and initiatives led by African Americans (for example, local chapters of the NAACP and Urban League or ministerial alliances and partnerships, like the various Industrial Areas Foundation–affiliated organizations active in communities across the nation).[9]

As I thought about these tasks, it occurred to me that what Thurman was describing might be understood as hospitality. The Civil Rights Movement addressed the fact that African Americans, quite literally, did not have a seat not only at lunch counters, but also at a number of economic, political, social, educational, religious, and cultural tables in U.S. society. In many ways, the role of white people was to recognize that lack of access and imagine what that would be like, begin talking about it privately and publicly, and join hands with African Americans, as Thurman says, "in sharing of life and resources at their deepest level."

As I began to think more about what Thurman suggests, it struck me that inviting and assuring a place at the table to persons previously left out struck me as a hospitable thing to do. I remembered that Paul somewhere identified hospitality as a spiritual gift, so I went to a concordance to find out what he had to say. What I found amazed me. Near the end of Romans 12, in which Paul addresses life in the Body of Christ, he says, "Let love be genuine; hate what is evil, hold fast to what is good. . . . Contribute to the needs of the saints, practice hospitality" (Romans 12:9-13). The word translated as "hospitality" in the Revised Standard Version is *philoxenian*—"love of the stranger or other." It is the opposite of xenophobia—fear of the stranger or other. That sounded like what Thurman was talking about. Rather than fearing the other who has been forced to the other side of a social firewall, the appropriate response was to love them. That is, to use one's imagination, voice, and energies to move across, to transcend, the "dividing walls of hostility" (Ephesians 2:14) and find our way out of the social isolation imposed by the external social walls and the internal self-alienation they cause.

It also struck me that this kind of love is not primarily a feeling (though feelings are involved). Rather, it is a commitment to act in ways that, at least at first, sometimes seem contrary to what comes naturally or feels right to us. If one's town is residentially segregated, it might feel uncomfortable, even scary, to drive into the predominately African American part of town for the first time to attend a meeting in an African American church. But one does it anyway, because that is what justice requires, and it is where healing is to be found.

Several years ago, I did an academic presentation about the aspect of the men's movement that encouraged mostly white men like me to go into the woods, outside the heavy responsibilities of our institutional duties, to find "sacred space" to heal. After listening patiently, my colleague, Alton Pollard—an African American—said, "Steve, all you have to do is drive over to East Winston [the predominately African American part of our town]." And he was right. Shortly afterward, I began driving over to the Emmanuel Baptist church to attend meetings of a local biracial organization, Citizens United for Justice. Weekly, I and others in the group heard person after person come and talk about what had happened to them in our city's courts, police stations, schools, and businesses. What I heard changed my life. I realized that those who came were more like me than not. They, like I, wanted opportunities for a good education and meaningful work; freedom from violence—at the hands of persons on either side of the law; health care; and good, life-giving relationships with others, including me. I discovered that much of what I had believed about African Americans, to the extent that I thought about them, was not true; it was the product of projections of those in my own communities. My fears of violence in the neighborhood, of hostility, of not being accepted, of feeling like an alien, were unfounded. In fact, in a very short time, I felt very much at home at the church, in the meetings, and with folks I met there.

Also, what I heard convinced me that some of what African Americans experience can only be changed in partnership with people like me. For example, in our school district, expulsions and suspensions are meted out to African American students—males in particular—at a rate disproportionate to the population. There are several reasons for that. One is that there is often a disjunction between what a white teacher may expect in terms of classroom behavior and the usually more expressive norms of behavior young African Americans learn in their homes and churches. Also, a white teacher, interpreting silence as insolence, may simply be projecting his or her fears onto an African American student. To any white person who begins to understand some of these dynamics, it becomes apparent that in order for these dynamics to change, other white people (for example, teachers, principals, and so forth) must learn to see African American students more clearly. For that to happen, white people who have begun to see more clearly must speak up in our own communities and share what we have learned; we must report what we have seen, heard, and experienced—"without," as Thurman says, "regard to prejudgments of private or collective fears."

The seeing and reporting leads us into collaboration—colaboring—with others on both sides of the firewall, in order to share "of life and resources at their deepest level." And there are many, many opportunities for exciting, life-giving partnerships.[10]

As I have moved to enter such partnerships, I have come not only to feel more at home in my city with increasing numbers of people like and unlike me, but I feel more at home with myself. This is also an important piece of what happens. Down deep somewhere, we know that it is the right thing to do. For those of us on the privileged side of one of these firewalls, what Thurman counsels us to do are simply things we would want others to do if we sat where they sit. It is simply to love our neighbor as ourselves.

From my vantage point now, I can see that the challenge my colleague, Alton, presented me with almost ten years ago has led me to a number of healing places—what Garth Kasimu Baker-Fletcher has called Xodus-spaces

(Baker-Fletcher 1995). Because one good Samaritan, among others in the ensuing years, stopped on the road to attend to me lying bleeding and half-dead, I who was blind, mute, and lame can now see a little better, speak a little more audibly and truly, and walk a little more steadily as a partner in the co-creation of the world as God intends it.

And then the last word Jesus spoke to the teacher of the law—and to me and men like me—was and is, "Go and do likewise." Go and approach the walls from your side, extend yourself to those on the other side, and the kingdom of God—the Beloved Community—may just come in the midst of you.

Bibliography

Baker-Fletcher, Garth Kasimu. 1996. *Xodus: An African-American Male Journey*. Minneapolis: Fortress Press.

Boyd, Stephen. 1997. *The Men We Long to Be: Beyond Desperate Lovers and Lonely Warriors*. Cleveland: Pilgrim.

Conroy, Pat. 1987. *The Prince of Tides*. Toronto: Bantam.

Keen, Sam. 1991. *Fire in the Belly*. New York: Bantam.

Meeks, Wayne A., et al. 1993. *The HarperCollins Study Bible*. New York: HarperCollins.

Suchocki, Marjorie. 1994. *The Fall to Violence: Original Sin in Relational Theology*. New York: Continuum.

———. 1990. "A Feminist Re-interpretation of the Doctrine of Original Sin." Robinson Lectures. Wake Forest University.

Thurman, Howard. 1989. *The Luminous Darkness: A Personal Interpretation of the Anatomy of Segregation and the Ground of Hope*. 1965. Reprint, Richmond, Ind.: Friends United Press.

West, Cornel. 1993. *Race Matters*. New York: Vintage Books.

Wink, Walter. 1992. *Engaging the Powers: Discernment and Resistance in a World of Domination*. Minneapolis: Fortress Press.

———. 1986. *Unmasking the Powers: The Invisible Forces That Determine Human Existence*. Minneapolis: Fortress Press.

———. 1984. *Naming the Powers: The Language of Power in the New Testament*. Minneapolis: Fortress Press.

Notes

1. I want to thank David Schoeni for his editorial suggestions to this article.

2. All passages from the Scriptures come from the New Revised Standard Version in Meeks et al.

3. The sermon, "The Loadedest Question," was given at Wake Forest University, February 24, 2000. Williamson is the Pastor of the First Baptist Church, Granville, Ohio. I am grateful to him for both the experience of hearing the sermon that day and for sharing a copy with me.

4. In Boyd 1997, I have argued that much of masculine socialization for a man like me involves violence and results in profound isolation.

5. Keen observes that one of the well-kept secrets of many men is the degree to which our emotional lives revolve around one woman—whether she is the first one (our mothers) or the current one (a wife, or significant other). See also Boyd 1997, 41–68.

6. This is not to say that there is not lack of understanding and prejudice against white people among African Americans. But because African Americans have had to learn about and adapt to white culture out of economic necessity, they tend to know much more about the dominant white culture than most white people know about African American culture.

7. See Lee H. Butler's "Xodus to the Promised Man: Revising our Anthropodicy" in this volume for an analysis of the role of projection in the "colorization" of good and evil and the destructive effects of its introjection in the lives of African American men.

8. I am grateful to Alton Pollard for suggesting Thurman's work generally and this book in particular, and to the members of the Joint Book Discussion of the First Baptist Church, Highland Avenue, and the Wake Forest Baptist Church of Winston-Salem for their insights and companionship in our common journey over the last several years.

9. Examples of local organizations affiliated with the I.A.F. are H.E.L.P. of Charlotte, North Carolina, B.U.I.L.D. of Baltimore, and the Nehemiah Project of Brooklyn.

10. For a white person, the best place to start would be the local affiliate of the Urban League, the city's African American ministerial association, or the local chapter of the NAACP.

4

Responsible Forgiveness within a Relational Church Community

David J. Livingston

Portraits of Forgiveness Unresolved

A misty morning in the city of Florence, October 12, in the year 968. The day is dreary, and out of the gray, impenetrable mist rises the eerie call of the Order of Penitents. Not quite a chant, not quite a cry, this plea, this begging call, is meant for the ears of those treading through the fog of the gloomy morning on the way to the Cathedral of Florence. Those on their way to Mass are familiar with the call for forgiveness and readmittance. The call comes from a group of men about fifty yards away from the entrance of the church; they hope that they will someday be walking into the damp nave to hear of the forgiveness of God, rather than being outside members of the community of believers.

This tenth-century picture of Christendom may appear harsh and unchristian, but it does represent an important historical model of how Christians have responded to the reality of sin and violation within the church community.

North side of Chicago. It is Saturday night and people are lining up for confession; the year is 1954. A young man stands waiting for the confessional door to open, wondering what he should confess this week. Finally, an elderly woman slowly exits the booth and he moves into the small closet and sits down. The panel slides back and he begins, "Bless me, father, for I have sinned, it has been two weeks since my last confession. . . ." This scene, though unfamiliar to many non-Catholics as well as most contemporary

Catholics, is nonetheless preserved in the minds of Catholics who were adults before the sixties. It is also a scene preserved in many Hollywood depictions of Catholicism. Catholic Confession, as it is classically portrayed, involves an individual identifying his or her flaws in private, and the penance required of the individual remaining a secret between the penitent individual and the confessor.

These two scenes are like single frames taken out of a full-length movie. They reveal only a meager outline of the two models of reconciliation, which Catholic Christianity adopted throughout its history. Yet in spite of the simplicity of these pictures, they present the viewer with some important images. The Order of Penitents shows a community's response to sin in its midst. The response is one of ostracizing the sinner, while at the same time maintaining contact with the sinner and offering the outsider/penitent the opportunity to someday be readmitted. The Order of Penitents becomes the symbol of a flock of scapegoats, which never completely leave the community to roam in the wilderness, but instead linger, bleating for forgiveness and reconciliation. Sin cannot be condoned within the community, yet grace is an ever-present possibility.

The second scene is also an unfinished clip of the penitent in the process of reconciliation, yet this picture, in contrast to the first, emphasizes individuality, not community. The second frame is one that focuses on privacy, not public humiliation. The second also implies confidentiality, whereas the first offers no such solace for the sinner. Like the picture of the Order of Penitents, the young man in the confessional booth offers the onlooker of the post-feminist church insights and warnings: Beware of removing the violation from public view or you may create a system of corruption, collusion, and abuse! Martin Luther named this abuse, and yet it continues in a myriad of other forms. Don't forget that privacy and confidentiality should be respected, for the public is hungry for news of the latest scandal, and public confession is often more of a charade than a sign of a contrite heart. In this case as well, sin cannot be condoned, but grace flows weekly from the confessionals into the streets of cities and villages.

The reflections below are an attempt to clarify the importance of forgiveness and reconciliation in contemporary church communities. I write as a white male raised in the Roman Catholic tradition. With all its flaws (and it has many related to gender and masculinity), the Roman Catholic tradition remains a rich resource that should be mined for its insights. I will show that the two primary models of reconciliation in the Catholic tradition offer warnings and guidelines for how men in the twenty-first century might take seriously the need to be involved in the journey of ongoing conversion, which the church, in its varied manifestations, attempts to call forth from its members.

The movement from a community-based understanding of reconciliation, the Order of Penitents, to an individual-based understanding of forgiveness, the private confession, parallels the movement of the patriarchalization of Christendom. As Christianity developed it became increasingly individualistic.[1] I would like to show that through the formation of the Catholic sacrament of reconciliation (Confession) and the Protestant rejection of the sacrament in favor of the personal relationship with Jesus and the altar call, the movement to a mechanistic and individualistic understanding of forgiveness has been foisted upon twentieth-century Christians with equally destructive, though very distinct, impacts on men and women. If we retrieve the example of the early Christian community and supplement it with a relational anthropology that has been emphasized by contemporary feminist theology, we will discover a means of re-enchanting and embracing reconciliation as a powerful ritual for contemporary male spirituality and ecclesial participation. As men in the twenty-first century, we often run the risk of taking the negative components of this model of violation and reconciliation instead of its positive components.

A History of Christian Models of Reconciliation

During the first five centuries of Christianity in and around the Mediterranean center of Rome, the penitential rite developed as a public display of contrition and responsibility connected to sin. The "Order of Penitents" developed as a group of "sinners" chosen by the Bishop to participate in public forms of penance. Once one was a member of the Order of Penitents, one remained so for life. There were substantial penalties that went along with one's entrance into this order. One was "barred for life from clerical service. In many churches, he was forbidden to marry, or if he was married, he was enjoined not to use his marital rights. In the civil society, access to public and honorable offices was closed to him" (Orsy 1978, 32). The severity of the penance imposed made it clear that this was to be an order for only a select few. Though everyone within the Christian community sinned, only a few individuals, involved in the most grievous cases, would be forced into the Order of Penitents by the bishop. One's conscription as a penitent was always a public affair. The repentance present in the Order of Penitents was referred to as "second repentance" in order to distinguish it from "first repentance," which was the repentance required of one prior to baptism.

We will discuss the dynamics of exclusion and reconciliation exemplified by the Order of Penitents as the Mediterranean model. The Mediterranean model has three primary elements. First, penance was communal throughout; the penitent was publicly claiming his sin and asking the community to assist him in his conversion.[2] The penitent was "re-conciled" when he received membership into the community after his separation. The term reconciliation comes from the Latin "to rejoin the *concilium.*" To *re-concile* meant to enter anew the community of faith. Therefore, reconciliation is linguistically a community-based term and is focused on this world and being a part of a community.[3] One can see parallels here to the prodigal son and the lost sheep/coin discourses in the Lukan community material (Luke 15). It is the very act of rejoining the community, a community that has aided in the process of claiming responsibility and making satisfaction, that one recognizes that reconciliation has finally occurred.[4]

The second aspect of the Mediterranean model is duration, the focus on time. There is a process to reconciling with the church community. One cannot confess one's sins and immediately find that one has been welcomed back into the community. The importance of duration is central to authentic reconciliation. It takes time to address the source of sin, to achieve satisfaction, and to be fully accepted by the community.

A third important feature of the Mediterranean model is the issue of permanence. The penitent will always be known as a member of the Order of Penitents. Once one joined the Order of Penitents, one could never completely erase that connection. One could fully rejoin the body of the church, but one could never remove the reality of being a penitent, just as one can never fully remove the scar tissue one receives from a very serious injury.[5]

These three characteristics of the Mediterranean rite may help in reconstructing reconciliation in reference to contemporary forms of violation. With a focus on *community, duration,* and *permanency,* we can now begin to see how the contrasting claims of the Irish Penitential Books offer moderation as well as some problematic tendencies. The Mediterranean and Irish, or Celtic, models collided most forcefully in the Middle Ages (Orsy 1978, 39). In the end, it was clear that the Irish rite would be the enduring form of the sacrament of reconciliation.

The Celtic Model

When Patrick arrived in Ireland, he came to a region that had never been a Roman colony, and so brought its own customs and practices to the table as it became a Christian land. There remained a pagan sensibility in the Irish people that could be contrasted with the cultural hegemony of the

Roman colonies. The Roman world had been the evangelical soil of the first five centuries of Christendom. It was in the fifth century that Patrick traveled to the Irish society, finding many small kingdoms that were primarily tribal in nature (Connolly 1995, 3). The religious culture that Patrick encountered in Ireland was referred to as Druidism. The Druids, prophetic men and women, filled many roles in Celtic society, from historian to teacher and physician to prophet.[6]

The monks would be able to enter into the Celtic society because they functioned like the Druids in many ways. The monks did not have an immediate responsibility to the bishop or the pope. The monks often lived in small communities eking out a living, as did the people of the Irish countryside. The way the Irish monks would come to address issues of sin and reconciliation offered a markedly different vision than that of the Mediterranean model of the Order of Penitents. The monks were to overcome sin and failure through confronting and naming their weaknesses. Many of the monks who wrote the penitential manuals maintained an understanding of sin in medicinal terms. As a sickness, sin was not an issue which could be solved one time and therefore be eliminated for life; instead sin was to be addressed regularly, as one needed to be constantly aware of one's health. "To do this, however, the vice, which was the root of the cause of the sickness, would have to be correctly identified and diagnosed. The young monk was obliged throughout his life to make full and regular confession of his faults, whether in thought or in deed" (Connolly 1995, 14).

The laity would eventually use the monastic life of consistent naming and confessing as their model of the penitent life. The focus on individuality and one-to-one encounter in which one regularly confesses one's sins is a very important revision. The regularity of confession in the Irish world can be seen in the saying: "As the floor is swept everyday, so is the soul cleansed everyday by confession" (Connolly 1995, 15).

There are three characteristics of the Celtic model of penance. First, penance has no public character. The Order of Penitents did not exist in Ireland, nor was there a sense of public accountability of shame. There was no group to join or community to be a part of; instead the individual penitent was given an individualized set of activities to be accomplished before absolution of sins would take place. Second, the reconciliation or healing was private rather than public. Confession and reconciliation occurred in private after all or a portion of the exercises demanded had been achieved. Third, the process of contrition, confession, satisfaction, and absolution was repeated regularly, usually weekly, but sometimes as often as daily.

The Celtic system confronted the Mediterranean system in the sixth century, and the conflict continued through almost five centuries of the church's history. The disputes centered on the main characteristics of each system, which we have outlined above: community, duration, and permanency in the Mediterranean model, and individuality, privacy, and repeatability in the Celtic practice. There was a central claim to the necessity of addressing the reality of violation and the need for healing in both systems, but the means by which these were achieved varied considerably and created the conflict within the evolving church.

These two systems offer insight into the ways in which violation can be addressed and healed in a meaningful way, but they also offer warnings for how attempts to reconcile can be perverted and corrupted. We will now turn to a contemporary example of violation, and the ways in which the models above can be used to clarify the common distortions of the process of forgiveness. The example will also offer a practical guide to the potential for healing within the context of a church community.

Multiple Violations in the Web of Relationality

The red numbers on the clock, which sat on the bed stand, read 2:14 as Jason entered the bedroom. His clothes smelled of smoke from the Green Lantern Inn, which he had left two hours ago with a woman named Susan. At her apartment they had sex. Sex was the best way to describe the actions that occurred, since love seemed to have little to do with it for either Susan or Jason. Jason looked over at his wife Diane as he peeled off his shirt and crawled into bed. Diane woke and turned to him, "Jeremy's teacher called. She wants us to come in to meet her. She says Jeremy is harassing other students and failing three subjects." Nothing more is said; Diane rolls over and pretends to go back to sleep.

Jason is not an aberration. He has had an affair; estimates claim that over half of married men have an affair at some point during their marriage.[7] He is also verbally and physically abusive to his son Jeremy. His wife Diane is scared of her husband. Though he has never hit her, he often threatens to do so and has grabbed her by the arm on several occasions. Domestic violence and the use of threats and intimidation are also more common than we would hope.[8] Jason and his family attend church regularly, and many of his friends and fellow parishioners suspect abuse and neglect, but no one wants to say anything, because they "don't want to pry," and "it really isn't any of their business."

Jason's case raises issues central to this essay. In situations where men are abusive and neglectful, the response of the church community tends to fall into one of two areas. The first is to avoid any recognition of the problem, and the second is to demonize the perpetrator. People avoid the situation by minimizing, denying, and blaming.[9] Friends often minimize the behavior by assuring themselves that whatever is going on is "not that bad" and that it will surely improve soon. They would rather not see, so they deny all the signs and the subtle requests for intervention. Instead of confronting the perpetrator of violence, there is a tendency to blame the victims. For example, if his son would just focus on school, then Jason wouldn't have to be so tough on him: "You have to keep kids in line somehow." Or, "Work is really tough for Jason right now; he is under a lot of pressure." Minimizing, denying, and blaming function together as a set of responses which avoids any action on the part of the church community. Avoidance harms both the victims and the perpetrators and slowly erodes the foundation of the church community.

A second set of responses, which falls on the opposite extreme, involves gossiping, demonizing, and destroying. These behaviors lead to community action, but the goal of the action, which appears to be justice and the protection of the victims, is actually a means of avoiding responsibility and placating a need for vengeance. This set of behaviors often begins with members of the community talking about Jason and his family in private and forming a consensus on how horribly Jason is behaving. After the consensus is formed, there is often a period in which the perpetrator is increasingly viewed through the lens of distrust, disappointment, and disgust. The demonization of the perpetrator, Jason in this case, occurs through a process of building up evidence about how horrible he has been to his wife and child. Once Jason has done enough to fully justify his status as an evil man, the community can justify its desire to ostracize, destroy, and remove Jason from the community. Out of a sense of justice, the community works to remove Jason from the community. This may or may not involve the criminal justice system. Sometimes it is only a matter of making public the sins of the family. In some of the most disturbing reactions by the church community, the family members are told that they must leave the abusive partner, and if they refuse to leave, they are blamed for any future problems. In the end, the entire family unit is sometimes ostracized from the community. The community wants to punish Jason and remove the ugliness that he has brought into the community, even if this requires the elimination of the entire family.

Both sets of behaviors described above fail to address the fundamental issues with which the community should be concerned: safety, edification, and healing. Safety, edification, and healing represent the goal established in almost every religious tradition and specifically within the Judeo-Christian tradition. Safety of the victims is an essential first step in any communal response to violence and violation. Edification of all members involved in the violation involves the complex task of discovering what is going to enhance the well-being of each individual, while at the same time recognizing that each individual functions within a set of relationships that are mutually interdependent. Healing of the individuals as well as the relationships is the goal of building the kingdom of God on earth. In some situations, relationships cannot be healed, but the goal of healing must never be abandoned by the church community.

Both the avoidance complex and the demonizing complex represent failures on the part of the church community to embrace the power of the symbols of forgiveness and reconciliation. Avoidance behaviors of minimizing, denying, and blaming have similarities to the Irish confessional tradition in that they attempt to hide the sin away from the community. This usually perverts the goal of confidentiality, which is to protect the perpetrator from the tendency of the community to demonize him or her. But by failing to claim the violations within a community-based context of respect, responsibility, and support, the community ignores the reality of the violations that occur to all the relationships involved, especially the intimate relationships within the family. The second complex, which demonizes the perpetrator, is similar to the Order of Penitents in its desire to have a person or persons who represent evil for the community. By naming the evil and pushing it out of the community, the members of the church feel clean and pure. This vicarious healing through ostracizing is similar to the scapegoat used in classical Jewish healing, though in this case it is a member of the community who functions as the scapegoat. As in the Order of Penitents, once the perpetrator is identified, a further infraction calls for the permanent removal from the community and carries the equivalent of damnation in the minds of many members of the church.

The question now must be raised, what is the alternative to these two modes of addressing violation? I believe it lies in a relational understanding of the self and a focus on the healing power present in each of the traditional responses to sin. Over the last three decades, feminist thinkers in various disciplines have introduced the importance of relationality as a primary component to understanding what it means to be human.[10] Feminist theologians have shown that there has been an overemphasis on the individual in Christian theology during the last two thousand years. It is the individual who is saved. It is the individual who sins and must seek forgiveness. Individuality runs like a deep stream through most of the classical Christian symbols. This focus on individuality is not the only interpretation of these symbols, and it often runs counter to the Judaic roots of Jesus as well as the focus of the early Christian communities, yet it has ascended to the place of preeminence within the tradition. Feminists insist that the hermeneutical lens of relationality is one that returns certain themes and symbols of the Jesus movement to the center and pushes other themes, like personal salvation and redemption, to the periphery.[11] I wish to use these insights to pull out of the two classical models of reconciliation the key elements that can provide a community with the ability to heal. Even more importantly, these insights offer men the capacity to claim their own brokenness, responsibility, and place within a caring community.

A Relational Response and the Interconnection of Men

Carol Gilligan, in her classic work on moral development, *In a Different Voice*, claims that the focus of women in making moral decisions is the web of relationships that will be affected by these decisions. She contrasts this to a justice-based ethic found within traditionally male ethics, which turns to an established rule or norm to assess the justice of an action. As complex as the rule might be, Gilligan maintains that an ethic of care, which focuses on the relationships involved, alters the decision-making process and guides women to different assessments of the morally appropriate action to be taken.

If we return to the story of Jason and examine it through a relational lens, we discover that Jason's actions affect an almost endless list of relationships: his relationship with his wife, son, sex partner, his son's teacher, his son's friends, his wife's friends, his friends, members of his church community, his pastor, his coworkers, his wife's coworkers, and so forth. This list goes on and on, and though the relationships become increasingly distant, they remain affected by his actions. In physics, this type of deep relationality is discussed in terms of the butterfly effect. Systems that are highly dependent on initial conditions can have radically different outcomes based on the smallest of changes within the system. Thus some scientists have claimed that a butterfly flapping its wings in Hawaii may contribute to a thunderstorm in Iowa (Young 1996). The sensitivity of relational systems is not simple; in fact, there is no way of measuring the multitude of ways in which a family system, a church community, or a school may be affected by the behaviors of one person. It is possible that Jason's choice to demean his son on a regular basis may create a situation in which his son Jeremy no longer feels he can perform well in school. His son Jeremy becomes increasingly disruptive in class, which causes two other children who were having difficulty with their ability to read to fall further behind their peers. The inability to read well may influence them the rest of their lives. There is clearly no cause-and-effect situation when it comes to human behavior, but we fail ourselves and those around us when we dismiss as unimportant the depth of the relationships in which we are always already enmeshed.[12]

What can we pull from the two classical models of reconciliation that can offer us a relational response to violations that avoids the negative tendencies of avoidance and demonizing? First, we should recognize the importance of a community devoted to the well-being of all its members. If a community is committed to the possibility of *metanoia* (conversion) of the individual who is harming the web, one takes an important first step toward the healing of the community as a whole. The problem is that even this language betrays an individualistic tendency, which has a place, but should not be overemphasized. It is Jason who has emotionally and physically abused his son, and Jason who has slept with a woman other than his wife, and Jason who intimidates his wife as a form of manipulation. If the community around Jason is going to try to heal all of the wounded relationships, it must not isolate and demonize Jason. At the same time, it must hold Jason responsible for his actions. This is one of the primary philosophical difficulties facing feminist anthropologies; they want responsibility and relationality at the same time.[13] Relationality implies complex causation, and responsibility implies the ability to identify the party who caused the violation and hold him or her responsible. It is easier to claim that one has found the problem, and eliminate it. As we have shown above, this is one of the distortions of the desire for justice. Demonizing leads to a scapegoating that does not address the complexity of relationships. Diane may want or need to be separated from her husband Jason, but she also may want to have a healthy supportive relationship with Jason. Jeremy may hate his father, but at the same time, there may be nothing more that Jeremy wants than for his father to appreciate him and love him. Ostracizing Jason does not heal the wounds that Diane and Jeremy suffer. And, at the same time, Jason may need to be separated from Jeremy and Diane, but not separated from a community that supports him while still holding him responsible.

Here we must raise two of the most important insights found in the Mediterranean rite: duration and community. The Mediterranean rite recognizes that healing takes time and that the community must be supportive of the penitent. If Jason is forced to claim publicly the ways in which he has harmed his wife Diane and his son Jeremy, while simultaneously knowing that he will be supported by the community in his attempts to change his behavior, he may be more willing and able to do the difficult work of self-transformation and accountability. The church community must embrace those who violate others among us and not ostracize them. Models for this kind of behavior can be found in Alcoholics Anonymous groups and other twelve-step programs. They can also be found in the work on reconciliation being done in South Africa. Therapists who work within a family systems approach use this model as well. In all of these varied circumstances, it is becoming increasingly clear that societies and groups that work with the perpetrators develop more long-lasting healing than those that either demonize the perpetrator or ignore the violation.

The Irish rite also offers valuable insight for responsible healing. It is important to remember that the idealistic view I have addressed above of a community filled with support is rarely the case for an entire church community. More often than not the community falls into the habit of demonizing. For this reason, the ancient church saw private individual confessions as preferable to the public displays of condemnation into which the Mediterranean rite often dissolved. It may be necessary to form an intermediary group, which takes on the responsibility of holding the violator responsible and at the same time supporting him or her. Again one finds similarities to the twelve-step programs. The problem with the twelve-step program as the model program is that these programs require all the members of the group to have a shared experience of being an alcoholic, a drug addict, or an adult child of an addict. The church community must be able to embrace and promote these groups, while at the same time taking on the challenge of healing the wounds of members within the church community who do not fall into narrow definitions of preestablished national groups.

My fundamental conclusions are that forgiveness and reconciliation should involve the entire community as a supportive base. Men within the community need to hold other men responsible for their behaviors without demonizing them. Privacy and confidentiality should remain a hallmark of the reconciling community, but it should not be a privacy that allows for denial of responsibility. Instead, it should be a confidentiality that lives out of the respect for the lives of the violated as well as the violator. At times the violations must involve the criminal justice system, but when this occurs it calls for an equally intense prison ministry by the church community. The criminal justice system is often dehumanizing. The answer is not to protect criminal behavior from public scrutiny but to reform the criminal justice system so that it moves more and more toward a model of restorative justice instead of retributive justice.

A church community should be respectful of the members within its community who are violating others, but never allow the respect for the violator to deny safety and respect for the victims. Men must take a leadership role alongside women, calling for accountability without demonizing. We all share the gifts of God's grace, and we are the instruments of this grace. Grace involves forgiveness as well as the creation of right relation where relationships have been violated. Men will become agents of grace within their homes and their church communities as they continue to develop a sense of interconnectedness and realize that Martin Luther King Jr. was right in his powerful statement from Birmingham Jail:

> We are caught in an inescapable network of mutuality,
> Tied in a single garment of destiny. (King 1985, 431)

Bibliography

Anderson, Megory, and Philip Culbertson. October 1986. "The Inadequacy of the Christian Doctrine of Atonement in Light of Levitical Sin Offering." *Anglican Theological* Review 68:4, 303–28.

Connolly, Hugh. 1995. *The Irish Penitentials: And Their Significance for the Sacrament of Penance Today*. Portland: Four Courts.

Cooper-White, Pamela. 1995. *The Cry of Tamar: Violence against Women and the Church's Response*. Minneapolis: Fortress Press.

Duluth Curriculum for Batterers, available at Domestic Abuse Intervention Project, Duluth, MN, 55806.

Dutton, Donald. 1995. *The Domestic Assault of Women: Psychological and Criminal Justice Perspectives*. Vancouver: Univ. of British Columbia Press.

Federal Bureau of Investigation Web site: <http://www.fbi.gov>.

Fisher, Helen E. 1992. *Anatomy of Love: The Natural History of Monogamy, Adultery, and Divorce*. New York: W. W. Norton.

Gilligan, Carol. 1982. *In a Different Voice: Psychological Theory and Women's Development.* Cambridge, Mass.: Harvard Univ. Press.

King, Martin Luther, Jr. 1985. "Letter from Birmingham Jail." *Afro-American Religious History: A Documentary Witness.* Ed. Milton C. Sernett. Durham: Duke Univ. Press. 430–45.

Omerod, Paul. 1998. *Butterfly Economics: A New Theory of Social and Economic Behavior.* New York: Random House.

Orsy, Ladislas. 1978. *The Evolving Church and the Sacrament of Penance.* Denville, N.J.: Dimensions.

Ruether, Rosemary. 1983. *Sexism and God Talk: Toward a Feminist Theology.* Boston: Beacon.

Sands, Kathleen. 1994. *Escape from Paradise: Evil and Tragedy in Feminist Theology.* Minneapolis: Fortress Press.

Schneider, Laurel. 1998. *Reimagining the Divine: Confronting the Backlash against Feminist Theology.* Cleveland: Pilgrim.

Young, Karl. 1996. "Deterministic Chaos and Quantum Chaology." *Religion and Science: History, Method and Dialogue.* Ed. Mark W. Richardson and Wesley J. Wildman. New York: Routledge. 227–42.

Notes

1. The gradual transformation and multiple influences on this transition to an individualistic anthropology (sense of self) are too complex to explore in any detail. In spite of this complexity, one sees this turn away from communal accountability in Protestant individualism, Enlightenment Deism, and the Catholic turn to the individual's soul and its journey through purgatory and on to union with the divine. Some of this has been traced out in Ruether.

2. I use the masculine pronoun here exclusively because men were the people involved in the Order of Penitents. This was the case almost without exception because of the role of women in the Western Christian society of the time.

3. An excellent discussion of the communal aspect of the term reconciliation, especially as it is connected to domestic violence, can be found in Cooper-White 1995, 261–62.

4. It is important to note here the connections to the way in which the Judaic tradition understood atonement as a communal process. Judaic use of sacrifices and scapegoats to atone for sin necessitated the action of the sinner in some form of repaying of the debt to the person violated. This is also true of the Catholic ritual of reconciliation, which involves four steps: contrition, confession, satisfaction, and absolution. The Judaic process, most notably seen in the Yom Kippur service, is important as a foundation for understanding the issues present in Christian

attempts to make sense of sin and forgiveness. See Anderson and Culbertson (1986).

5. Though there may be some controversy surrounding any desire to permanently mark certain people as perpetrators or penitents, this issue is one that merits careful attention by the church. If one were found to be a pedophile, rapist, or batterer, the social-scientific research would enjoin us to recognize that these situations are not aspects of our personalities that are easily discarded or changed.

6. The Druids' doctrinal system was threefold in structure: "Three rules had to be adhered to in order to insure harmony between mortals and the divine: (a) Adore God; (b) Do no wrong to anyone; (c) Act justly toward everyone. Similarly, Druids shared three great fears: offending God; contravening the love of another; unduly accumulating riches" (Connolly 1995, 3).

7. Though there will never be definitive figures on the number of extramarital affairs, there are several studies that suggest a figure between 40 percent and 70 percent. See the discussion of recent studies on marital infidelity in Fisher 1992, 84–87.

8. There are many good studies on the prevalence of domestic violence; one important work is Dutton (1995). For current statistics, consult the Federal Bureau of Investigation's Web site: < http://www.fbi.gov>.

9. A complete discussion of the use of behaviors used by abusive men can be found in the Duluth Curriculum for Batterers.

10. There are many feminist theologians who have contributed to this thesis, including Rosemary Radford Ruether, Elizabeth Johnson, Rita Nakashima Brock, and Marjorie Hewitt Suchocki. It is also important to note that this focus is also present in classical claims about humanity. One finds recognition of the fundamental role of community life in Plato's *Republic,* the Hebrew claim of a covenant people, and the monastic traditions of Christianity. Contemporary examples include Martin Luther King's "Letter from Birmingham Jail." These examples do not alter the importance of the new emphasis added by feminist thinkers.

11. Note Ruether's discussion of the major Christian symbols in her *Sexism and God Talk* (1983).

12. In his new book, Paul Omerod has made an argument for chaos and complexity theories helping to understand equally nuanced and relational issues.

13. Nonfoundationalist metaphysics, as well as the challenges of postmodern thinking combined with the ethical mandates of feminism, have presented contemporary feminist thinkers with serious philosophical difficulties. These difficulties are being addressed by several young feminist theologians. Two important new books that struggle with this issue are Sands (1994) and Schneider (1998).

5

Don Quixote as Moral Narcissist: Implications for Mid-Career Male Ministers

Donald Capps

In *Myths of Modern Individualism* (1996), Ian Watt focuses on the emergence of "a new type of self" in sixteenth-century Europe, one attributable to the Renaissance emphasis on individuality and the Protestant emphasis on one's responsibility for one's own salvation (that is, "work out your own salvation with fear and trembling"). According to Watt, Protestantism and the Catholic Counter-Reformation both emphasized the price one will pay for developing one's individuality, for living according to one's own wants and desires. These movements warned that it is altogether possible that one will have to pay for such individuality with one's very soul.

Watt explores the three myths of modern individualism that were created within this crucible of Renaissance liberation (on the one hand) and Protestant-Catholic caution (on the other). These myths center around the figures who personified them, including Faust (1587), Don Quixote (1605), and Don Juan (c. 1620). A fourth myth, that of Robinson Crusoe (1719), shares certain commonalities with the other three, but emerged in a different era. Significantly, the earlier three reappeared in nineteenth-century Romanticism, and were recreated as far more admirable, even heroic, than in their earlier representations.

The three myths of Faust, Don Quixote, and Don Juan may appear to have little if any bearing on the life and career of the very late twentieth-century pastor. The goal of this essay is to show that they are, in fact, very relevant. As my discussion unfolds, it will become evident that I am especially interested in the Don Quixote myth, particularly for its relevance to the struggles of the mid-career (which usually means middle-aged) minister.

Two observations at the outset: First, it should be noted that all three myths involve males. This being the case, I cannot in all honesty claim that they have direct relevance for women ministers. My hope, however, is that this will not be reason alone for women to avoid reading this essay, for inasmuch as women ministers are often affected by the decisions of their male colleagues, it can be quite useful to know why these men do what they do, and especially why they do things that women find odd, puzzling, exasperating, or downright reprehensible. This essay, in other words, is not written in a spirit of male exclusivism, much less triumphalism, but is instead an attempt to take an honest, searching look at the male pastor, especially in light of the myths that he, for the most part unconsciously, lives by.

Second, the very fact that I am taking these myths of "modern individualism" seriously may seem odd to most readers, if not perverse. The enormous influence of Robert N. Bellah's *Habits of the Heart: Individualism and Commitment in American Life* (1985) has created a climate in which "individualism" is viewed as the most serious threat that churches face in our times. If one picks up virtually any issue of *The Christian Century*, for example, one will find at least one, often more, articles that use "individualism" (often with the adjective "rampant" attached) to explain why churches are in decline and why such-and-such social problem exists. Individualism has taken the place formerly ascribed to racism, classism, and sexism—to name only a few—as the primary evil facing churches in our day.

I have discussed this tendency to scapegoat individualism in another context (Capps 1993b) and will not repeat that discussion here. I will simply note that whatever one may think, pro, con, or some of both, about individualism, it helps to know what one is talking about when one uses the term. Watt's book is especially helpful in identifying the early origins of individualism, enabling one to appreciate that it is a long-standing cultural influence and is associated, in a complex way, with the emergence of Protestantism in the sixteenth century.

The argument that I wish to make here is that the young male minister lives out the Faustian myth for the first twenty to twenty-five years of his ministerial career, and then, in mid-career, is faced with a critical decision between the two remaining myths, that of Don Juan or Don Quixote, to guide his subsequent career. I assume, however, that even as the Faustian myth is dominant in the early years of his career, one or the other of the other myths is already present, influencing the way in which the Faust myth is carried out. Its emergence in mid-career is therefore not unanticipated.

In light of what I have already written on the problem of clergy sexual misconduct (Capps 1993a, 1997b), my advocacy of Don Quixote over Don Juan should come as no surprise to the reader. What may cause surprise, and requires justification, is that I would advocate for Don Quixote. I do so, however, on the grounds that one does not have many options if one intends (unlike Robinson Crusoe) to live in the "real world" and make the best of what may appear to have been a rather bad, or at least ambiguous, bargain. I suggest that with the Don Quixote option there is hope, and where there is hope, there is reason to get up in the morning and greet the new day with at least some amount of anticipation and maybe even a trace of enthusiasm.

The Myth of Faust

The Faust myth, based on an actual historical figure, Dr. George Faust of Heidelberg, was created and popularized by Johann Spies, whose *Faustbuch* appeared in 1587, and by Christopher Marlowe, whose *Doctor Faustus* was written in 1592, one year prior to his violent death. It was later revived by Johann Wolfgang von Goethe, who worked on his *Faust: A Tragedy* off and on for sixty years. He completed Part 2 in 1831 and it was published posthumously the following year. The myth reappeared in the twentieth century in Thomas Mann's *Doctor Faustus*, published in 1947.

Watt discusses the Faust myth in considerable detail. Here, I will briefly identify the major characteristics of the sixteenth- and nineteenth-century versions. In its earlier form, these included:

1. The excitement of going beyond the current limits of knowledge. Marlowe's Faust is a genuine intellectual.
2. The exercise of free choice insofar as career is concerned. Marlowe's Faust is not forced into a career he doesn't want. He becomes a scientist.
3. His education raises expectations that cannot be realized. As a young man in his twenties, he realizes that the future looming before him is either a demeaning job or dependence on a patron for his livelihood. Thus, he is caught between high expectations for himself and chilling disillusionment.
4. There is not enough time to realize his career objectives if he is going to be tied down to social obligations, such as the struggle to make a living, marriage and family obligations, and so forth.

The only solution to his problems as reflected in three and four, what Watt calls "the hell of the real world," is some kind of magic. This is realized through a pact with Lucifer. He gets exactly twenty-four years to be what he wants to be, and then Lucifer is rewarded with his soul in perpetual damnation. Watt calls this "the solitary ego against time." He also notes that Faust does not commit any crimes but is punished for wanting to meet expectations that he does not consider unreasonable. Thus, in Watt's view, Faust was individualism's scapegoat: "During a period of great ideological tension he became the symbolic figure upon whom were projected the fears of the anarchic and individualistic tendencies of the Renaissance and the Reformation; his damnation was the Counter-Reformation's attempt to anathematize the hopes that a more optimistic generation had cherished and that history had disappointed" (Watt 1996, 46).

Goethe's nineteenth-century Faust is depressed over his career. He has grown weary of the old refrain, "You must do without." So he enters into a pact with Mephistopheles. But, unlike the earlier sixteenth-century version, he escapes, for the heavenly angels carry off his soul before Mephistopheles can get hold of him. In Goethe's Faust, however, we get some idea of what is both positive and negative about Faustian individuation. The negative features are: (1) he is free of family constraints (only his father is briefly mentioned) but has no lasting personal relationships; (2) he travels widely but is unable to settle down; (3) he has little interest in religion, and unlike the original Faust, the threat of the loss of his soul does not concern him; and (4) while he affirms democratic beliefs he does not live by them, but is autocratic in his interpersonal dealings. The more positive features are: (1) he continues to search for some kind of happiness; (2) he rarely admits to defeat or discouragement, but keeps trying; and (3) he thinks like a pessimist but acts like an optimist. The paradox of this romantic form of Faustian individualism is that he is restless, in a kind of perpetual motion, and this restlessness of spirit is both his weakness and his strength. As Watt puts it, his individualism is "a ceaseless and active search for experience, for the deed; he knows there is no final peace in sight, and apparently welcomes this sad fact" (Watt 1996, 206–7). His punishment is not the loss of his soul but the fact that all his effort seems to get him nowhere in particular. What is all this striving for? What is the goal? He doesn't know and no one else seems to either.

Mann's twentieth-century Faust is a faint shadow of the sixteenth and nineteenth-century Fausts. He is aloof to the point of offensiveness, he is entirely self-absorbed, he is irritatingly dogmatic, and he pays for his narcissism by contracting venereal disease and living the final ten years of his life as a vegetable. While this version of the Faust myth provides opponents of modern individualism with all the ammunition they could possibly need, it fails to register the inherent paradoxes of Faustian individualism, its strengths as well as its weaknesses.

As I have suggested, I view male ministers as essentially Faustian in the first two or so decades of their careers. I do not mean to imply that they have literally entered into a pact with the devil for which they must subsequently pay, but that they exhibit many of the characteristics of the Faustian character in both its sixteenth and nineteenth-century forms. Like the sixteenth-century Faust, the minister is typically an intellectual (three or more years of graduate study make him so), he has chosen the ministry (and has not been forced to become one by parents, economic circumstances, lack of other career options, and the like; his "call" is also deeply personal); he has high expectations that are, at some juncture in the course of the next two decades, usually earlier than later, subjected to significant disillusionment; and he experiences a constant struggle between career responsibilities and familial obligations. Additionally, he manifests all of the more positive features of the nineteenth-century Faust and some of the negative ones. He seeks happiness in and through his work, he rarely admits defeat, and, while prone to pessimistic thoughts, always acts like an optimist. While it may be questioned whether these are actually positive traits, for, after all, they may well be the perfect prescription for burnout or worse, these traits are, in fact, valued by those for whom he works and are likely to be both rewarded and, for the most part, rewarding.

The negative features are part of his profile as well. True, he is not free of family constraints, but he is likely not to have lasting personal friendships. He is usually thinking about moving on and has a restlessness of spirit about him, which, while suggesting adaptability, may also contain an element of avoidance and escapism. He affirms democratic processes and values, but, frustrated by the inaction of the laity, is often sorely tempted to act autocratically, and sometimes succumbs to this temptation. While it appears that he has great interest in religion, it is often the case that he has gotten rather weary of religion over the years, as it is too much a part of his everyday reality, and he often seeks refuge in other interests and envies men who are in other professions. By and large, he has long since ceased worrying about the fate of his soul, either because he doubts that he, as a minister, could ever lose it (if anyone has been working out his salvation with fear and trembling, surely he has), or because the issue of his soul has been demystified by virtue of his certified insider status, as one who knows how religion works, an expert practitioner of its inner workings. Soul matters, but he is certainly not worried to death over it.

In my view, the key features of Faustian men are the following three. They may not apply uniformly to the young male minister, but to the extent that he can identify himself, now or later, as fitting the profile, he is, like it or not, a Faustian individualist:

1. As a Faustian, the man lives with a deep, usually unarticulated, sense that he is a condemned man. He has committed no great crime, but to the extent that his early years have been reasonably successful, he does not have any great confidence that this will last, and is, in fact, prepared for a major downturn in his prospects in his middle-to-late career, a situation from which only retirement will bring relief. Even if his situation does not deteriorate in his later career, the commitments of his early years are a shackle from which he knows no freedom. The future, by and large, is not a happy prospect.

2. As a Faustian, the man is actually well-adapted to "postmodern" society because his inherent restlessness coheres with the ever-changing face of society. But because the myth of Faust is modern, not postmodern, the Faustian man does not feel right about his restlessness, and cannot unreservedly throw himself into a post-modern society, for to do so would make him feel tremendously guilty. He is restless, but he tells himself that he ought not to be, that he should be satisfied with where he is now and able to love what he already has, not lusting for the new and the novel.

3. As a Faustian, the man is ever-optimistic and rarely admits to discouragement or defeat. A crushing defeat is viewed as a temporary setback. Others know that he can be counted upon to continue his search for happiness, his drive for adulation, or whatever his personal goal may be, and they often exploit this knowledge by taking advantage of him. His optimism thus becomes the basis of his vulnerability, as others know that he will never give up, no matter how many difficulties or obstacles are put in his path. He is a romantic in this regard, and a romantic can easily be played for a sucker.

While viewing male ministers as Faustian may seem to place them in an unnecessarily negative, even pejorative light, this nonetheless enables us to identify at least some of the grounds for the mid-career crisis that many ministers experience when, in effect, their whole life begins to feel very much like a pact with the devil. Of course, there are many ministers for whom such a crisis never occurs, and many others for whom it is brief, quickly surmounted, and readily forgotten. I am not, however, writing this essay for them, but for those for whom the Faustian myth hits uncomfortably close to home and captures some pervasive, even deep and troubling perceptions and feelings.

But now I want to complicate the picture and suggest that, if Faust is, as it were, the master myth within which most male ministers live their lives, at least for the first two decades, the Don Juan and Don Quixote myths represent subtypes of this master myth. Thus, like a zoom-lens camera, they enable us to further delineate the profile, to identify more adequately the personal differences within it, and to explain how, at mid-career, ministers who appeared to be quite similar to one another in the beginning take very divergent paths. As noted earlier, I believe that the two options for the male minister at mid-career are either the myth of Don Juan or the myth of Don Quixote. This prospect may itself be disheartening, for most of us would like to believe that we might, at some point in our careers, do without myths altogether, and begin to live out our lives in the bright light of reality, realizing how things really and truly are, not just how they may seem to be.

On this point, however, I want to register a strong cautionary note. In *The Psychology of Adaptation to Absurdity: Tactics of Make-Believe* (1993), Seymour and Rhoda L. Fisher cite several research studies showing that contrary to popular belief, depressed individuals are more realistic than nondepressives in a number of respects. For example, they are more realistic in areas of perceived control over external circumstances, in appraisals of one's own social behavior, and in response to catastrophic threat. The Fishers conclude that those who are non-depressed surround themselves with "an illusory glow," that whereas "depressives' thoughts are painfully truthful," nondepressives are "unrealistically positive" (Fisher and Fisher 1993, 8). They argue that our sense of well-being seems to require that we develop a repertoire of defenses against the reality of the situation in which we find ourselves, that we need to believe that things are better than they are, and that in order to get through life, we need to develop the capacity to shut out awareness of the unpleasant and to be "opportunistically obtuse and simple-minded" (196). They cite the adaptive uses of pretense, which has its origins in early childhood, enabling one to cope with otherwise overwhelming or debilitating anxieties and fears.

In other words, we need our myths and, as I now want to argue, to the extent that one can choose the myth he lives by, the myth of Don Quixote is to be preferred to the myth of Don Juan as one undergoes further individuation in mid-career (on the issue of individuation, see Levinson et al. 1978, 209–44). This is not to say that the myth of Don Quixote is all sweetness and light. As we will see, it has its obvious and not so obvious downsides. But one purpose of this essay is to alert the reader to these very features of the myth, so that in being aware of them, he can minimize the deleterious effects both on himself and on those involved in his particular enactment of the myth.

The Myth of Don Juan

Why favor Don Quixote over Don Juan? In spite of the fact that Don Juan is the prototypical philanderer (see Pittman 1993, 32), we should not dismiss the myth out of hand. It was initially created by the Spanish monk, Fray Gabriel Tellez, in his early seventeenth-century play, *The Trickster of Seville and His Guest of Stone*, and was further developed in the nineteenth century by Molière, Mozart, Byron, and Zorilla. Ian Watt's description of the original seventeenth-century Don Juan indicates that he possessed an extreme individualism characterized by an "antonimian egocentricity," a "conscious strategy of deferred moral responsibility," "not the faintest indication that he feels any qualms of conscience for the sufferings he causes," and "total imperviousness to the impact of his actions on other people" (Watt 1996, 108–12, 117).

In the nineteenth-century portrayals, he is less subject to retributory justice for his crimes, including his exploitation of women, but the central tenets of his character remain unchanged. He "always declines to commit himself convincingly," he is "patently insincere," he exhibits a hypocrisy of "professed belief and actual skepticism," and betrays an "internal void" (Watt 1996, 209–10, 212). And yet, Kierkegaard praises Mozart's opera, *Don Juan*, for its portrayal of "the energy of sensual desire"; and Byron, in his poem *Don Juan*, turns the traditional story inside out, making Don Juan the *object* of female seduction, the innocent boy who is used by aggressive women (211–13). Moreover, in Zorilla's play, he actually falls in love and is thereby redeemed. Yet, even in these more appreciative portrayals, he remains highly egocentric and, in Watt's view, Zorilla's redemption of his hero is "implausible," as it undercuts the moral force of the original ending with "romantic pieties" (218).

A more nuanced view than Watt's, however, is offered by James N. Lapsley's essay on the Don Juan of the Mozart opera (1995), focusing on the rise of charm as a virtue. While emphasizing that Don Juan's charm may be, for us today, a stand-in for the traditional virtues that seem to be in abeyance, Lapsley makes a qualified case for the virtue (or "pseudo-virtue") of charm, noting our "need for charm and its soothing intimations of bliss as a legitimate part of our humanity in an age characterized by acerbity in public and private discourse" (Lapsley 1995, 329). What funds this need is the fact that charm has its origins in songs of enchantment, which possess the power to lull one into relaxing vigilance in sleep, and also has an alluring, attractive quality that may either be altogether benign or deeply sinister. Its very power to allure, however, reveals to us our own vulnerability and longing: "Perhaps this full acknowledgment of our vulnerability is the positive virtue we need to learn from Mozart," a teacher "whose metier is suffused with charm, thus making this hard lesson easy, but not to be confused with the lesson itself" (330). While Lapsley does not enthusiastically endorse the Don Juan figure himself, noting Don Juan's willingness and capacity to use his "compelling attractiveness to entrap his victims," he takes an appreciative view of the opera's "message" of the essential ambiguity of charm, one benefit of such ambiguity being that "modern audiences with predominantly narcissistic character structures" may thereby experience Don Juan "as an aggrandizing self-object, to use Heinz Kohut's term for another person experienced as a part of oneself" (328). That is, at least for some members of the audience, the opera affords self-recognition, and does so by representing Don Juan as much more than "a rather wicked seducer," for he also represents "the nurturing comforts" of charm.

As noted earlier, my moral concerns regarding clergy sexual misconduct prompt me toward an advocacy of Don Quixote over Don Juan, whose identification with sexual seduction is too central to the character to be overlooked. In this regard, I share Peggy Noonan's assessment (quoted by Lapsley) of President Clinton's character: "You can move a country with charm, you can use charm to achieve your purposes, but charm isn't a belief, it isn't a guide; it can't tell you where you want to go, it can only help you to get there" (Lapsley 1995, 329). Also, as we will see, Don Quixote is not lacking in sexual passion; the difference between him and Don Juan in this regard is that he has found a responsible, if ultimately tragic, way to sublimate it. In the distinction I employed in one of my essays on the subject of sexual misconduct (Capps 1997b), Don Quixote developed a tolerance for the nonfulfillment of sexual desire by holding it in limbo. *Limbo*, originally a religious term, was, in contrast to purgatory, the place for human beings not weighted down by any personal sin but only by original sin (for example, children who had died without benefit of baptism or righteous souls who predated Christ). For these, limbo was conceived as the bosom of Abraham, a place, like a mother's womb, of calm and tranquil peace. If Don Quixote more successfully sublimated his sexual desire than Don Juan, however, such sublimation was not without its difficulties. I do not, therefore, wish to uphold him as a perfect image for the mid-career pastor to emulate. I identify him, however, as an alternative to Don Juan, and as one who is not without a certain charm of his own, a charm owing to his rather attractive capacity to be "opportunistically obtuse and simpleminded," especially in his commitment to two-hundred-year-old chivalric ideals.

The Myth of Don Quixote

In exploring the uses of the Don Quixote myth for the mid-career minister, I will first focus on Watt's portrayal of Don Quixote and then introduce some further considerations—complications derived from psychoanalytic studies. Watt notes that, unlike Faust, Cervantes's *Don Quixote* (1995) was not based on an actual historical person. Cervantes's wife's uncle may have believed that the romances of chivalry were true, but identification of the hero of the story with an actual historical person is speculative at best. The basic premise of the story is that a poor *hidalgo*, a member of the lowest order of the Spanish nobility, who lives in an out-of-the-way province, La Mancha, has been reading books of chivalry until it becomes an obsession. So much so that, at an age "bordering on fifty," he hits upon the idea of making himself a knight-errant, roaming the world in full armor on horseback in quest of adventures. His goal is to right the wrongs suffered by the poor and the vulnerable, and he is inspired in his quest by Dulcinea, the lady of his imagination, who supports him in his battles and gives focus to his longings.

Watt suggests that any attempt to evaluate Cervantes's achievement in Don Quixote must begin with the apparent contradictions in the hero's character (Watt 1996, 69). First, there is the obvious fact of his madness, evident in the very idea that he takes romances seriously. But he is mad "only in the colloquial sense of 'crazy'; his behavior is markedly obsessive, but only in a defined and limited range of matters." As the narrator points out, "he only talked nonsense when he touched on chivalry, and in discussing all other subjects he showed that he had a clear and unbiased understanding" (70). Moreover, he seems, in Watt's view, "to negotiate a very fine balance between truth and his darling fictions" (70). He is even able, at times, to acknowledge that Dulcinea may be a creation of his imagination, confessing, for example, that "God only knows if the world does or does not contain anyone like Dulcinea, or whether she is or is not a mere phantasm, nor are these issues which can be settled with absolute certainty" (Cervantes 1995, 521). This confession, however, occurs late in the novel and cannot be separated from a general sense of disillusionment that has begun to overtake him, and will, by the end of the book, leave him in total skepticism about the whole knight-errancy business.

A second contradiction is that Don Quixote could and did fall short of the chivalric ideal of exemplary courage and selflessness: "He has some of the self-centeredness of a solitary old man, and this often makes him capricious and domineering" (Cervantes 1995, 72). Still, on the whole, he "has no more faults and weaknesses than are needed to make him seem real and human," and nowhere is his character "more convincing than in his fear of mockery," for those who engage in mockery "make the ordinary mental and social norms by which they live seem," by comparison, "dull, cautious, and selfish" (72). In effect, his folly *is* his charm, and it is highly contagious, for time and again, the reader is led to marvel at his capacity "to protect his delusions from the realities that would expose them," and identifies with him, hoping that he will triumph over reality. The reader even breathes a sigh of relief, not without envy, "when he succeeds, time and time again, in making everybody else play his own game merely by his obstinate refusal to play any other" (73). At the same time, "we find the narrator's mockery of Quixote gratifying, because it helps us acknowledge the feeble caution of our own irresolute attempts to live the life of our dreams" (73).

Watt also comments on Cervantes's brilliant device of creating a companion for Don Quixote in the form of Sancho Panza. Unlike Faust and Don Juan, Don Quixote and his squire, Sancho Panza, have become visual myths, embodying many of the contrasts between the ideas they represent—basic physical differences between thin and fat, tall and short, but also psychological polarities of spirit and flesh, brain and belly, dream and reality, the introvert and the extrovert, the solitary and the gregarious, the confirmed bachelor and the husband with children. They represent many of the dualities that comprise humanity as a whole, and reflect the inherent contradictions of the middle-aged male, with aspirations toward heroism or saintliness on the one hand, and instincts for self-preservation on the other. Significantly, the two men are not mere opposites, for in the course of their relationship, they adopt each other's traits: "The sad veracity of the whole third [and final] expedition, especially, can be seen as a dialectical process whereby Sancho's faith in his chivalric role slowly rises, while Quixote's assurance in it declines. . . . For, as the book proceeds, Sancho's thinking is more and more dominated by his role as squire; it becomes a second nature in which he finds more satisfaction than he had ever before experienced as a peasant farmer. But the change in Don Quixote is more ambiguous; it owes less to Sancho and more to the way in which his own increasing doubts about himself are reinforced by his failures" (Watt 1996, 78). What Quixote has done, in effect, is give Sancho a reason to believe in himself even as he himself is increasingly beset by self-doubt.

Watt acknowledges that the ending of the novel, with its account of Don Quixote's repentance for his folly and his death, has disappointed many of its readers, even as it leaves Sancho Panza heartbroken, trying to the end to rally his master's chivalric spirit, arguing that "the most foolish thing a man can do in this life is to let himself die without rhyme or reason, without anybody killing him or any hands but melancholy's doing him in" (Watt 1996, 81). But, disappointing as this ending may be, the reader cannot but be impressed by the subtle irony in Sancho's contention that accepting disillusionment and the melancholia this produces is the "most foolish thing" that Don Quixote could ever do. Does Cervantes himself share Sancho's pain at seeing his friend die, albeit in a perfectly lucid state, at the end of the novel? Watt suggests that this is very difficult to tell, for Cervantes distances himself from his hero by means of the device of a narrator who is identified as someone other than Cervantes himself. Yet, he "surely shared Don Quixote's nostalgia for the golden age and the heroic past, the triumph of good over evil, the exciting life over quotidian boredom, inspirational dream over everyday reality, madness over prudence" (89). Moreover, "the complexity of the narrative suggests that it was, perhaps, no more than a dream, or a game; but it answered the need to express how the association of values of a long-gone world with the rewards of human fellowship in a common purpose could endure even amid the insoluble contradictions and brutalities of their contemporary world. As the myth still does in ours" (89). The story is oddly inspirational in spite of its ending.

Watt discusses Romantic appropriations of the Quixote myth, noting that Johann Herder, a lifelong student of *Don Quixote*, was at first put off by Cervantes's mockery of his hero, but later came to appreciate Sancho Panza's realism, for Don Quixote is one of those relics of history "who are still riding in broad daylight without realizing that their hour is past" (Watt 1996, 221). While Herder was generally unsympathetic to Don Quixote because of his effort, as an isolated individual, to create order and stability for himself, without due regard for the established laws of state and society, most English, French, and German Romantic writers saw Don Quixote "as a pure and genuine fighter for social equality and for an ideal" (224; also Paulson 1998). In Dostoevsky's *The Idiot*, Don Quixote lives in the person of Myshkin, who, despite his childishness and folly, was "a perfectly good man." More than this, he is, in Watt's view, "a fine example of the Romantic reinterpretation of Don Quixote as an ego-ideal: a figure that, though defeated by the demands of real life, still suggests a firmer model of human aspiration than does mere adaptation to the demands of ordinary existence" (Watt 1996, 226).

As for his own assessment of the myth of Don Quixote, Watt concludes that Faust, Don Juan, and Robinson Crusoe "are not nice or friendly people. . . . The exception to the unattractiveness of our four mythical heroes is Don Quixote. . . . He is, in his own way, a 'do-gooder,' and although he is often defeated, his example makes us feel better about the human lot. He has a further positive aspect; his relationship with Sancho Panza demonstrates his capacity, uniquely among our four, for a friendship which, however asymmetrical it might be, is devoted and enduring" (Watt 1996, 175). Thus, if Don Quixote is one of the "myths of modern individualism," his is an especially compelling form of individualism, and a challenge to communitarians like Bellah et al., for he evidences a powerful desire to "do good," to effect greater "social equality," and is capable of "devoted and enduring friendship." Thus, he bears little resemblance to the asocial and self-aggrandizing individualist depicted in *Habits of the Heart*.

And yet, as we begin now to explore the psychoanalytic readings of Don Quixote, we will discover that there is a greater depth and complexity to the Quixote character than Watt's discussion reveals. When these complexities are revealed, we may well feel that Don Quixote's image has been diminished. However, my own view is that, all in all, the psychoanalytic readings enable us to recognize the inner suffering that his comic persona tends to disguise, with the result that his nobility is not diminished, but enhanced.

Psychoanalytic Portraits of Don Quixote

While Sigmund Freud did not write a full-scale essay on Don Quixote, he was deeply interested in Cervantes's hero. As a teenager he learned Spanish in order to read the novel, and he carried on a ten-year Cervantine correspondence, often in Spanish, with his closest friend, Eduard Silberstein.

During his engagement to Martha Bernays, he was unable to write her a proper love letter, being too involved in his reading of Cervantes:

> Forgive me, dearest, if I so often fail to write in a way you deserve, especially in answer to your affectionate letter, but I think of you in such calm happiness that it is easier for me to talk about outside things than about ourselves. And then it seems to be a kind of hypocrisy not to write to you what is uppermost in my mind: I have just spent two hours—it's now midnight—reading Don Quixote, and have really reveled in it. (quoted in Farrell 1996, 100)

Continuing, he relates the episode involving Cerdenio and Dorothea with Quixote in "the enchanted tavern," and comments that he "cannot remember ever having read anything so satisfactory which at the same time avoids exaggeration . . . ; none of this is very profound, but it is pervaded by the most serene charm imaginable. Here Don Quixote is placed in the proper light through being no longer ridiculed by such crude means as beatings and physical maltreatment but by the superiority of people standing in the midst of actual life. At the same time he is tragic in his helplessness while the plot is being unraveled" (Farrell 1996, 100). No doubt aware that as a recently engaged young man he was not unlike Don Quixote in his quest for his own Dulcinea, Freud indicates to Martha that he cannot help identifying with Don Quixote: "Before we were so fortunate as to apprehend the deep truths in our love we were all noble knights passing through the world caught in a dream, misinterpreting the simplest things, magnifying commonplaces into something noble and rare, and thereby cutting a sad figure. Therefore we men always read with respect about what we once were and in part still remain" (96).

In *Jokes and Their Relation to the Unconscious* (1963a), Freud has a footnote reference to Don Quixote, describing him as a figure "who possesses no humor himself but who with his seriousness offers us a pleasure which could be called humorous" (232). He notes that the Don Quixote character evolved into something infinitely more than Cervantes originally intended, for at first he is "a purely comic figure, a big child"; but "after the author had equipped this ridiculous figure with the deepest wisdom and the noblest purposes and had made him into the symbolic representative of an idealism which believes in the realization of its aims and takes duties seriously and takes promises literally, this figure ceased to have a comic effect" (232). This does not mean, however, that he ceases to be humorous, for "just as in other cases humorous pleasure arises from the prevention of an emotion, so it does here from the interference with comic pleasure" (232). This footnote occurs in a discussion of the humorous pleasure derived from sympathy. In the case of Don Quixote, it is sympathy evoked by a man who is idealistic and believes in faithfulness to his ideals. The humor is in the fact that he is totally void of cynicism and honestly believes that his ideals are realizable. To an audience that has long since relinquished the idealism of youth, Don Quixote, a middle-aged man, is an anomaly. The audience is incredulous. Given all the evidence to the contrary, how can he still believe in "all that stuff" and even act on these beliefs? He is much more than the ridiculous, comic figure Cervantes set out to create.

Narcissist with paranoid features. Given his identification with Don Quixote, his sense that Quixote is something he once was and in part still remains, Freud's failure to "psychoanalyze" Don Quixote, to assign him a "Freudian" label, is not surprising. John Farrell argues, in fact, that the "convergence of vision between Freud and Cervantes is remarkable," and "psychoanalysis is a somewhat unwitting but nevertheless strategically deployed imitation of Quixotic satire universalized in the language of science" (Farrell 1996, 116–17). Unfortunately, I cannot pursue Farrell's intriguing argument here, as we need to focus our attention on psychoanalytic interpretations of the Don Quixote character itself. Farrell's own view is that he is a "pretentious paranoid." He develops this view by first noting Quixote's narcissism, which is reflected in his confusion of his own megalomaniac wishes with reality, and his creation of Dulcinea as a "pure projection of 'narcissistic' wish," an ideal woman who exists for him and him alone (102). His "belief in Dulcinea is a test of faith, or of 'narcissistic' potency. She infuses her strength into the being of Quixote; his exaltation of mind furnishes the proof of her exalted nature" (103). The narcissistic quality of his fixation on Dulcinea ensures that his way of thinking and behaving will stand in absolute contradiction to reality.

This, however, creates the very conditions for paranoia. In order to sustain his tenuous intellectual coherence, the belief system within which he thinks and acts, he must call the real world into question. But the real world does not mirror his narcissistic ideal construct, and "the incongruity between his sense of what should be and his experience of what is terrifies and galls him to the same degree that it amuses and delights the reader. So arises his slightly self-pitying sense of persecution, a sense which, nevertheless, confirms his grandiose self-image" (Farrell 1996, 104). But this shoring up of his grandiose self-image through a sense of persecution eventually gives way as the novel unfolds. As Farrell explains, his ability to blame his defeats on external forces (enchanters) becomes increasingly tenuous, and he begins to take all responsibility on himself. His paranoid sense of the meaningfulness of every element of his experience has not left him, but he now blames himself for his defeats: "Psychoanalytically speaking, we might say that the 'narcissistic cathexis' has been transferred from the 'ego' to the 'ego ideal' or 'superego,' so that what was formerly a tendency toward absolute freedom from responsibility, absolute independence of the self, becomes an absolute responsibility, shame, and guilt. The self-punitive trend in Quixote's psychology ends in his death" (106). Farrell concludes that "Cervantes's portrait of paranoia has all of the features of the complaint that Freudian psychology has taught us to recognize. It is a madly unqualified form of self-aggrandizing idealism that requires a suspicious overcoming of ordinary appearances and a theory of persecuting enemies to keep it in place. Grandiosity and suspicion animate and sustain each other. The paranoid inhabits a world in which everything is significant and demands decoding with specific relation to him" (108). Thus, narcissism and paranoia feed one another.

Quixote as sexual being. In a brief discussion of Cervantes's own intentions, Farrell notes the vulgarity of the episode where Don Quixote finally meets Dulcinea (who is a saucy village lass whom Sancho Panza has represented to be Dulcinea). While Don Quixote is able to attribute her less-than-ideal appearance to the interference of the enchanters, he nonetheless complains that they robbed her "of that prime characteristic of all noble ladies, namely their lovely scent, which they acquire naturally, spending so much of their time among perfumes and flowers. Because I have to tell you, Sancho, that when I went to help Dulcinea back onto her palfrey—which is what you say the animal was, though to me it looked like a plain she-ass— I was struck by a blast of raw garlic that almost snuffed me out and poisoned my heart" (Cervantes 1995, 401). In Farrell's view, Cervantes's intent is that "the self-idealizing pretensions of the paranoid delusion should be confronted with the vulgarity it falsely denies, and this vulgarity finds its expression preeminently in the life of the body. . . . In order that the true character of Quixote's delusion be revealed, its false idealism must be reunited with all of the embarrassments of corporeal existence; knightly asceticism must be exposed as a form of self-frustration that serves no other end than to deny the exigencies of physical life" (Farrell 1996, 111).

Carroll B. Johnson's psychoanalytic approach to Don Quixote explores these "embarrassments of corporeal existence" further, and precisely in relation to Don Quixote's creation of Dulcinea. In his reading (1983, 1990), these embarrassments are sexual. Johnson notes that many readers of *Don Quixote* have proposed that Quixote throws himself into his reading of chivalric romances because his own life is so dull; then, as he reads, he gets so enthralled by the stories that he wants to live them out. Johnson, however, proposes another hypothesis. He suggests that Quixote turns to the reading of chivalric romances as "a defense against environmental pressure, a defense that proves inadequate and has to be abandoned," leading him to the more desperate measure of leaving his home and going out to live the life of a knight-errant (1990, 111–12). What is this environmental pressure? Johnson believes that it is the fact that Don Quixote's niece, who lives in his house, has emerged "as a desirable young woman at precisely the worst time in his life," when, as a middle-aged bachelor, "he is reliving the unresolved psychosexual conflicts of an earlier period," these being his inability as a young man to act, owing to shyness, on his sexual feelings for a village lass named Aldonza. Thus, Johnson also challenges the standard interpretation that Dulcinea is an idealization of Aldonza on the grounds that this does not explain his need to leave home, to "put real distance between himself and whatever (or whoever) is bothering him" (1990, 112). Moreover, he has seen Aldonza only four times in twelve years, and by his own account she is ugly and masculine. In contrast, Dulcinea is remarkably beautiful. In Johnson's view, this forces us to focus on the home "and to locate the intolerable environmental stress that has driven him to psychosis precisely there. The only kind of stress powerful enough to call forth a response as drastic as psychosis is something like the threat of incest. The gradual accumulation of boredom, for example, pales beside it" (1990, 113).

In support of his theory that the niece, who has ripened into a young woman over the last couple of years before his very eyes, is responsible for Quixote's precipitous departure, Johnson cites recent research on men in midlife that indicates, among other things, that the middle-aged male is experiencing a crisis over his masculinity together with a deepening appreciation of and capacity for intimacy. When viewed from this interpretive perspective, many incidents involving Don Quixote's relations with women begin to make greater sense. They reflect his "paradoxical combination of terror of women and attraction to them" (Johnson 1990, 114). Johnson is not alone in noting Don Quixote's attraction and terror toward women. Edward Abood notes that "He is dedicated to protecting women in distress but is terrified of any real contact with them; having vowed total fidelity to the elusive Dulcinea, he repeatedly represses potent sexual urges" (1983, 59). His "meeting" with Dulcinea reveals this conflict, for in his inability to respond adequately to her expression of need, which ought to have evoked a chivalrous response, he is overcome by "a fantasy of impotence. The fear of not having what is required when the moment of truth arrives may be just a manifestation of middle-age insecurity, but it is also another barrier Don Quixote erects between his desire and the threat of having to act on it. He makes action impossible" (Johnson 1990, 116). Given Johnson's thesis, it is noteworthy that it was Don Quixote's niece who, early in the novel, put forward the enchantment theory to "explain" why his books (removed by the priest and barber to save him from his delusions) had disappeared. Thus, she was not only the object of his delusion but the means by which his disillusionment was tempered. In the end, he includes her in his will with the proviso that she marries a man who "has no idea what books of chivalry might conceivably be about" (Cervantes 1995, 731).

For Johnson, however, a more crucial episode than Don Quixote's "meeting" with Dulcinea occurs in his encounter with a young woman named Altisidore. In spite of protestations to his prior commitment to Dulcinea, Altisidore expresses her love for him, feelings that Don Quixote appears to reciprocate. While this episode begins as pretense, as play-acting, it takes on a reality of its own, and Don Quixote finds himself unable to reject Altisidore without a struggle. But somehow, "perhaps because of his recent defeat in battle, perhaps through the passage of time, he has been cured of his infatuation. His rejection of her is serene and final. . . . From his point of view, his experience with Altisidore has allowed him to work through and overcome his feelings toward his niece. When he is cured of Altisidore he is also cured of that other woman Altisidore represents. He can go home now and face his niece in a different way" (Johnson 1990, 118).

Johnson concludes that his Don Quixote "is a sexual being, whose identity, whose story and whose interest for me as a reader ultimately depend on his sexuality" (Johnson 1990, 118). The tragedy of the story lies in the fact that when he is cured of Altisidore and can go home to face his niece, no longer the object of forbidden desire, he no longer needs to be Don Quixote. Now, however, he finds the boredom and drab routine of a country hidalgo so overwhelming that he can't take it anymore, and he retreats, "into the only space remaining for him, a transitory new identity [as a repentant man] and death" (1990, 119). Thus, the boredom thesis is not so much wrong as misplaced. It is not what propels Don Quixote into his reading and then acting out the life of the knight errant, but the fate that awaits him when he is "cured" of his forbidden desire.

In his earlier treatment of Don Quixote, Johnson discussed his resources on men in midlife in greater detail, citing the work of Erik Erikson, Daniel Levinson, George Vaillant, Roger Gould, and others. He cites Vaillant's observation from his studies of middle-aged men that 30-year-old men have fun bringing up their grade-school children, "but at age forty fathers often acted as if there were no kinship to their adolescent children at all. They were unaware that the heightened sexuality that so frightened them in their daughters was often a projection of their own forbidden wishes toward their suddenly attractive children.... The adolescent has the capacity to get under our skin, rekindle old flames, and to stimulate parents in parts of their innermost selves, that they had forgotten existed" (Johnson 1983, 82–83). Johnson follows this with a quote from psychoanalyst Roger Gould, who writes in "the more colorful parlance of Los Angeles": "As fathers, we do what we can to avoid staring at our daughters' curves or their friends who make a game out of seducing us; we do what we can to keep our wives from knowing" (Johnson 1983, 83).

While Johnson is the most concerned among contemporary authors to emphasize Don Quixote's sexuality, his view of Quixote as "a sexual being" is not new. Six decades ago, Helene Deutsch (1937) picked up on Freud's indication that Don Quixote was "a big child," and suggested that his behavior marked a regression to the onset of sexuality in puberty. Regressing to adolescence, he renews his fascination with romantic literature and thereby finds a way in adulthood to compensate for his lack of sexual experience. Whereas the boy at puberty ordinarily abandons the world of magic in favor of reality, Don Quixote reverses the process, playing out "the depths of a still longer forgotten past, into the practice of a magic whereby the young child . . . is himself able to cast a spell over the things of the natural world, and himself believes in this enchantment" (Martin 1988, 82).

Quixote as fictive personality. Noting that Deutsch's unidimensional view of Quixote minimizes the fact that he is also "a noble hero with the wisdom of the ancients," Jay Martin views Don Quixote as a quintessential "fictive personality," and therefore the model for what he has witnessed in several of his patients, who adopt such a personality "in order to give themselves a 'temporary inner structure'" (Martin 1988, 78). A fine example of the "fictive personality" is provided by Erik H. Erikson in *Identity and the Life Cycle* (1959), where he tells about his work with a high school girl of Middle-European descent who secretly kept company with Scottish immigrants, carefully studying and easily assimilating their dialect and social habits. With the help of history books and travel guides she reconstructed for herself a childhood in an actual township in Scotland. Erikson says that he "went along with the story, implying that it had more inner truth than reality to it. The bit of reality was, as I surmised, the girl's attachment, in early childhood, to a woman neighbor who had come from the British Isles; the force behind the near-delusional 'truth' was the paranoid form of a powerful death wish (latent in all severe identity crises) against her parents" (141). He notes further that "the semideliberateness of the delusion was indicated when I finally asked the girl how she had managed to marshal all the details of life in Scotland. 'Bless you, sir,' she said in pleading Scottish brogue, 'I needed a past'" (141).

Martin notes that the creation of a fictive personality is often a defense against the very feeling that reality is a fantasy. As Jacques Rousseau acknowledged, the motivation for his novel, *The New Heloise*, was to defend against the feeling of the fictiveness of his "real" life: "The impossibility of reaching real creatures threw me into the land of fantasies . . . which my creative imagination soon populated with creatures after my own heart. . . . [I made] an enchanted world" (Rousseau 1997, 83–84). This raises the question with regard to Alonso Quesada's transformation into "Don Quixote the knight errant": Was the fictive personality more real than the so-called real personality? This seems to be Sancho Panza's point at the end of the novel, when he confronts Don Quixote with the paradox that the most foolish thing he could do is shed his fictive personality, for in doing so he leaves himself vulnerable to melancholy and death itself. In this sense, the "cure" achieved through resolute reality-testing is hardly a cure, but is reminiscent instead of the familiar joke, "The operation was a success, but the patient died."

Quixote as moral narcissist. This brings us back to Farrell's view that Don Quixote is a narcissistic personality, a judgment also shared by Andre Green (1980–1981), who distinguishes three types of narcissism: bodily narcissism (which centers on the display of the body), intellectual narcissism (reflecting absolute self-confidence in one's intelligence), and moral narcissism (which turns morality into an autoerotic pleasure in which the pleasure itself is suppressed). Emphasizing the suppression of the pleasures that accrue from acting morally, Green links moral narcissism to masochism. Freud wrote of "the true masochist" that he "always turns his cheek whenever he has a chance of receiving a blow." Paraphrasing Freud, Green says that "the true moral narcissist always volunteers himself whenever he sees a chance of renouncing a satisfaction" (247). Thus Don Quixote, whom Green views as a moral narcissist, inflicts upon himself privations and cruelty for an idealized image (of Dulcinea) which, of course, he cannot possess. In the end, he comes to a "destitution of himself and of his individuality," and on his deathbed, he rebuffs Sancho Panza's entreaties not to relinquish his fictive personality with, "No more of that, I beseech you, all the use I shall make of these follies at present is to heighten my repentance" (Cervantes 1995, 267).

Quixote as narcissist with melancholic features. Noting that "Quixotism and narcissism are almost the same thing," Bela Grunberger (1989) sees Dulcinea as the means by which Quixote will establish his reputation and "win glory for himself." Thus, she is "a narcissistic ideal who has to be kept apart and protected from any hint of carnal desires" (131). But unlike Johnson, who associates her with the niece, Grunberger notes that Dulcinea's "name betrays her maternal origins, as it suggests *dulce* and *dulzura* ('sweet', 'sweetness') and perhaps the *dulzura* of milk" (131). She is, then, the maternal figure of his primary narcissism, going all the way back to his infancy. His "narcissistic project" is to get "others to recognize the absolute validity of his image (by recognizing the image of Dulcinea, who is in a sense a repository of his own image)" (131). In other words, his existence depends upon her existence, in much the same way that an infant is wholly dependent on his mother. As Don Quixote puts it: "She fights and conquers through me, and I live and breathe and have my life and being in her." When he loses her, he loses all reason to live, and he succumbs to what is, in effect, "the suicide of the melancholic" (135). After the encounter with Dulcinea, he may "well seem to have recovered and to be behaving as a sane and sensible family man, but that merely disguises his unconscious decision to do away with himself, and it is because he has taken that decision that he can act so serenely" (137). Grunberger adds: "When a narcissist decathects his object, he rejects it and begins to despise it. . . . When Don Quixote dictates his will he shares out his modest possessions, forgetting no one, but he makes no mention of Dulcinea. It is as though she had never existed. Don Quixote has no illusions left" (137). But "one final and supreme narcissistic act remains to be performed," that of the ultimate renunciation of a life "which has been drained of all its cathexis" (137–38).

Taken together, these psychoanalytic readings place Don Quixote's idealism in a very different light from that of Ian Watt, as they present a case for his narcissism, paranoia, and masochism. In my view, however, these readings, far from pejorative, are quite sympathetic. Rather than demeaning him, they testify to his nobility, the very point that Martin makes in his objection to Deutsch's view of Don Quixote as a comic figure. As Theodore Roethke, the American poet who was in and out of mental hospitals throughout his life, writes in his poem, "In a Dark Time," "What's madness but nobility of soul at odds with circumstance?" (1971, 79). Precisely because they are concerned with identifying the roots of Don Quixote's pathology, the psychoanalytic readings certainly have a more sympathetic view of him than that of his creator, Miguel Cervantes. In fact, as Simon Leys (1998) has noted, the novel's power is due in large part to the fact that Cervantes makes no effort to evoke sympathy for his protagonist. Thus, "When we reproach Cervantes for his lack of compassion, his indifference, his cruelty, for the brutality of his jokes, we forget that the more we hate the author, the more we believe in the reality of his world and his creations" (34). This also means, however, that Don Quixote's loneliness is all the more pervasive, for when he loses Dulcinea, he is confronted with a totally disenchanted world, one that is wholly indifferent to him. Cervantes's indifference to his hero is the "world" within which Don Quixote's moral narcissism flamed, flickered, and eventually extinguished itself, leaving him utterly destitute in a universe that did not give a damn.

The Mid-Career Minister as Moral Narcissist

What, then, is the relevance of Don Quixote for the mid-career male minister? I suggest that Green's view of him as a *moral narcissist* provides the interpretive bridge between this fictional character and the mid-career minister. Green's view of the moral narcissist as one who "always volunteers himself whenever he sees a chance of renouncing a satisfaction" is an apt description of many ministers, especially those who cannot fashion themselves after the Don Juan myth of a potentially sinister (read: seductive) charm.

A research study supporting this view of the minister as moral narcissist, and specifically as one who volunteers himself whenever he sees a chance of renouncing a satisfaction, is Reinard Nauta's "Task Performance and Attributional Biases in the Ministry" (1988). Nauta hypothesized that "self-presentation of modesty and self-protection against loss of face will govern [ministers'] explanation of performance outcomes in the ministry" (612). The study generally supported these expectations. Nauta notes that "the attribution of positive outcomes to variable causes, especially in combination with a transcendental explanation of these outcomes as dependent on

God's guidance, can be conceived of as a modesty-inspired self-presentation, i.e., the self-serving bias of a serving self. Within a theological doctrine
of divine grace and human fallibility, taking all the credit personally for
positive outcomes would be considered hubris. To avoid doctrinal incon-
sistencies . . . modest counter-defensive attributions are made" (619). In
contrast, "negative outcomes are attributed to stable factors, in particular to
task difficulty." Nauta suggests that the meaning of this attribution is
ambiguous. On the one hand, it "reflects the difficult nature of the tasks at
hand, but it may therefore also articulate the self-sacrificing meaning of
personal effort in fulfilling the tasks and duties of ministry." On the other
hand, attributing negative outcomes to task difficulty enables one to present
"effort expenditure" as "an act of heroic stature, i.e., to work hard is to hope
for effect against all odds" (619). Thus, if the minister renounces the satisfaction of claiming his efforts as the sole, or primary, reason for success, he
avoids blame for failure on the grounds that the task was virtually doomed
from the start. It is interesting to note, in this connection, that Don Quixote
copes with his failures *until he begins to accept personal responsibility for
them*, at which point his downward spiral of disillusionment begins.

So these contemporary Don Quixotes go forth, fortified by the belief that
they are empowered by the mother (who is either their literal mother, the
women in the church on whom one's honor depends, or "the Church" herself), knowing that his existence depends on her existence. The "blows" that
he suffers are proof that she is behind him, empowering him, as they testify
to the reality of his enchanted world. He lays himself open to derision, however, because he is alone in his idealism, in his commitment to duty, in
his literal belief in promises, his own and those of others. In effect, he is
the token believer, the one who embodies the conviction that all this
play-acting makes a significant difference, and his bruised and battered
body is evidence of such embodiment of ideals that the others may share,
but surely would not allow to frame their very existence. That he has been
set up to be the token believer, the idealist among realists and cynics, creates a situation in which paranoia is virtually inevitable; and to be sure,
from time to time he succumbs to a self-pitying sense of persecution that
nevertheless confirms his somewhat grandiose self-image. He reasons, "I
would not be suffering so, were I not doing something that is important
and worthy."

Like Don Juan, he is a sexual being, but unlike Don Juan, he has learned
to sublimate his sexuality in noble causes, and his ability to resist "forbidden desires" further suggests his moral narcissism, as he takes refuge in the

honor that he has renounced, a satisfaction to which his Don Juan colleagues have fallen prey. As "moral narcissist," he is always in danger of succumbing to depression, which is implied in Cervantes's own portrayal of Don Quixote as the "knight of the sad countenance," and of an even deeper threat of melancholia. As I have argued in other writings (Capps 1997a), the religious male is especially susceptible to melancholia which, as Freud points out (Freud 1963b, 164–79), has greatly to do with the loss of the object of one's original love, which is then introjected and attacked in what becomes a self-punitive hate.

Then there is the feeling, fleeting for some, more persistent for others, that one is a character in a novel whose creator is indifferent and lacking in compassion. Only here, in this case, the creator is God, who, as Leys points out, is Cervantes's model for his own refusal to express a single word of compassion for his hero, or one word of blame for the vulgar bullies who relentlessly mock and persecute him (Leys 1998, 33–34).

I assume that mid-career male ministers, at least those who are somewhat more likely than others to read this essay, have experienced much of the disillusionment that Don Quixote, in the second part of the novel, eventually experienced. The original idealism with which they entered ministry in their 20s, and was sustained through sheer persistence in their 30s and early 40s, is now, in their late 40s and 50s, showing signs of wearing thin. For Don Quixote, the series of defeats to which he was subjected began to take their toll. Moreover, his delusions were especially evident when he tried to assess the progress of his enterprises, and here, according to Leys, "the hoaxes to which he fell victim played a fatal role: they gave him a false assurance that his undertaking was really feasible, they confirmed his mistaken hope that he might eventually succeed. Thus, these hoaxes artificially prolonged his career" (Leys 1998, 35). Even his successes, therefore, were suspect, and would have been viewed as such by a man who was more in touch with reality, as I assume is the case with the reader of this essay (who would not, after all, be preconditioned to read through the glow of chivalric romances).

So the question is: What is a man to do once he, a confirmed (if not confessed) moral narcissist, has become divested of his illusions? Is there life after disillusionment? I would suggest that Don Quixote perceived there were essentially two options for him. One was to succumb to cynicism, the other was to become melancholic. He chose the latter as the more honorable choice, as being more congruent with his noble sense of himself, and as being more consistent with the moral narcissist's disposition to volunteer himself whenever he sees a chance of renouncing a satisfaction (in this case, the satisfactions that accompany the spirit of cynicism). But the question is whether there is a third way. Here, Heinz Kohut's view (1985, 97–123) that in midlife there is the possibility of the transformation of narcissism is quite relevant. He does not say that the narcissist may become something else entirely, but that within the narcissistic self structure, transformation may occur. The indications of such transformation are new expressions of personal creativity, empathy, acknowledgment of one's finitude, capacity for humor, and wisdom. While Kohut discussed Don Juan types, noting that their sexual exploits have "the air of counteracting a sense of self depletion or of forestalling the danger of self fragmentation" (Kohut 1971, 119) or "the attempt to provide an insecurely established self with a continuous flow of self-esteem" (Kohut 1977, 194), it is unfortunate that he did not discuss Don Quixote in light of his theories of narcissism. Still, his themes of transformed narcissism can be applied to Don Quixote types, including ministers who share something of the Don Quixote complex. I will not attempt a detailed application of Kohut's five themes of transformed narcissism here. But, drawing implicitly on them, I suggest that they would manifest themselves in the following self-realizations:

1. Recognize that you have inspired Sancho Panza, who now thinks of himself as more squire than peasant. To become melancholic or cynical would let down your friend, who believes in you, in spite of, or perhaps because of, your hopeless failures. Have you no feelings for him?
2. Recognize that your successes were real, and that you accomplished them without the help of Dulcinea or the special favoritism of God. If they occurred because someone was playing a hoax on you, so what? It doesn't matter how they happened, but that you were the indispensable element in the fact that they did happen.
3. Recognize that you represent to others a "world" that no longer exists, if it ever did. Your value to others was not your ability to imagine a better future, but to represent a golden past. As Erikson's "Scottish" girl recognized, we all need a past. You are a palpable, unforgettable reminder of what once was, whether real or imagined. In your role as minister, you embody nostalgia.
4. Recognize that in an age in which the "real" world is so ephemeral, your "fictive personality" was, oddly enough, the only thing that felt real to others, even as it felt real to you. Was this

mere impersonation? I do not think so, because you truly embodied the role that you played. If it seems all too phony now, think of the phoniness of the "world" that is said to be the "real world." Your phoniness is the most real thing going.

Would these words of encouragement be enough to get Don Quixote back on Rocinante, his aging and weather-beaten horse, for a fourth expedition? I wouldn't know. But I do know that the moral narcissist has a longstanding habit of volunteering himself whenever he sees a chance of renouncing a satisfaction, and as the comparison of Don Quixote to Don Juan reveals, some difficult-to-break habits are less harmful than others to the health of oneself and others. In fact, for all his madness, Don Quixote was a rather harmless old guy, and despite the indignities to which he was subjected, carried himself with a certain infectious nobility. May he never repent of his illusory glow.

The author wishes to express special appreciation to Allan Cole, who assisted him in finding materials for this essay, and to Andrew Chaney for drawing his attention to the Simon Leys article.

Bibliography

Abood, Edward. 1983. "Don Quixote in Search of a Self." *Psychological Perspectives* 14, 54–67.

Bellah, Robert N. 1985. *Habits of the Heart: Individualism and Commitment in American Life.* Berkeley: Univ. of Calif. Press.

Capps, Donald. 1997a. *Men, Religion, and Melancholia: James, Otto, Jung, and Erikson.* New Haven: Yale Univ. Press.

———. 1997b. "Power and Desire: Sexual Misconduct Involving Pastors and Parishioners." *Women, Gender, and Christian Community.* Ed. J. D. Douglass and J. F. Kay. Louisville: Westminster John Knox. 129–40.

———. 1993a. "Sex in the Parish: Social-Scientific Explanations for Why It Occurs." *The Journal of Pastoral Care* 47, 350–61.

———. 1993b. *The Depleted Self: Sin in a Narcissistic Age.* Minneapolis: Fortress Press.

Cervantes, Miguel de. 1995. *The History of that Ingenious Gentleman Don Quixote de la Mancha.* Trans. B. Raffel. New York: W. W. Norton.

Deutsch, Helene. 1937. "Don Quixote and Don Quixotism." *Psychoanalytic Quarterly* 6, 215–22.

Erikson, Erik H. 1959. *Identity and the Life Cycle.* New York: W. W. Norton.

Farrell, John. 1996. *Freud's Paranoid Quest: Psychoanalysis and Modern Suspicion.* New York: New York Univ. Press.

Fisher, Seymour, and Rhoda L. Fisher. 1993. *The Psychology of Adaptation to Absurdity: Tactics of Make-Believe*. Hillsdale, N.J.: L. Erlbaum.

Freud, Sigmund. 1963a. *Jokes and Their Relation to the Unconscious*. Trans. J. Strachey. New York: W. W. Norton.

———. 1963b. "Mourning and Melancholia." *General Psychological Theory*. Trans. J. Riviere. New York: Collier. 164–79.

Green, Andre. 1980–81. "Moral Narcissism." *International Journal of Psychoanalytic Psychology* 8, 243–69.

Grunberger, Bela. 1989. *New Essays on Narcissism*. London: Free Association.

Johnson, Carroll B. 1990. *Don Quixote: The Quest for Modern Fiction*. Boston: Twayne.

———. 1983. *Madness and Lust: A Psychoanalytical Approach to Don Quixote*. Berkeley: Univ. of Calif. Press.

Kohut, Heinz. 1985. "Forms and Transformations of Narcissism." *Self Psychology and the Humanities: Reflections on a New Psychoanalytic Approach*. Ed. C. Strozier. New York: W. W. Norton. 97–123.

———. 1977. *The Restoration of the Self*. New York: International Univ. Press.

———. 1971. *The Analysis of the Self: A Systematic Approach to the Psychoanalytic Treatment of Narcissistic Personality Disorders*. New York: International Univ. Press.

Lapsley, James N. 1995. "The Rise of Charm as a Virtue: Don Giovanni as its Vehicle, and Some Implications for Theological Anthropology." *Pastoral Psychology* 43, 319–31.

Levinson, Daniel J., et al. 1998. *The Seasons of a Man's Life*. New York: Knopf, 1978.

Leys, Simon. "The Imitation of our Lord Don Quixote." *The New York Review of Books* 45, 32–35.

Martin, Jay. 1988. *Who Am I This Time? Uncovering the Fictive Personality*. New York: W. W. Norton.

Nauta, Reinard. 1988. "Task Performance and Attributional Biases in the Ministry." *Journal for the Scientific Study of Religion* 27, 609–20.

Paulson, Ronald. 1998. *Don Quixote in England: The Aesthetics of Laughter*. Baltimore: Johns Hopkins Univ. Press.

Pittman, Frank. 1993. *Man Enough: Fathers, Sons, and the Search for Masculinity*. New York: Berkeley.

Roethke, T. 1971. *The Far Field*. Garden City: Anchor.

Rousseau, Jean-Jacques. 1997. *The New Heloise: Letters of Two Lovers Who Live in a Small Town at the Foot of the Alps*. Trans. Philip Stewart and Jean Vach. Hanover: New England Univ. Press.

Watt, Ian. 1996. *Myths of Modern Individualism: Faust, Don Quixote, Don Juan, Robinson Crusoe*. Cambridge: Cambridge Univ. Press.

6

Discovering Creative Depth Within

Mike Bathum

God writes the Gospel, not in the Bible alone, but also on trees, and in the flowers and clouds and stars.

—Martin Luther

In a small highland valley in south central Montana lies the community of Livingston, an important railroad town surrounded by four mountain ranges. To the south lie the dramatic peaks of the Absaroka-Beartooth wilderness that flank the northern approach to Yellowstone National Park. To the west and northwest of the town, the Gallatin and Big Belt mountains help shape the eastern slopes of the Rocky Mountains as they snake their way north to the Canadian border. To the northeast lies a lesser-known group of mountains called the Crazies.

During the early history of the area, First Nation Sioux and Crow tribes considered the mountains sacred, and warriors from each tribe made frequent trips into the heart of the peaks during each summer season for "vision quests." It was their version of what we would call a sabbatical: a time to refresh, reflect, find solitude, and gather spiritual strength surrounded by the area's natural beauty. The Indians called the mountains *awaxaawippiia,* or "mountains of the crazies!" Early settlers in the area found it almost impossible to pronounce the Indian name for the mountains, and coupled with the knowledge that Indians traveled into the forests and lakes of the area for strange rituals to commune with nature, the settlers, out of ignorance, simply called the region the Crazies.

Searching for Spiritual Direction

For most Christian men today, the idea of a vision quest—the discovery of a personal spirituality within—seems like a strange or crazy idea. In my experience, men who take up residency in the church pews on Sundays find solace in seeking out activities that fulfill their needs for comfort, peace, and refreshment; but in most cases you won't hear them define this as a spiritual quest. The disguises they use are often activities that are equally acceptable to other men. For all their identity in society as competitive and individualistic, men flock to participatory activities with others that bring acceptance and comradeship. Even though a man's identity is firmly in place in church, the idea of a spiritual awakening is a unique and individual experience. Fortunately, God moves silently and mysteriously in the hearts and minds of men who seek a personal invitation or a deeper identification with spirituality.

The spirit moves within each man in truly unique ways. Transformation begins with a series of steps that are both revealing and unnerving. God has a way of feeding us with spiritual nourishment. This feeding is not forced, but it allows a man's will to accept or reject what God has to offer. Spiritual transformation gains its strength from a deepening commitment to personal prayer, worship, and theological education. A Christ-centered metamorphosis can begin to grow up and out into the world of action—from the pew to the street! The man hanging on each Sunday in church will begin to experience new stirrings of faith-moved-to-action.

Steps toward Spiritual Movement

Let's look at some of the steps that may or may not influence our introduction and movement to spiritual depth. Keep in mind that the steps I describe are subjective feelings and experiences that have influenced my own spiritual development, but each man's interior movements may differ.

First, men are affected by tangibles versus concepts. We arrange our lives around activities that have logical beginnings, middles, and ends. Through the results of the work we do, the relationships we develop, and the sports scores we keep track of, we are personally fulfilled, and our lives are gratifying. But each Sunday men sit in church and are faced with a structured worship service that deals with concepts, things we are not altogether sure of or comfortable with. The themes of Sunday worship are presentations of things we cannot see. We have not seen God, and we know of Jesus only through biblical stories in the Scriptures or through the liturgical art that adorns the sanctuary. We are comforted with the idea of living by faith that is reinforced over and over again by the theme expressed in Second Corinthians: "For we fix our attention, not on things that are seen, but on things that are unseen. What can be seen lasts only for a time, but what cannot be seen lasts forever" (2 Corinthians 4:18). If men are prepared to trust and believe in what they cannot see, then God's authority and the spirit can begin the groundwork in men toward inner spiritual development.

Second, as the spirit moves, our lives become filled with questions. These questions don't necessarily have or require answers, but they are asked in a rhetorical sense as a reflection upon the movement of the spirit within. The questions create a sense of wonder and a challenge for each of us to grow. Take heart: the Gospels are filled with questions!

Third, spiritual development requires downtime. Recently I was driving down the freeway, following a car with a bumper sticker that read: "KILL YOUR TV!" While I think the remark was a demonstration of revolt against the noise and complexity of society, it still reflected the idea that the spirit requires our attention beyond the earthly distractions that fill our minds with noise, sensation, and information overload. The word I would choose to demonstrate downtime is solitude: the chance to be alone, to take a deep breath, to leave the mind open, to listen and reflect.

Spiritual work requires time away from the usual activities so that the heart and soul can link together for sustenance and strength. The coming together of soul and spirit is a restlessness that takes our energy and demands our time for development. This theme is reinforced by Roman Catholic theologian Ronald Rolheiser in his book, *The Restless Heart*: "To creatively come to grips with "restlessness-loneliness" each of us must travel inward, to meet ourselves, and to meet the infinite love and riches of God dwelling inside of our beings" (Rolheiser 1988, 166).

Fourth, one must be careful here in thinking that the restlessness-loneliness experience is always uplifting. Sometimes the exercise of spiritual enlargement may bring distress instead of refreshment. What happens if we open our souls by viewing a vast landscape and find nothing there? There is a loneliness factor involved here that can cause an interior terrorism of the spirit. The loneliness of the physical environment can register with a similar interior desolation, and we may run from the landscape. But as Rolheiser reminds us, loneliness too draws us closer to God in love and creativity.

In the midst of this potential problem I believe that aloneness should be complemented with community. The individual should not be left alone;

friendship and church are important elements to assist the person in self-discovery. A community, friend, a spiritual guide, or a therapist can be the companion along the way. Loneliness can be a path to aloneness, and aloneness a path to solitude, and solitude a companion on the pathway to soul enlargement and spiritual depth.

Fifth, solitude takes its place in our being by way of the wildness that can be found in nature. Jesus took time for himself in the wilderness, and we all need the same experience for spiritual-soulful strength. Nature has the capacity to accept us where we are in our lives. The uncluttered landscape has much to teach us. A liturgy of the wind can be heard as it bends the trees in its rhythm and the spirit catches us in its action. As we watch the seasons change, we become aware that life, like nature, is a period of adjustments. A tree grows in spring, develops leaves in summer, gives up its leaves in fall, and becomes dormant in winter, with the promise of life again the next season. Our spiritual development follows the same sort of path, both busy and quiet in our seasons of life.

Listen to the passionate words of Terry Tempest Williams as she names the spirit's empowerment within her, describing the natural surroundings of the Great Salt Lake Desert:

> Once out at the lake, I am free. Native. Wind and waves are like African drums driving the rhythm home. I am spun, supported, and possessed by the spirit magnet that will not let me go. Dogma doesn't hold me. Wildness does. A spiral of emotion. It is ecstasy without adrenaline. My hair is tossed, curls are blown across my face and eyes, much like the whitecaps cresting over waves. (Williams 1991, 240)

Finally, each of us is an artist in one form or another. We have the capacity to see creatively in two ways. We see clearly the tangible view that is in front of us as well as the conceptual imaginative view played out in our mind's eye. By our creative action we blend what we see into images that were only ideas in our minds. When we relate this same imaginative concept of shaping our spirituality through God's view, we begin to see with fresh eyes the reality of God's tangible action in the men who sit in the pew each Sunday. As the spirit moves in our hearts and minds, we suddenly become aware that men are clearly displayed as part of the same partially painted canvas. At this point we become cocreators. But it takes courage to produce a piece of artwork, just as it takes courage to be a companion along the spiritual way. Rollo May suggests, in his book *The Courage to*

Create, "If you do not express your own original ideas, if you do not listen to your own being, you will have betrayed yourself" (May 1975, 3).

Using Nature and Fine Art Themes to Shape Spirituality

The sincerity and movement of spirituality is shaped by three distinct themes: aesthetics, insight, and performance. The igniting of these themes is set in motion by an openness to view nature and to interpret what is seen in artistic form, to listen to music, which opens an attentiveness to be present to spiritual consciousness, and to nurture the intellect to be present and active to the mystery of God. Within the context of these three themes, a deeper clarification and understanding of spiritual shaping is called for.

The first theme is linked to aesthetics, which I describe as soul awareness. The question shaped by this heading is: What messages are being transmitted between nature and the soul that profoundly affect a person's position of faith, worship, creativity, relationships, justice, prayer, and discernment? In the presence of nature, a stillness is formed within the heart that nurtures the soul to attention. The soul needs and is energized in the wildness of nature to activate the spirit of each person. In this context, nature represents a visual and sacred platform in which God speaks words to each man's heart that are felt rather than heard.

Following this first question is a second taken from the Roman Catholic Ignatian contemplation exercises used for shaping deeper spiritual awareness. As much as I am able to receive, God will share all of what the Creator possesses. A spiritual response would be: What can we give of ourselves in return? We give of ourselves through the quiet acceptance of our hearts, and we find the words to say yes with courage and conviction. It is a yes that has always been present in our hearts, waiting for God's call to come to us. With the availability of nature and the visual and performing arts, God softens our stony hearts with a blending of sight and sound through the avenues of our soul and spirit. Soul awareness is the understanding of movement through God's operative grace.

A second theme is the insight understood as the "truth quest." The question that best fits a man's individual inquiry is: How do I process the visual information for growth and integration through the action of being in nature, church, and community? A person's developing spiritual experience adds a second and deeper question as the Lord dwells in the breadth and depth of that bounty. Within a sacred space, do we dwell in God and make use of our giftedness by appreciating nature and participating in the arts and worship? An understanding of the truth quest is the interpretation of movement through spiritual discernment.

A final theme is performance in the shape of spiritual mentoring. Here two additional questions are asked. How can we transform both the messages and the processed information into avenues of guidance that will help other men, sitting confused and stony-faced in the Sunday service, in issues of spiritual growth and development? God is active and working for good every moment of every day. The spirit within inquires: Are we developing our gifts for ministry as we recognize that God's power is with us? The distinction becomes service to others through faith in action.

Our spirituality is very active, seldom passive or quiet, and is shaped by the presence of active viewing, determining information, and heartfelt action. It is the way of seeing ourselves as being "fully alive." My personal understanding of movement from one stage to the next is best expressed by Parker J. Palmer in his book *The Active Life: Wisdom for Work, Creativity, and Caring.*

> In the stage of integration we learn that contemplation-and-action are so intertwined that features we associate with one are always found at the heart of the other—just as the Chinese symbol of yang harbors a dark spot of yin, and the symbol of yin harbors a light spot of yang. Action becomes more than a matter of getting from here to there, but a contemplative affair as well, a path by which we may discover inner truth. Contemplation becomes more than a luxury to be indulged when the worries of the world are behind us, but a way of changing consciousness that may have more impact on the world than strategic action can have. Contemplation-and-action are integrated at the root, and their root is in our ceaseless drive to be fully alive. To be fully alive is to act. The capacity to act is the most obvious difference between the quick and the dead. But action is more than movement: It is movement that involves expression, discovery, reformation of ourselves and the world. I understand action to be any way we can co-create reality with other beings and with the spirit. (Palmer 1990, 16–17)

Defining Spirituality

Before I go further, developing ideas whereby men can seek out tangible statements for spiritual development, I think it is important to construct a spiritual definition. Despite the fact that the term *spirituality* is a slippery word to interpret, I believe it is essential to encapsulate the word in its own skin, to give the word a life of its own as a way of discovering a starting point for the journey that is to follow.

I offer here two definitions of spirituality: one academic and complex, the second lay-friendly and practical. My first interpretation is a broad and technical view of my understanding of God's action in each person. I define spirituality as the intimate and active participation of God's Holy Spirit, moving through human reality to embrace a meaningful life for individuals through the practices of prayer, worship, and personal unification in the social community. God transcends the human spirit and bestows self-empowerment so that individuals may become fully alive through transformation and growth, seeking an authentic life through a search for meaning and finding a creative vision of self in the world.

The second definition is much more practical and is formed from the words of M. Robert Mulholland Jr. in *Invitation to a Journey: A Road Map for Spiritual Formation*.

> I want to share with you what may appear to be a rather simplistic definition of spiritual formation: Spiritual formation is a process of being conformed to the image of Christ for the sake of others. Upon closer examination, however, you will discover that this definition encompasses the essential dynamics of spiritual formation and effectively counters cultural dynamics that work against holistic spirituality. (Mulholland 1993, 12–13)

The first definition of spirituality will help each man to understand the broad movement of God's presence and purpose in the world: to witness the shaping of Jesus in the lives of others through divine power, might, wisdom, and strength. The shorter clarification of spirituality helps all of us stay focused on the intent of God's directives for developing wholesome relationships, prayer, worship, creative outlets, and professional work. Interestingly enough, both definitions are intertwined for private inspiration and public service. Being conformed to the image of Christ is a process of God's nurturing deep within, remaining open to the probing of our character, unearthing personal traits, and coming to terms with our hindrances to growth—all for the purpose of spiritual maturity and for the sake of others.

A Personal Journey

During the month of June 1993, my son Aaron and I traveled to New Zealand to visit friends in Auckland and had a few days to refresh ourselves by skiing in the South Island snowfields of the Remarkable Mountains. Between skiing and visiting friends, I drove to one of my favorite places, the Tangarapapa Regional Park. The park contains an area of sacred Maori ritual grounds that sits high on a bluff with sweeping views of the Hauraki Gulf Islands, the Coromandel Peninsula, and the South Pacific Ocean. The land is blessed with smooth rolling hills, pine trees, giant ferns, pampas grass, bamboo clumps, tall and graceful poplars, wild Japanese iris, and flowering bird-of-paradise. Sheep and whiteface cattle roam the hills, grazing on the lush, dark green grass. The sun shines brightly over the multicolored land, and the pastel blue-green water sparkles as the ocean waves roll along the beach.

As I walked through the open fields, I loaded my camera to take pictures of the terrain as resource material for future paintings once we returned to the U.S. I became aware, as I stood motionless on the grassland, that there were tears running down my face. I had opened myself to a healing and spiritual experience. I felt one with my natural surroundings and had a deep sense that God was expressed in everything. I felt that the trees, the flowers, and the grass grew up to bear witness and allegiance to God. What impressed me was the understanding that the natural world is the continuous cycle of God's creation. I didn't want to change it, but to observe its order and structure as it moved in the wind and to hear the sound of it as the ocean waves met the shore. Then I was aware of how much we, as humans, try to rearrange the order to fit our own needs. Part of my tears were shed in realizing how we have failed God's creative order and how it has had an impact on our lives, not for something better, but for our own self-indulgence.

As I probed the unusual spiritual expressions of the New Zealand countryside, a question formed in my mind. What was I being called to understand in the silence of the landscape? The answer came in three parts. The first was soul awareness. What messages are being transmitted between nature and my soul? A primary answer came clearly to mind: we are invited to dialogue with God through the observation of nature, and we are asked to respond to what God is saying to us.

The second response was truth quest. How do I process the visual information for growth and integration? This is an act of acknowledging that God wants us to interpret what we see and feel into a language that we can understand.

The final rejoinder was spiritual mentoring. How can I transform both the messages and the processed information into avenues of guidance that will help people, particularly men, in their growth and development? In the words of Rosemary Roney, framed from her essay "Discernment," this is "where adoration in freedom finds its completion in consent and action" (Roney 1994, 3).

After carefully considering each point, I have reached a further conclusion. Soul awareness, truth quest, and spiritual mentoring are the ways I process spiritual material through the continuous action of discernment. It is discernment that leads me to levels of prayer and worship formulated from the basis of my awareness of nature. Roney is very clear about the act of discernment:

> Discernment is a way of life. To live a discerned life is a commitment to a way of being. It is to stand before God and other persons somehow holding what I value most from what I have learned from life in such a firm yet gentle grasp that it does its work for me; yet I can let it go to be fashioned further. Discernment is not something to be turned on and off—to be pulled out at decision time and then to be filed away again. Commitment to discernment is fidelity to a way of life in which I sift through the movements I feel within myself. Through this process I gradually experience a congruity which I recognize. (Roney 1994, 6)

A Closer Look at Spirituality

Let's take a closer look again at the three points I have raised. The first is soul awareness. When I stand in the presence of an immeasurable landscape, I believe that the vastness of the scenery resonates with the vastness of my soul. My crying is the outer manifestation of the joyful union between nature and my spirit. My artistic ego is put on hold while my true being is energized by visual pleasure. I say, "Thank you, God, for the gift of seeing your creation," without the ego's interference to try to manipulate or rearrange the landscape for self-indulgent reasons. I also sense that my personality is engaged in the process of soul-enlargement. The larger the landscape before me, the more my soul can take it in! My primary act of worship is privately conducted as a panentheistic identification of God with the various forces and workings of nature. That reflection of God, through nature, is reinforced in the community of believers in church worship through the signs and symbols of the sacraments: water for baptism, the lighted candle as the spirit of God, the wood of the cross, and the bread and wine that grew from the earth and represent the Body of Christ.

I also believe that my soul is expanding to grasp and understand the truth about myself: to meet the giftedness of my individuality and identify with it as unlimited inner energy. This enveloping energy yearns to be freely expressed through words of comprehension or expressions in action. It means to be reflective, to penetrate illusion and touch the reality of who God created me to be. It means to take more risks and be more creative. As the saying goes, we should not go to our graves with our music still inside us. It means personal transformation through a fulfilling life!

In Marsha Sinetar's book *Ordinary People as Monks and Mystics: Lifestyles for Self-Discovery*, she speaks to the issue of truth:

> There is a truth within the self which yearns to be known, and the expression of this truth makes a person exist, be real, in her own eyes, ultimately in the eyes of others. The collective wisdom of mankind holds a deep and abiding belief in the idea that there is, within each person, some substantive truth waiting to be known, waiting to be expressed. When psychologists speak about someone as having an "authentic personality," they mean that the individual has managed to express what is genuine, truthful and real about himself to others. (Sinetar 1986, 17)

Finally, and most importantly from an artistic point of view, soul-enlargement is an act of courage! Getting in touch with our fullness and the depth of our being takes tremendous daring. The outer environment, as well as the inner surroundings, can become polluted and closed to view. For individuals to look at and face the inner turmoil and sludge that clog the spiritual pipes of the soul, they need to be, as Rollo May suggests in his *The Courage to Create,* "rebels of personal transformation. Courage . . . is the foundation that underlies and gives reality to all other virtues and personal values. Without courage our love pales into mere dependency. Without courage our fidelity becomes conformism" (May 1975, 4).

This is an act of encroachment upon the inner being to recognize creativity, giftedness, and inner visions of what each is meant to be and do. In this context, we can be transformed by God's vehicle of courage that carries our individual spirit into new arenas of soul development: to see, to feel, and to touch the inner power that we all possess if we are willing to stand before beauty and let it shape us.

On a deeper level, courage can lead us to the center of soul awareness through the act of prayer. Visual stimulation through nature, music, and the presentation of the Eucharist in corporate worship can become an active ingredient in spiritual dialogue with God. Quite often a prayer life can be static in petitions but active in visual sensations, tears, and creative energy. This is an important time to give reverence and thanks to God for all the soul-stirrings taking place within each person.

Beyond prayer, music affects our inner sensitivity to hear God. Combined with how each person views God in nature, the two experiences can, from time to time and in the process of prayer, form messages in our minds that are not of our own making. Each message is preceded by selected music that, I believe, opens a space in the soul, allowing the spirit of God's communication to come through. Unlike viewing a landscape that enlarges the soul, music fills the inner void with words, visions, signs and symbols. When inspiring music is played, all this richness bubbles and percolates from the vast soul-space of the inner person and rushes into consciousness. The physical manifestation is expressed much like David dancing before the Ark of the Covenant!

I am moved deeply but joyfully by Jean Sibelius's *Symphony No. 7*. This is his last symphony and is twenty-four minutes of restless and powerful music. Sibelius did not set out to compose this work as sacred music, but it clearly speaks to me of the Easter Passion. Music is an active ingredient in my spiritual development, especially as a way of nurturing a deep sensitivity that emanates from my stomach and chest. I feel comforted and at peace as the music opens deep visual images that I can't come in contact with in any other way. Consequently, listening to the music, I am transformed into an exercise of weeping that registers as an affective prayer activity. Tears of compassion often outweigh the need for words in prayer! The expression of crying speaks to the nature and depth of each person's personality.

Music stirs the strong feeling and intuitive side of our being and blends it with our creative energy. While the music plays on, the energy is released through tears. Then we become aware that music is a catalyst for personal understanding and spiritual transcendence. The outcome is a person who loves deeply, as well as a person who grieves deeply as the music we choose for inspiration carries us into prayer, and through images of our own pain, to the pain and suffering of the entire world.

Inner Truth Can Be Found in Many Ways

The second point in my thesis concerns the theme of the truth quest. This portion of the writing centers on my personal spiritual truth discovered in a Seattle University classroom, based on the Myers-Briggs Personality Type Indicators. This story may or may not have implications for another individual's spiritual journey, but it gives clues to the ability each man has to determine spiritual development using personality measuring indicators that we are all blessed with.

Until recently I never understood completely how I processed information through my intellect. How did I arrive at important decisions? How were personal self-discovery issues formed? What interactions were taking place when I framed natural elements together for paintings and drawings? How did I practice cognitive learning to arrive at a determination? Finally, how did I understand and critique the experiences of being in nature and feeling the depth of spiritual encounters?

The mystery was solved while participating in a graduate course called "Psycho-Spiritual Development" taught by Father Pat Howell, S.J., at Seattle University's School of Theology and Ministry, to complete my master's degree in spirituality. One afternoon Father Howell deviated from the normal class material to begin a discussion centered on the Myers-Briggs Personality Indicators to give some index of how we process tangible and conceptual information. Father Howell went to the blackboard and drew a cross with the chalk. Above the cross, and at the left side, he wrote an "I" for Introverted. To the right of the cross he wrote an "E" for Extroverted. In straightforward fashion he wrote the letters "S" for Sensate in the upper left quadrant of the cross, "N" for Intuitive in the upper right corner, "T" for Thinking in the lower corner, and "F" for Feeling in the lower right corner of the cross. Below the cross he placed the letters "P" for Perceiving and "J" for Judgment.

"I" (Introverted)	"E" (Extroverted)
"S" (Sensate)	"N" (Intuitive)
"T" (Thinking)	"F" (Feeling)
"P" (Perceiving)	"J" (Judgment)

Father Howell randomly chose a personality indicator for a hypothetical individual and began to describe how that person processes information. I was immediately focused on the letter indicators because they so closely resembled my personality. He wrote on the board: ENFJ. During the next hour of class he lectured on this fictitious individual's style of mental adaptation. Father Howell chose to talk about what it is like for a man with personality indicators that are strong in Extroverted, Intuitive, Feeling, and Judging qualities to walk about in an arboretum and be immersed in the natural surroundings. As he talked I was immediately transported back to New Zealand, viewing the landscape and crying before the beauty of creation.

Father Howell took each letter indicator through four stages. The first stage of development was the Intuitive (N). A strong intuitive takes in the natural beauty without the use of rational processing. There is a clarity of immediate knowing and understanding of nature, a feeling of oneness with the creator and creation. The first stage is acted out in extroverted form because the person is physically active in the process. This was very clear to me, because I took an active part in viewing: walking, praising, weeping, voicing my appreciation, and taking pictures.

The second stage of development moves to the Feeling indicator (F). The active intuitive person takes the expressions into an affective state of consciousness through emotions and desires, and works with them from the inside of the personality, from the introverted perspective. I stood in the openness of the fields of New Zealand and expressed my feelings through the active participation of tears. I was expressing my deepest feelings and tender emotions of love for what I saw. I believe that this stage was the door opening from my consciousness to the vastness of my soul. The vastness of beauty spoke to the vastness and goodness of my spirit, and I rejoiced.

The third stage develops with the transference of the feelings to the Sensate side (S). I take my tender emotions and place them within the objects of beauty. I extend my being through a capacity to appreciate or understand what I am seeing. Nature becomes a creative way of worship: seeing God in all things in the environment. The spirit of God moves in the wind, and I feel it and move with it. The branches of trees sway in the breeze, and I can prayerfully dance with them. Waves roll along the ocean beach, and I am creatively painting as I become part of the water. The clouds roll along the sky, and I can play in their shapes. I look to the horizon, stretch myself into the distance, and hear God's call to a hopeful and productive future. In the sensate stage I can live in the doctrine of panentheism. During this stage I process quietly and alone, with the introverted self, desiring not to focus on spoken language, but experiencing the earth through sight and sound.

The final stage opens out again in the Extroverted personality (E). The quiet sensate who walked in the wilderness ends the journey as the thinking process begins. This is the time for active participation: to ask questions, to paint pictures, to make statements, to pray openly and worship freely, and make feelings felt—to self and others. My experience has been to record what I have seen with a camera and to adapt the landscapes to a painting or a drawing. The thinking process is then combined with my strong Judging indicator (J), which makes a discernment about what I have seen and felt. Now I can make an interpretation, a creative action, that affirms God's creation and my cocreative act to rearrange the elements in a unique way.

With Father Howell's explanation I am able to understand my own personality in cognitive and intuitive action. That understanding gives me a sense of power to go beyond my limitations and strike out in new creative territory. I can, at the same time, surrender to God's work within me, while being obedient to my giftedness and to the active yeast of spirituality deep within. I could not always be obedient to God and surrender my gifts at the same time, because I was confused and suspicious of my understanding of the process. Now I am comfortable in the new clarification of my personality type, and that knowledge assures me of a continuously creative future through a steady spiritual walk. Elizabeth O'Connor describes this notion in her book, *Eighth Day of Creation*. She writes about the consequences of our actions:

> We ask to know the will of God without guessing that His will is written into our very beings. We perceive that will when we discern our gifts. Our obedience and surrender to God are in large part our obedience and surrender to our gifts. This is the message wrapped up in the parable of the talents. Our gifts are on loan. We are responsible for spending them in the world, and we will be held accountable. Though it may seem that God leaves us and is not concerned with what we do with our lives, the parable makes it clear that this is not the case. Even though we feel He is away a long time—the absent God—we perceive His presence in the consequences of our action. (O'Connor 1971, 15)

There have been times when I thought that God was "away" for a long time. But now I seek God in the beauty of the landscapes, and I find the Creator in the trees and grass, water and clouds, flowers and lakes. With the Myers-Briggs Personality Type Indicators, I am anchored theoretically and rationally to the truths before me in the shape and volume of the landscape.

Sharing the Gift of Personal Spirituality with Others

Finally, let's look at the issue of spiritual mentoring. All men can use their sensitivity to nature as a source for spiritual awakening, as well as the understanding of the Myers-Briggs indicators, to process information in an artistic way and to assist people in their spiritual journey. Imagination plays a major role in this. Cissy McLane, a leader in the Ignatian Spiritual Exercises, is instructive on this point:

> What we imagine—while it is a very real way of coming to know something—is also subject to the scrutiny of discernment; is this true of God, or is it something else? This must always be asked in regard to our imagination. But imagination is a way of knowing; Ignatius used it constantly. It brings to our disposal what is not, in reality, available to us and gives us valuable information. Also, before a thing can ever be realized in our lives, we have to have first imagined it. (McLane 1994)

Shaping our true desire to assist individuals to a new spiritual understanding requires an imaginative way of knowing and a willingness to search for deep inner meaning. This is both a journey in solitude and a journey in community. Christians are given to both traditional forms of worship and creative outlets to actualize God's presence through ritual, sacrament, and visual forms. Part of the ritual in the customary sense is the need to be immersed in community. The church is a moving and dynamic social place where men find wholesome people sharing their strengths and weaknesses with a loving God. Bernard Cooke expresses this need clearly in his book *Sacraments and Sacramentality*: "Life experienced as a sharing in the real human community has quite a different meaning than life lived in isolation and loneliness. If my life is to be meaningful, it has to have meaning for someone" (Cooke 1983, 25).

In the midst of the fullness of community, however, is the solitude of community. At this point the thought arises: What do men give of themselves in this community life experience? The void men feel in church is sometimes the extension of our yearning to feel the love of the living God through people in the church. The conceptual image of God shaped through a man's spirit is reinterpreted into tangible love for those in community! It is the lonely search for God that activates the soul awareness, truth quest, and spiritual mentoring for the sake of others. So there are times that the spirit requires us to stretch ourselves and be vulnerable, to grow in the pain of loneliness, and to reach out to those in community with creative energy that is expressed in the Holy Communion: the same compassion that Jesus offers to us through his body and blood for redemption and the claiming of our giftedness.

Once again Rolheiser clarifies my point in his book *The Restless Heart*: "Looked at sensitively and through the eyes of faith, we see that our loneliness has a very clear generic aim. We are thirsty for love and community, for unity with God and others in the body, the body of Christ. Loneliness is God's way of drawing us into that body" (Rolheiser 1988, 143).

So we come to other questions in an effort both to understand our own behavior as we take our place in the pew and to mentor other men of faith. Do we dwell in God? Do we make use of our giftedness in acts of compassion and love for community? Our spirits are stirred to fullness when we feel that we are part of the shared expression of worship with those we know in the church community. In worship, we are able to see and receive all that God possesses through song, Scripture, and the Eucharist. We respond in prayer by offering ourselves to God in service, as God gave Jesus Christ as a sacrifice for us. That is a difficult reality to grasp at times, because belief in God is conceptual, not tangible. How can we believe what we haven't seen? It is the risen Christ that we see in the actions and movements of the Christian community. We rely upon our visual intelligence, the artist in each of us, to transpose the unseen image of Jesus working in the hearts of the men who sit near us in church. Thus it is the energized movement of the spirit within each of us that drives our devotions and actions toward individuals, as the image of Christ is fleshed out into reality.

In the reality of "fleshing out" the image of Christ, we feel as if we are working actively with God and bringing truth to the next questions: Are we developing our gifts as we recognize God's power working within us? Are we working for ourselves and for the sake of others? We can answer affirmatively from our artistic nature as the Spirit directs us in the action of being cocreators with the Lord. Lois B. Robbins states in her book *Waking Up in the Age of Creativity*:

> Some who look to traditional forms of worship find solace in them, but many do not, and these yearn for authentic ways of expressing the sacredness now livening our consciousness. David Spangler feels that art itself is the ritual through which the creative potential of humankind is manifested. We are now realizing that while we are not primitive people, there is much to be learned from them. One lesson is that an art-involved community, working with images in a fluid way, can be a healing context for the liv-

ing God. In ancient times, art and religion were one power field. Today, as we develop the creative and transpersonal side of ourselves, they again come together in our communities, and new rituals are born. (Robbins 1985, 166–67)

As an artist, my spirituality is the yeast found in the action of producing a piece of work. My soul-enlargement experiences are a beautiful gift of appreciation wrapped in images. Occasionally I have difficulty quieting myself to spend time with the Lord in traditional forms of prayer and worship. Creative energy makes it so, as I look for new ways to identify with the numinous, the mystery that is God. The crime of a noisy world is that it steals the energy from all of us to fully find time to be silent before God. What is called for is a mature attitude of asking God to be present with us throughout the whole day, asking that our actions be the Creator's actions, and that our thoughts and words be God's thoughts and words. In the end, we want to be a living prayer, allowing the image of Christ to move through our activities all day long.

Finally, consider what is found in the Gospel of Mark: "And what I say to you I say to all: Keep awake" (Mark 13:37). In the midst of the experience of soul-searching, let the landscape be a place to breathe deeply, to allow the individual to practice the presence of God. This will make our traditional form of prayer into a living prayer: a prayer that literally "keeps us alive" to ourselves in the presence of the environment that God gives us, all for the sake of creative worship. Each man's spirit quest takes him deeper and deeper into the world and out of himself, to act and to serve in the name of the Lord Jesus Christ. As we are moved by the Spirit, we find that our feelings are a wonderful vehicle for releasing inner energy. This psychogenic and incorporeal activity can shape our spiritual formation through insight by means of imagery: the kataphatic experience of God through mental inventions and metaphors. It can happen in the art studio! Perhaps in the concert hall! Surely in the Crazy Mountains! Certainly in the church pew on Sunday! As the song by the Lutheran composer, Marty Haugen, suggests: "My soul in stillness waits for you, O Lord, my soul in stillness waits, truly my hope is in you" (Haugen 1991).

Bibliography

Cooke, Bernard. 1983. *Sacraments and Sacramentality*. Mystic, Connecticut: Twenty-third Publications.

Haugen, Marty. 1991. "My Soul in Stillness Waits." *The Lutheran Book of Worship*. Chicago: GIA Publications, Hymnal Supplement #724.

May, Rollo. 1975. *The Courage to Create*. New York: Norton.

McLane, Cissy. 1994. "Notations on Spiritual Direction Supervision." Seattle University. Photocopy.

Mulholland, M. Robert, Jr. 1993. *Invitation to a Journey: A Road Map for Spiritual Formation*. Downers Grove, Ill.: InterVarsity.

O'Connor, Elizabeth. 1971. *Eighth Day of Creation: Gifts and Creativity*. Waco, Tex.: Word Books.

Palmer, Parker. 1990. *The Active Life: Wisdom and Work, Creativity and Caring*. HarperSanFrancisco.

Robbins, Lois B. 1985. *Waking Up!: In the Age of Creativity*. Santa Fe: Bear.

Rolheiser, Ronald. 1988. *The Restless Heart*. Denville, N.J.:Dimension.

Roney, Rosemary. 1994. "Spirituality Synthesis: Discernment." Synthesis Class, Seattle University. Mimeographed.

Sinetar, Marsha. 1986. *Ordinary People as Monks and Mystics: Lifestyles for Self-Discovery*. New York: Paulist.

Williams, Terry Tempest. 1991. *Refuge: An Unnatural History of Family and Place*. New York: Random House.

Part Three

Relationships

7

Masculinity, Competitive Violence, and Christian Theology

James Newton Poling

Male Violence as a Theological Problem

I became interested in the topic of male violence for professional reasons when I started hearing stories from my parishioners and students about their experiences of violence, and for personal reasons when I realized the presence of incest in my extended family. Some of my pastoral clinical experience for the last fifteen years has been with fathers from working-class and poor backgrounds who have engaged in incest—fathers, step-fathers, and live-in boyfriends who engaged in inappropriate sexual behaviors from fondling to intercourse with boys and girls from ages five to sixteen. I have also worked as a therapist in groups for men who have battered women, usually their wives, girlfriends, ex-wives, and ex-girlfriends, and often their children. All of these men, the fathers who engaged in incest and the batterers, were in counseling because they had been convicted of crimes, and their attendance in therapy or group reeducation was a condition of probation. In all cases, there were other professionals involved with the victims and survivors who were watching out for safety issues. I consulted frequently with other therapists to ensure that my work was not increasing the danger to vulnerable children or women. In most cases, the men were separated from their families by the court during counseling or group education.

I work as a victim-advocate, which means that I work self-consciously to prevent male violence in myself and others, and I hold myself accountable to the community of survivors and advocates who are trying to prevent interpersonal violence in the United States. Feminist and womanist analyses of male power and violence are, in my opinion, the most profound and comprehensive theories available today.[1] Interventions with male abusers are significantly different from usual pastoral counseling and psychotherapy. Most counseling is based on a premise of motivation and honesty, that is, the person wants to change and tries to be honest with the therapist. With perpetrators of violence, an awareness of manipulation, denial, and dishonesty as conscious and unconscious patterns always influences diagnosis and treatment. The art of therapy with this population is finding some ambivalence in the men that can be a basis for a therapeutic relationship inside a container of external coercion: the risk of going to jail if treatment is terminated. Often, the ambivalence of men who make progress in therapy is generated by a fear of the consequences for their illegal and stigmatized behaviors *and* a genuine wish to be good husbands, parents, citizens, and/or Christians. This kind of counseling sounds impossible within the history of pastoral care and counseling theory, but I believe it is possible based on my experience (Poling 1991, 1996).

Pastoral counseling has failed to respond adequately to the pastoral care needs of victims, survivors, and perpetrators of family violence. The problems of family violence have been overlooked, minimized, misdiagnosed, and mistreated by most pastoral counselors. I am beginning to develop a hypothesis about why this is true. In one sentence, I believe that too often pastoral counseling is a "love theory" that is naive regarding issues of power in human families. The historical reasons for this are complex and beyond the scope of this essay, though related to the influence of Sigmund Freud, Erik Erikson, and Carl Rogers, and the historical development of liberal and progressive theologies. I am interested in René Girard, because he is developing a theory of human relationships that includes power alongside love. In his system of thought, power and violence play a central role in the diagnosis and treatment of human sin. My work with perpetrators of violence confirms this hypothesis about the centrality of power and violence. In this essay, I explore Girard's theory in relation to my experience of pastoral counseling with male perpetrators of violence.

How does a power-love analysis challenge traditional pastoral counseling in its misunderstanding of family violence, and how can pastoral counseling be revised in order to take power into account? Even as I ask this question, I remind myself that I am a pastoral counselor—a product of pastoral counseling training and practice. Therefore, I believe in the power of love; I believe that attachment has transformative potential. Attachment is a primary dynamic between parent and child, between partners in marriage, between student and teacher, between client and counselor. So I will be asking this theoretical question: How can we develop a form of pastoral counseling that adequately takes into account both love and power as primary forms of sin and redemption in human life?[2] In this chapter, I can only develop the beginning of such an argument, but I hope it will be a helpful exercise and stimulate us to further thinking.

Girard's Theory of Male Violence

As I reflected on Girard's theory of the origin and cure of interpersonal and social violence in relation to my clinical experience with perpetrators of family violence, I discovered that I share several assumptions with Girard.

First, Girard says that power and violence are a nearly universal part of human experience, not only an infrequent and unfortunate side effect of the search for love. Violence is a root cause of many other social and religious problems, not just a symptom that occurs when social systems break down. Therefore we need to understand power and violence in order to improve the quality of human life.

Second, Girard says that one of the main functions of religion is to sanction "good violence" and condemn "bad violence." By this he means that Christianity and other major religions do not oppose all kinds of violence, but only certain kinds of violence by certain people. For example, religious priests frequently have blessed acts of war by nation-states, capital punishment, and police actions for the sake of social order. According to Girard, violence must be understood in relation to a dynamic he calls "the sacrificial crisis," which occurs when an innocent person or group is injured, killed, or banned by official sanction of the nation or community. The purpose of the sacrificial crisis is to solve another problem that threatens the harmony of the community.

Third, Girard believes that the lie of the sacrificial crisis and its violence must be honestly confronted in order to create social systems that are healing and redemptive for all persons. As long as the dynamics of the sacrificial crisis are hidden by ideologies of necessity and truth, the resulting violence will be impossible to stop.

My work with perpetrators validates these three assumptions, and I hope that the details I provide will add evidence in its favor. This chapter is organized into five sections to guide my reflection on Girard's theory in relation to male violence. In each section I ask how my clinical experience with perpetrators of violence confirms aspects of Girard's theories and/or raises questions for further development of the theories. What does Girard's theory disclose and what does it obscure? René Girard is a complex social scientist and I am no expert on the complexities of Girard and the social science context in which he works. What I can do is test what I know of Girard against my experience as a practical theologian and a pastoral counselor and hope that my questions will be useful to others in their work.

Question #1: Sin and Diagnosis

To what extent does Girard's concept of "mimetic violence and surrogate victimage" explain what is wrong with men who have been violent and incestuous within families in United States society? In simpler words, "mimetic violence and surrogate victimage" is competition between men that often selects women and other innocents as substitute victims for their battles with one another. An example is the batterer who kills his partner because he is jealous of another man's interest "in my woman."

> Once his basic needs are satisfied (indeed, sometimes even before), man is subject to intense desires, though he may not know precisely for what. The reason is that he desires BEING, something he himself lacks and which some other person seems to possess. The subject thus looks to that other person to inform him of what he should desire in order to acquire that being. If the model, who is apparently already endowed with superior being, desires some object, that object must surely be capable of conferring an even greater plenitude of being. It is not through words, therefore, but by the example of his own desire that the model conveys to the subject the supreme desirability of the object. (Girard 1977, 146)

"In this light sin appears as mimetic rivalry with God" (Hammerton-Kelly 1992, 92). My understanding of Girard is that persons seek to grow into maturity and be fulfilled by imitating the desires of someone who seems to be more mature and more fulfilled, such as a child imitating a parent, a student imitating a mentor, or a younger sibling imitating an older sibling. In order to be like the admired person, one imitates the form of that person's desires. By desiring the same objects as the admired one, the person hopes to become like the one admired and to decrease the distinctions between them. The possibility of violence erupts at the point when the social distinctions actually begin to dissipate. This loss of distinction creates mimetic or competitive rivalry from both directions. The parent feels threatened by the growing strength and beauty of the child, and the child begins to feel competitive with the parent. The mentor feels threatened by the knowledge of the student, and the student begins to feel desire for the privileges of the mentor. The older sibling notices the growth of the younger sibling and fears the loss of domination as the younger sibling begins to savor the possibility of having the objects of the older sibling. Since both persons cannot have the same desired objects at the same time, one or the other feels he must dominate and win. In the Oedipal struggle between father and son described by Freud, the father usually wins and the son learns to seek other objects. But the son also learns what it feels like to lose and be humiliated by the greater power of the powerful father. This memory of loss provides motivation for competitive violence in the future.

In situations of potential peerage, between student and mentor or between siblings (in blood or social status), such violence threatens to escalate and destroy the fabric of the community itself. In the midst of such a threat, the sacrificial crisis emerges. At the crucial time, when the dangers are most high, the persons in competitive rivalry discover the mechanism of scapegoating: the possibility of destroying objects of desire instead of each other. When this discovery is made, almost as if by magic, the violence between them dissipates and they turn against the scapegoated person. Scapegoating becomes the mechanism whereby mimetic violence is projected onto a (un)deserving object, and after the sacrifice of that victim, peace is restored. After the scapegoats are destroyed, they are elevated to sacred status to alleviate the guilt with the excuse that they saved the relationship or community from violence. Ritual reenactment of the sacrificial crisis helps the community to remember the dangers of mimetic violence but obscures the universal responsibility for violence.

The question this description raises for me is this: To what extent does "mimetic rivalry and surrogate victimage" explain the intergenerational transmission of violence (Girard 1977, 174ff.) and its corollary of arbitrarily constructed guilt?

The violent men I have worked with seem to learn their violence from two sources: a) their own experiences of observing or experiencing violence during childhood; and b) the power, privilege, and encouragement they get from race, gender, and class ideologies about dominance as a way of being. That is, race, gender, and class ensure that everyone will have some object to exploit in exchange for the abuse they endure from others. Even an abused child will be able to kick the dog, chase the cat, or mutilate the doll.

To take the first point first, most violent men I have seen in pastoral counseling have witnessed or experienced violence during childhood. Men with violent experiences in their childhood who do not become abusers are an important group to study for how intergenerational violence can be prevented. My clinical experience confirms Alice Miller's view from her earlier books, that violence is often passed on from one generation to another by actual experience (Miller 1984). George was sexually abused by his older brother and two friends when he was twelve years old. At first he thought it was exciting sexual play, but when they forced him to perform oral sex, it stopped being fun and he became the scapegoated object for the older boys. Sam was rescued from a violent home of drug addicts when he was only four, only to be beaten with a bullwhip in a foster home and then forced to tolerate emotional abuse, including watching his sister be sexually abused during adolescence. Phil was the excluded child in a family where his father engaged in incest with his younger sister; he was forced to grow up in the streets where he got into all manner of trouble. All three of these men were arrested for fondling their adolescent daughters. If they hadn't been stopped by being arrested, their abuse would have proceeded to intercourse, by their own testimony.

This experience confirms Girard's thesis that the mimetic rivalry of one generation is taught to the next generation in an unending cycle. If we could trace it back, we would find centuries of intergenerational abuse. My own clinical experience has uncovered three and four generations within some families. Witnessing or experiencing abuse as a child gives one the primal injury that leads to mimetic rivalry with other adults and the choice of children by some men as available scapegoats. Girard does not emphasize the importance of prior injury as a motive for mimetic rivalry, but it seems to be true in my clinical experience.

The second point is that social oppression by race, gender, and class set up the structural dynamics of mimetic violence. In the stratified, oppressive, capitalistic society in the United States, everyone is exploited by someone. The silent agreement in operation is that no matter how exploited one is, there is someone more vulnerable to be exploited. In therapy I heard constant stories from the men about humiliation and injury at work. If the men cannot compete and win at work with bosses and peers, then they surely can be dominant at home, and they can hate other scapegoated social groups such as the poor, African Americans, immigrants, and women (Culbertson 1994, 35–41). Abusing children made them feel powerful in spite of the injuries from work. The sexual gratification that came with the abuse became a strong positive reinforcement for the abuse.

One of Girard's corollary theories is what I call "Constructed Guilt." He says: "Anybody can play the part of the surrogate victim. . . . It is futile to look for the secret of the redemptive process in distinctions between the surrogate victim and the other members of the community. The crucial fact is the victim is arbitrary" (Girard 1977, 257). Survivors of family violence are often relieved and enraged when they discover that their victimization was arbitrary. They are relieved because it assuages their own guilt that they deserved or wanted the abuse. They begin to see that even their attempts to manipulate the adult abusing them in order to survive does not make them guilty for the abuse. Working through the consequences of the abuse is enough without also feeling guilty for causing the abuse. On the other hand, arbitrary guilt makes survivors enraged because there is no justification for what happened. Their abuse is without cause or meaning. Such anger can be healing because it often leads to action to protect other innocent victims. Discovering that their abuse was arbitrary discloses the lie of the scapegoating mechanism. Murray Anselm Strauss's (1980) answer to why men batter is "because they can." One molester's answer to his daughter when she asked why was "because you were there." There was no other reason. The scapegoat was innocent. Therefore the violence of scapegoating is evil and should be stopped.

Theories of diagnosis of perpetrators of violence are divided into theories of power and control and theories of gratification, especially sexual gratification. Some programs challenge the abuser's need to dominate others, while other programs prescribe therapy, drugs, or even castration to diminish the sex drive. Power and control seems to be a primary motive for abusers I have known in pastoral counseling. Girard's theory takes a clear position on the side of power, for example, when he says, "The hidden basis of myths is not sexual; it cannot be, for that motif is openly revealed. Nonetheless, sexuality is important insofar as it stimulates violence and provides occasions for it to vent its force" (Girard 1977, 188). I agree with Girard that power has been vastly underestimated as a motive for sexual and physical violence. Theories of love (misdirected as sexual desire) cannot adequately explain male violence. But, as our theories become more complex, we need to integrate theories of power and love. Men who sexually abuse children are trying to make up for narcissistic injuries from childhood and from experiences of exploitation in society. They seek domination, that is, power and control over someone to make up for a fragmented self. They also receive sexual gratification and pseudoconnection with another human being that is a substitute for being loved. It will require much theoretical and theological work to understand how power and love can be combined in one complex theory of pastoral counseling. Until we do, we will be unprepared to work with perpetrators of family violence.

In summary, Girard's theory does help to interpret sin and diagnose personality deficits when working with perpetrators of family violence by emphasizing power and mimetic rivalry and the arbitrary choice of scapegoats. His theory probably underestimates the importance of direct gratification as a motive for abuse.

Question #2: Redemption and Healing

To what extent is demythification (truth-telling) an adequate theory of redemption and healing for men who have been incestuous and violent in their families? Demythification is defined as dissent by way of "retelling the story from the point of view of the victim, exposing the lie, and revealing the founding mechanism. . . . We can no longer ritualize or rationalize our violence. . . . We are thrust into a time of absolute responsibility" (Hammerton-Kelly 1994, 38–39). In common language, truth-telling undermines the power of scapegoating by revealing the lie that supports it.

Girard's theory of redemption and healing is radical honesty about our own participation in violence, solidarity with victims, and acceptance of full responsibility for changing the communities in which we live. A corollary principle must be a changed social consciousness and a life of resistance to the rituals and rationales that make mimetic violence and surrogate victimage work.

This viewpoint describes much of what must go on in therapy and reeducation groups with perpetrators of violence. For most of my clients, at least those with enough self to be candidates for therapy, being arrested and having their violence disclosed creates a crisis at the core of their being. The art of therapy with abusive clients is how to sustain their internal crisis over enough time that a premature resolution is prevented. Premature resolutions can take two forms: a) overidentification of oneself as a victim; b) rationalizing and minimizing the damage one has caused.

Since many perpetrators of violence have witnessed or experienced violence during childhood and also have experienced exploitation because of race or class, the therapist can get caught in seeking healing only for the victimized self of the past. Significant time must be spent listening to the stories of injuries and modeling from the past; these stories are real. But the client who is an abuser is not only a victim, but also a victimizer. The shame around the injury done to others is usually greater and harder to explore than experiences of being a victim. One reminder I use is to make sure that issues of being an abuser get half of the attention in each session. In this way I agree with Girard that absolute honesty in facing one's complicity with violence is part of the redemptive process.

Some therapists make the mistake of joining the client in rationalizing and minimizing the damage done, that is, finding excuses and ignoring the consequences for others. Many abusers feel entitled to the dominance they have established and the power and sexual gratification they obtain from that dominance. They will say things like: "A father has a right to educate his child however he wants. My father beat me and I turned out okay. It is better for my daughter to learn about sex from me than from some rapist out in the streets." There are many versions of such entitlement that men use to justify their abuse, but it all has the same effect—it refuses to face the actual consequences of violence on the victim. Therapists who have not faced their own history as abusers may unconsciously join the client in minimizing the effects of violence on others.

Girard's theory helps me to understand the delicate balance involved in therapy with perpetrators. "Absolute responsibility" means facing the terrible reality of one's own participation as a perpetrator of violence. "Identification with the victim" means more than locating my own experiences of being a victim. It means knowing in detail how the particular victim's life was affected and damaged by my behaviors. Healing for perpetrators is a difficult road that balances empathy and ethical responsibility.

Taking absolute or full responsibility for abusing another person, in my theory of pastoral counseling, is only possible within a relational context of love and power. That is, the perpetrators of violence in therapy slowly change when they begin to trust a counselor who displays sufficient empathy for their pain and enough strength to hold out an alternative ethical vision without being abusive (Winnicott 1984; Kohut 1971). The person who depends on violence to prop up his fragmented self and fill up his empty self is not capable of the "absolute responsibility" Girard calls for, even though it is eventually necessary. What is needed is therapy based on loving attachment within a power structure that protects others from victimization. Love and power must find a proper relational balance—"Fierce Tenderness," as some of my feminist friends call it (Hunt 1991; Ramsay 1998). Fierce reminds us of the strength required to love those who are abusive; tenderness reminds us of the warmth we must have for each human being within their circumstances. Where in Girard's theory is the role of loving and powerful attachments that serve as positive models for change, actually the mirror image to mimetic violence? Unless I am missing it altogether, Girard does not attend sufficiently to the role of love and empathy. Girard helps us a lot in describing the distortions of aggression on a personal and social level, but he underestimates the power of eros and love as healing agents.

Pastoral counseling theory is deficient in its understanding of the relationship of power and love. Empathic bonding with a perpetrator without external control of his or her abuse of others is nearly useless. The inability to address the power dimension is a form of collusion with perpetrators who feel entitled to continue their abuse. But love and empathy do play a crucial role in transformation of abusers into ordinary sinners.

Question #3: Gender and Violence

Does competitive violence and the search for scapegoats work the same for men and women under patriarchy? Are men more violent than women? If so, is it because of nature, learning, or social class?

> At the core of the Oedipus myth, as Sophocles presents it, is the proposition that all masculine relationships are based on reciprocal acts of violence. . . . Both parties in this tragic dialogue have recourse to the same tactics, use the same weapons, and strive for the same goal: destruction of the adversary. (Girard 1977, 48)

Girard himself suggests that his theory is primarily a description of male violence. By use of male authors, male examples, and focus on women as victims, Girard seems to agree with some feminist theories that the structures of violence are primarily male.

> The preponderance of women in the dionysian cult remains a subject of conjecture . . . We may therefore wonder whether the preponderance of women does not constitute a secondary mythological displacement, an effort to exonerate from the accusation of violence, not mankind as a whole, but adult males, who have the greatest need to forget their role in the crisis, because, in fact, they must have been largely responsible for it. They alone risk plunging the community into the chaos of reciprocal violence. . . . The woman qualifies for sacrificial status by reason of her weakness and relatively marginal social status. (Girard 1977, 138–41)

Girard's theory fits some of the data about family violence and feminist and womanist theories of male power and violence. In terms of battering, men are arrested for battering adult women three times as often as vice versa; women are three times more likely to be murdered by a present or former intimate male partner than vice versa; women are three times more likely to seek emergency-room treatment for violence inflicted by a man than vice versa. In terms of sexual abuse, girls are three times more likely to be sexually abused than boys, and the perpetrators of sexual abuse of both boys and girls are ten times more likely to be men than women (Koss 1994, 41–67). This imbalance of male violence over female violence in research statistics and health care programs has led to the creation of many programs to support female victims and survivors but almost none for men, and of many programs to treat male perpetrators of violence but almost none for women. The data seem to support Girard's assumption that mimetic violence is a problem of patriarchy, and that women are more likely sacrificial victims than perpetrators.

However, there is literature and anecdotal material from opposing viewpoints. Within feminism itself there is a vigorous debate about whether and how women socialize children into patriarchy and acceptance of its violence (Benjamin 1988). Child-welfare programs have always had programs of therapy and reeducation for mothers of young children who cause many serious injuries to children. The increase of drug addictions like cocaine and heroin seem to increase the rate of neglect and violence perpetrated on children by women. In my own clinical experience, it is not unusual for male clients to report severe physical and sexual abuse by mothers, older sisters, and adult women in the community.

Girard himself does not present his theory as gender-specific, nor does he use feminist or womanist theories of male power. Girard implies that the mechanism of mimetic rivalry, violence, and scapegoating are at work in most social systems, even when women are in leadership positions. Whether the mechanism works independently of gender or in some complex interaction with it is, of course, a matter for further research and development of theory. I follow the work of Catherine MacKinnon, who has a similar view as Girard, that power and violence are more basic than sexuality and gender, and once in place as ideologies, are influential on women as well as men. MacKinnon believes that "violence is sexy" in the sense that eroticism is defined by violence, though men are more likely to be sexually predatory and women to be victims of sexual violence (MacKinnon 1987; see also Russell 1993). The reversal of gender roles may be an illustration of the power of mimetic violence to make victims and victimizers of anyone who is vulnerable, regardless of gender.

The intriguing question, though, is whether women, who have been oppressed for millennia under patriarchy, have developed a subversive wisdom through their resistance to the consequences of patriarchy in their lives. Patricia Hill Collins makes an argument like this regarding black women. While black women are sometimes perpetrators of violence in the family, they have survived gender, race, and class oppression through resistance (Collins 1990). Much scholarship is being done by womanist scholars to retrieve the wisdom and resources of resistance from the oral traditions of the past. Perhaps it is not necessary to see women as innocent of the violence Girard identifies (Brock 1993). Rather, it is important to identify the subversive traditions of resistance that make possible "retelling the story from the point of view of the victim, exposing the lie, and revealing the founding mechanism" (Hammerton-Kelly 1994, 38).

Recently, with the help of a new generation of women scholars, pastoral counseling has addressed issues of gender asymmetry in its theories and practices (Glaz and Moessner 1991; Moessner 1996; Graham and Halsey 1993). Making a power analysis of gender central to pastoral counseling is crucial for doing something about family violence. Male violence is a major ethical and theological problem in Christian families that has been overlooked. A theory based on love alone too easily falls into blaming victims for being abused and minimizing the exploitation that men impose within their families. As we have explored the power dimensions of our theory, pastoral counselors must integrate these insights with a theory of empathy, attachment, and transference.

Question #4: Race and Violence

Does Girard's theory help explain the persistence of classes of permanent scapegoats in the United States, such as African Americans and other ethnic groups, women, children, and the poor?

> The sacrificial crisis—a repetition of the original, spontaneous "lynching" that restored order in the community by reestablishing, around the figure of the surrogate victim, that sentiment of social accord that had been destroyed in the onslaught of reciprocal violence. . . . If my thesis is correct, the pharmakos, like Oedipus himself, has a dual connotation. On the one hand he is a woebegone figure, an object of scorn who is also weighted down with guilt; a butt for all sorts of gibes, insults, and of course, outbursts of violence. On the other hand, we find him surrounded by a quasi-religious aura of veneration; he has become a sort of cult object. This duality reflects the metamorphosis the ritual victim is designed to effect; the victim draws to itself all the

violence infecting the original victim and through its own death transforms this baneful violence into beneficial violence, into harmony and abundance. (Girard 1977, 95)

The above quote from Girard seems to describe racism in the United States fairly well. African Americans, foremost in the public mind among the minority ethnic groups, serve as objects of projection for every form of violence in our society—murder, rape, drugs, gangs, child abuse. At the same time, African American images in sports and music create a "quasi-religious aura of veneration." The paradox is startling: 5 percent of the population (black men) make up a huge percentage of superheroes in the major sports of football, basketball, and baseball, and at the same time make up more than 50 percent of the United States prison population of 1.7 million persons.

According to Girard, the need of a society for a class of permanent scapegoats indicates a firm commitment to the sacrificial crisis of scape-goating. I feel uncomfortable with Girard's observation that modern Western societies are less captivated by the sacrificial crisis (Girard 1977, 15–27). The complaints of ethnic and immigrant groups seem to provide evidence that scapegoating is a mechanism for social order in many parts of the United States.

Men who engage in incest and abuse within the family seem to be an accurate reflection of the larger social forces I have just described. Perpetrators of family violence act with greater impunity whenever their chosen victims are less valued in the larger society, and when protection for children is less likely to be effective. For example, adopted and stepchil-dren are twice as likely to be sexually abused within families, and children with disabilities are four times as likely. Likewise, African American chil-dren are twice as likely as other children to be abused in families. There seems an inverse correlation between how much certain classes of children are valued and how much they are abused. The more vulnerable a child is, the more likely that child will be abused. With child abuse rates running between thirty to 50 percent, the vulnerability of children is high (Archer 1994, 195–232).

Girard's theory of the existence of a permanent class of scapegoats begins to make sense of the role of children, women, and oppressed eco-nomic groups in the United States. Whenever race, gender, and class accu-mulate to increase vulnerability, the possibility of social protection diminishes.

An increasing literature from African American pastoral counselors in the United States is challenging our field to understand the oppression of race, class, and gender (Wimberly 1995; Smith 1997; Hollies 1992; Baker-Fletcher 1992). These power relationships create a different reality for some families, and have generated a subversive culture of resistance that must be respected as health-giving rather than pathologized. Their work discloses the collusion of pastoral counseling with the ideologies of the dominant white supremest culture. As long as pastoral counseling remains a theory of love rather than an integrated theory of love and power, its complicity in evil will continue.

Question #5: Jesus and Violence

How has Christ redeemed humanity from sin and evil? How has Jesus helped to disclose the sacrificial crisis, according to Girard, and liberate us from competitive violence and the need for scapegoats?

The central Christological question for pastoral counseling can be crudely stated this way: "What has Jesus done for me?" In more scholarly language, Christology is the question about how Jesus' life, death, and resurrection leads to liberation of human bodies, spirits, and communities when we believe and follow Jesus today.

The heart of Girard's argument, as I understand it, is that the sacrificial crisis—the sanction of violence by religion—depends on secrecy and lies. The community must believe that some violence is unavoidable and caused by forces outside the community—that is, most of those killed by violence are not innocent but deserve to be abused and killed. The community must believe that the deaths of certain persons or groups actually protect the community and restore nonviolence. The final step in his theory is that those who are killed need to be honored later to distinguish good from bad violence.

In Girard's Christology, Jesus' life and death help us to understand the lie of scapegoating because, in spite of his death, he was clearly innocent. Jesus lived and died in such a way that the scapegoating mechanism itself was exposed as pathological. Because of Jesus, we know that the violence in communities comes from the hearts of men, not outside forces, and that victims who are scapegoated are innocent. This disclosure of the lie by Jesus shows a way out of the sacrificial crisis: humans have the choice of "retelling the story from the point of view of the victim, exposing the lie, and revealing the founding mechanism" (Hammerton-Kelly 1994, 38). According to Hammerton-Kelly, St. Paul understood the sacrificial crisis and showed how faith in Jesus gives humanity a new religious and ethical choice.

> To leave the community of sacred violence is to refuse the una-
> nimity of conflictual mimesis. As soon as one dissents, one
> becomes a victim oneself. Such dissent is tantamount to identify-
> ing with the victim, because the group of conflictual mimesis
> needs unanimity to function and can treat dissenters only as vic-
> tims. Thus Paul is transformed from persecutor to persecuted, he
> is crucified with Christ. (Hammerton-Kelly 1992, 69)

By identification with Christ crucified, the innocent scapegoat, we dissent from the sacred violence of the community and join in the forces of
resistance to live in "absolute honesty" as free people within the love of
God. Girard's theory has a Christology—in Christ, humans have the
choice of dissenting from the sacrificial crisis. By believing in Jesus, that is,
believing that Jesus was an innocent scapegoat, and by following Jesus, that
is, following his way of nonacquisitive sacrificial love, we can find salvation
in our personal, interpersonal, and social lives.

In some ways, this is a Christology that describes good pastoral counseling with perpetrators. First, a pastoral counselor believes that all people are
capable of change given the right circumstances. A pastoral counselor is
willing to engage with perpetrators with a sense of hope, is not afraid of
using power in order to control evil, and is willing to engage in mutual and
sometimes sacrificial love for the salvation of his or her clients. This mechanism is similar to the needed spiritual transformation for the perpetrator
himself. A client in therapy must believe in himself enough to want change,
be willing to engage with the counselor, be willing to comply with the
imposition of external power and control to stop his abuse, and be willing
to engage in mutual and sometimes sacrificial relationships for the sake of
his own salvation and the protection of future victims. This deconstructive
and reconstructive task is complex given the many layers of defense against
such change and the terror of confronting his own emptiness. But the
promise of the gospel is that salvation is possible.

What image of God is helpful to perpetrators as they engage in such a
theological task? In my own thinking I have rejected both orthodox and liberal theologies, because they are naive about the power dimension of salvation. I have developed, instead, an image of the relational, ambiguous God
who is engaged in the world and does not shrink back from the ambiguity
involved in sharing responsibility for the evil of the world. Images of God as
unified, omnipotent, and perfectly loving, I believe, are counterproductive
for perpetrators of violence in their search for salvation.

I find support for my view in the work of Girard, especially his discussion
about fathers and sons:

> The "father" projects into the future the first tentative movements of his son and sees that they lead straight to the mother or the throne. The incest wish, the patricide wish, does not belong to the child but springs from the mind of the adult, the model. . . . The son is always the last to learn that what he desires is incest and patricide, and it is the hypocritical adults who undertake to enlighten him in this matter. . . . If the Oedipus complex constitutes an erroneous reading of the double bind, then we can say that those desires that the world at large, and the father in particular, regard as emanating from the son's own patricide-incest drive actually derive from the father himself in his role as model. (Girard 1977, 175)

In this passage, Girard clearly lays the responsibility for the sacrificial crisis first on the religious imagination of the father or mentor, that is, on the educational processes of the community. The father sees his son growing up with dreams of eventually taking his place in the marriage and in the world. The mentor sees his student gaining competence with hopes of replacing the mentor at the university. Competitive rivalry is actually introduced into the relationship by fathers and mentors before their progeny are aware of the dynamics of their relationship.

In theological terms, this means that mimetic or competitive rivalry is constructed by humans within our relationship with God. In the crucifixion, God reveals a full understanding of mimetic violence and also a capacity to abstain from its full implementation from the divine side. This means that God has the potential to engage in mimetic violence and the potential to abstain from it. Therefore God can engage humans in either violence or nonviolence. This is what I mean by the relational, ambiguous God. Every good or evil desire and behavior that is possible for humans is also possible for God. God is not limited to being good all the time, but has to decide over and over again to be good. In faith we pray that God will be good, but we know that our lives could be snuffed out in a moment if God chose to be evil.

This image of God is very important for pastoral counseling with perpetrators. When I counsel with a perpetrator of violence, I must know that I am potentially capable of whatever violence the client has imposed on others. We are no different at the level of potential good and evil. I am capable of whatever good and evil he has done, and he is capable of both good and evil. If this is not true, then there can be no empathy and no healing (Peck 1983).

In actual practice, I have met several perpetrators who so horrified me that I could not work with them. This does not mean that I am not capable of the violence they committed, but I was not capable of living for very long in the religious world they had created by engaging in such violence. One example was a pedophile who had been arrested for molesting a nine-year-old boy in Times Square, New York. After several sessions of therapy, I asked him whether he would mind if his own adolescent son were molested. He said he would not mind if his son were molested. At that point, I was unable to continue my work with him, and I hoped that someone else could help him. My own moral strength was not sufficient to enter into his world for the sake of therapy. In a second case, I did an assessment with a man who had violently raped a woman in Central Park, New York, in broad daylight. He had already spent eight years in prison for several rapes. I could not contain my own feelings of fear and revulsion enough to help him. As opposed to Scott Peck, who labels such persons as evil and beyond hope, I am cognizant of my own limitations. It was not their depth of evil that prevented healing, but my inability to have empathy for them in their life experiences (Peck 1983). Given my own development and maturity, these men were beyond my ability to cope.

However, my theological view is that God is not beyond understanding such violent men. The crucifixion reveals the unanimous consent, including the disciples, of a whole community to the death of God. God was not shocked by such a depth of evil, and God responded with nonviolent love and power in a way that changed the world. I believe in the God of Jesus Christ, and in his act of salvation for all people. I commit myself to believe in and follow Jesus in my ministry of pastoral counseling, to try to be a relational, ambiguous presence for perpetrators of family violence.

Toward a New Theory of Pastoral Counseling

I think Girard's greatest contribution to pastoral counseling is his brilliant description of the role of power in human relationships. Pastoral counseling has much to learn about power as an aspect of theory and practice, and I hope that attending to issues of power will help pastoral counseling to become a resource for victims, survivors, and perpetrators of family violence. I think pastoral counseling has a contribution to make to Girard in its insistence on the role of love and attachment in human relationships. In the end, I hope for a new theory of pastoral counseling that understands both power and love.

Bibliography

Adams, Carol, and Marie Fortune, eds. 1995. *Violence against Women and Children: A Christian Theological Sourcebook*. New York: Crossroad.

Archer, John, ed. 1994. *Male Violence*. New York: Routledge.

Baker-Fletcher, Garth Kasimu. 1996. *Xodus: An African American Male Journey*. Minneapolis: Fortress Press.

Benjamin, Jessica. 1988. *The Bonds of Love: Psychoanalysis, Feminism, and the Problem of Domination*. New York: Pantheon.

Brock, Rita Nakashima. 1988. *Journeys by Heart: A Christology of Erotic Power*. New York: Crossroad.

Collins, Patricia Hill. 1990. *Black Feminist Thought: Knowledge, Consciousness, and the Politics of Empowerment*. New York: Routledge.

Culbertson, Philip. 1994. *Counseling Men*. Minneapolis: Fortress Press.

Dobash, R. Emerson, and Russell P. 1992. *Women, Violence, and Social Change*. New York: Routledge.

Farley, Wendy. 1990. *Tragic Vision and Divine Compassion: A Contemporary Theodicy*. Louisville: Westminster.

Girard, René. 1977. *Violence and the Sacred*. Trans. Patrick Gregory. Baltimore: Johns Hopkins Univ. Press.

Glaz, Maxine, and Jeanne Moessner, eds. 1991. *Women in Travail and Transition: A New Pastoral Care*. Minneapolis: Fortress Press.

Graham, Elaine, and Margaret Halsey, eds. 1993. *Life Cycles: Women and Pastoral Care*. London: SPCK.

Hammerton-Kelly, Robert G. 1994. *The Gospel and the Sacred: Poetics of Violence in Mark*. Minneapolis: Fortress Press.

———. 1992. *Sacred Violence: Paul's Hermeneutic of the Cross*. Minneapolis: Fortress Press.

Harrison, Beverly. 1985. "The Power of Anger in the Work of Love." *Making the Connections*. Ed. Carol S. Robb. Boston, Beacon. 3–21.

Hollies, Linda, ed. 1992. *WomanistCare: How to Tend the Souls of Women*. Joliet, Ill.: Woman to Woman Ministries.

Hunt, Mary. 1991. *Fierce Tenderness: A Feminist Theology of Friendship*. New York: Crossroad.

Kohut, Heinz. 1971. *The Analysis of the Self: A Systematic Approach to the Psychoanalytic Treatment of Narcissistic Personality Disorders*. New York: International Universities.

Koss, Mary P., ed. 1994. *No Safe Haven: Male Violence against Women at Home, at Work, and in the Community*. Washington, D.C.: American Psychological Association, 41–67.

MacKinnon, Catherine. 1987. *Feminism Unmodified: Discourses on Life and Law.* Cambridge, Mass.: Harvard Univ. Press.

Miller, Alice. 1984. *For Your Own Good: Hidden Cruelty in Child-Rearing and the Roots of Violence.* New York: Farrar, Straus, and Giroux.

Moessner, Jeanne, ed. 1996. *Through the Eyes of Women: Insights for Pastoral Care.* Minneapolis: Fortress Press.

Peck, Scott. 1983. *People of the Lie: The Hope for Healing Human Evil.* New York: Simon and Schuster.

Poling, James Newton. 1996. *Deliver Us from Evil: Resisting Racial and Gender Violence.* Minneapolis: Fortress Press.

―――. 1991. *The Abuse of Power: A Theological Problem.* Nashville: Abingdon.

Poling, James Newton, and Christie Cozad Neuger. 1997. *The Care of Men.* Nashville: Abingdon.

Ramsay, Nancy. 2002. Personal Correspondence. Fierce Tenderness is the central metaphor for her new book on treatment of survivors of family violence.

―――. 1998. *Pastoral Diagnosis: A Resource for Ministers of Care and Counseling.* Minneapolis: Fortress Press.

Ramsay, Nancy and John McClure, eds. 1998. *Telling the Truth: Preaching about Sexual and Domestic Violence.* Cleveland: United Church.

Russell, Diana. 1993. *Making Violence Sexy: Feminist Views on Pornography.* New York: Teacher's College.

Schwager, Raymund. 1987. *Must There Be Scapegoats? Violence and Redemption in the Bible.* San Francisco: Harper and Row.

Smith, Archie, Jr. 1997. *Navigating the Deep River: Spirituality in African American Families.* Cleveland, Ohio: United Church.

Stevens, Maryanne, ed. 1993. *Reconstructing the Christ Symbol: Essays in Feminist Christology.* New York: Paulist.

Strauss, Murray Anselm, ed. 1980. *Behind Closed Doors: Violence in the American Family.* New York: Anchor.

Wimberly, Edward P. 1995. *African American Pastoral Care.* Nashville: Abingdon.

Winnicott, D. W. 1984. *Deprivation and Delinquency.* London: Tavistock.

Notes

1. The best source of information about family violence and religious issues is the Center for the Prevention of Sexual and Domestic Violence, Seattle, WA: <http://www.cpsdv.org>. My orientation of male violence depends on feminist and womanist analysis. See Carol Adams and Marie Fortune.

2. For further discussion of power in feminist theory, see Harrison; Farley; and Ramsay, 127–44.

8

Allies in the Sexual Healing Journey: Reflections for Partners of Women Who Were Sexually Abused as Children

Merle Longwood

During the past decade many of us have become increasingly aware of the ambiguity and complexity of our sexuality. In the best of circumstances, our sexuality provides the basis for our experience of intimacy, communion, and ecstasy. I agree with James Nelson, who observed in his deservedly widely read book, *The Intimate Connection*:

> Above all, sexuality is the desire for intimacy and communion, both emotionally and physically. It is the physiological and psychological grounding of our capacity to love. At its *undistorted* [emphasis mine] best, our sexuality is that basic eros of our humanness— urging, pulling, luring, driving us out of loneliness into communion, out of stagnation into creativity. (Nelson 1988, 26)

On the other hand, when it has become *distorted* by unfortunate circumstances, our sexuality may instead be the source of feelings of confusion, pain, guilt, shame, and even terror; and when we experience our sexuality in these latter ways, intimacy, communion, and ecstasy are rare phenomena in our emotional lives.[1] One of the most significant of these downside circumstances can occur when we as men, or our partners, have experienced sexual abuse (or perhaps more appropriately stated, intimate violence[2]) as children.

I was in a long-term relationship with a woman, Annette (not her real name), who was sexually abused as a child. I have chosen to write this essay to help myself understand more fully the dynamics of that relationship, even though it has now ended, and how I can learn from it to aid me in my continuing quest to nurture and heal "the intimate connection"[3] between my male sexuality and my body-mediated masculine spirituality. Early in our relationship, Annette told me that she had been molested by her father when she was a young child, but she never dwelt upon that experience and, for the most part, she seemed to pass it off as not all that significant. Consequently I, too, did not make much of this piece of information at the time, for I had no idea that it was really that important, though I was aware that she did not respect or trust her father. Now, several years later, I am convinced that many of the difficulties that emerged in our relationship, especially as we moved closer together emotionally and began to talk about making a commitment to marriage, had their origins in Annette's having been sexually molested by her father when she was a young girl, and my response to that abuse. Even more importantly, I now realize how ineffective I was in dealing with my own pain when she rejected my proposal that we work together toward mutual healing. As we stopped trying to negotiate the matters related to our intimate relationship, the complexities of feelings that emerged within me and between us never got sorted out very well; and we finally drifted apart.

Without going into great detail, I will say that because I was not able to deal with these issues within our relationship, I sought the counsel of a friend who is a therapist. I needed help to sort through my mixed feelings during this anguished time when it became apparent that there probably would be a separation between Annette and myself. I then began to make some connections between the deterioration of our relationship and the little bit of information Annette had shared with me years earlier about having been molested by her father. My friend introduced me to the concepts and the literature related to sexual abuse,[4] and she helped me interpret the confused signals I had been receiving from Annette as our relationship had grown close (including discussions about getting married) and then was blown apart by behaviors that are frequently manifested by women who have been sexually abused as children.

As I brought these interpretations back to Annette, I now realize how little I dealt with my own feelings, and how I completely missed understanding how Annette might have been resisting my assuming a role as a controlling fixer-of-the-relationship. For the most part, she denied, or at least minimized, the significance of her early experience of intimate violence. She did not want to talk about it with me or with the therapist whose counsel she sought to help her decide whether to move closer to me, or to stay in a relationship she had begun as "an affair" as she acted out her felt need to distance from me.

At the same time, Annette did arrange through her best friend to purchase for me a copy of a small booklet, written in a question-and-answer format, that interprets the experience of women who were sexually abused

as children (Spear 1988). This brief handbook provided a lot of basic information and perspective, including one of the most concise summaries of
the long-term effects of sexual abuse that I have read. Addressing husbands,
lovers, or partners of women who were sexually abused as children, the
author of this guide writes:

> There are a great number of issues that need to be dealt with, such
> as low self-esteem, poor body image, fear of not being in control,
> lack of trust, inability to know what she feels, difficulty in talking
> about feelings, anger, guilt, and denial—to name a few. In short
> the main messages children get from abusive, and other dysfunc-
> tional families are: "Don't Trust," "Don't Talk," and "Don't Feel."
> All three need to be reversed in order to lead a healthy adult life.
> (Spear 12)

Although I now believe this list identifies issues that may arise from a
variety of circumstances, at the time I recognized these as issues with which
I had seen Annette struggle during our years together, and apparently,
though we never talked in detail about the booklet after I received it, so did
she. I am now aware, also, that the emotional issues listed as consequences
of sexual abuse in this booklet are strikingly typical for many men in our
society, including myself.

One of the first things this booklet suggested, as well as other books I
subsequently consulted, is that a partner must learn about sexual abuse
(Bass and Davis 1993; Bass and Davis 1988; Davis 1991; Gil 1991; Lew 1990;
Maltz 1992; Maltz and Holman 1987; Warshaw 1988). So during the time
when the future of our relationship was unclear, but continuing after my
breakup with Annette, I immersed myself in the literature on sexual abuse.[5]
I realized then, as I understand even more fully now, that this was a com-
pensatory response, which I took because I was aware that I was not going
to have this learning and healing experience within the context of a continuing relationship with Annette. In addition, I began to bring the insights I
was gathering from my reading into the ethics courses I taught, as well as
into talks I presented in the community, and into conversations I had with
a number of men and women who are part of my circle of friends and
acquaintances. I approached other people not as an expert, but as one who
was trying to learn more about this phenomenon. I was amazed to discover
how many people were willing to share something about their own experience of either having been sexually abused as children or having had the
experience of relating to a partner who was sexually abused as a child. Thus

far, I have encountered far more women than men who acknowledge having been abused as children, and most men who have shared their experiences have done so as partners of women who have suffered abuse. But it may well be that we are at a very early stage in opening up these questions for men, and that more of us will share from our own experience as survivors of sexual abuse as we feel it is safe to do so.[6] I suspect there is much more abuse of males than we know about yet, though it is quite likely that it is not strictly sexual abuse, but emotional abuse.

Of the men with whom I talked, some, like myself, have gone through separation (or divorce) from partners who had been sexually abused; others have been accompanying their partners on a healing journey; and still others have continued to live with women who have not sought to engage in any deliberately focused sexual healing process.[7] The reflections that follow draw upon the insights shared with me by other men, a number of conversations I have had with professional therapists who have worked with women who have been sexually abused as children, and what I have digested from the readings I have done on this topic over the past several years.

In the literature I have read, there is no settled definition of what constitutes sexual abuse, but Wendy Maltz's concise working definition will serve as well as any for this discussion. She writes:

> *Sexual abuse is harm done to a person's sexuality through sexual domination, manipulation, and exploitation.* Sexual abuse is harm done that robs a person of any or all of his or her sexual rights, which characterize the relational and reciprocal relationships between people in community. When these rights are infringed on in the course of sexual abuse, the victim's sexuality, or sense of self as embodied, suffers harm. (Maltz 1992, 35)

This definition is particularly helpful if we view sexuality, as Nelson and many other contemporary writers on sexuality do, as involving a total sense of one's self as a bodyself. That is, sexuality is far more than "sex" as we popularly use the term to refer to sexual intercourse, although it includes that (see Nelson 1978, 17–18; United Church of Christ 1997, 12; Evangelical Lutheran Church in America 1991, 5). It is that integrated, individualized, unique expression of the self that may be manifested in a healthy manner when "sexual rights"—which Maltz describes by emphasizing their meaning not just in individual contexts, but as relational and reciprocal within community—are protected, enabling us to develop positive attitudes and behaviors to express our sexuality. These rights include:

> The right to develop healthy attitudes toward sex
> The right to sexual privacy
> The right to protection from bodily invasion and harm
> The right to say no to sexual behavior
> The right to control touch and sexual contact
> The right to stop sexual arousal that feels inappropriate or
> uncomfortable
> The right to develop our sexuality according to our sexual
> preferences and orientation
> The right to enjoy healthy sexual pleasure and satisfaction.
> (Maltz 1992, 35)

When these rights, which presuppose a broad definition of sexuality that includes bodily and emotional integrity, are infringed upon by perpetrators of sexual abuse, those who are exploited often become confused and develop feelings of powerlessness. The effects of such abuse are likely to have an impact on "how we feel about being a man or a woman; how we feel about our bodies, sex organs, and bodily functions; how we think about sex; how we express ourselves sexually; [and] how we experience physical pleasure and intimacy with others" (Maltz 1992, 2).

In the early stages of my reading, I ran across a popular article that expanded upon the list I had gleaned from the booklet I had been given by Annette's friend. This article listed a range of symptoms, when viewed from this distance perhaps too expansive and generalized, that survivors of sexual abuse may experience, suggesting to readers that they might want to consider joining a self-help group or seek incest counseling if they identify with more than four or five of the following experiences:

- Cannot remember large portions of your childhood
- Have an inexplicable aversion to certain family members or to
  being touched in certain ways or on certain parts of the body
- Have feelings of worthlessness, self-hatred, and/or low self-esteem
- Have addictions such as alcohol, narcotics, overeating, or
  compulsive spending
- Have feelings of disgust about your body
- Have inexplicable feelings of shame or guilt
- Are a workaholic or chronic underachiever
- Have a revulsion to sex or engage in obsessive sexual activities

- Feel isolated from other people
- Feel as though nothing you do will ever be good enough
- Have nightmares, flashbacks, or fear of going to bed, bathing, or taking a shower
- Are accident-prone or given to cutting yourself, burning yourself, or other forms of self-mutilation
- Are unable to express your feelings
- Disassociate from your body during sex
- Have trouble forming and maintaining intimate relationships
- Are afraid of having children or being alone with children
- Have inexplicable body aches, gastrointestinal troubles, muscle spasms, jerks, or twitches
- Have a sharp startle response and a fear of being touched
- Have sexual dysfunctions, such as impotence or frigidity
- Are subject to recurring depression
- Have a tendency to sexualize relationships, even when you don't want to
- Have a strong, inexplicable fear of people of the opposite sex or the same sex
- Feel powerless over people and situations
- Have a hard time knowing what you want or trusting your intuition
- Tend to get into destructive relationships (Raichlen 1989, 50)

In retrospect, I believe that many of the statements on this list cry out for a more nuanced interpretation and ordering, and that many of the items on the list relate to issues that are pervasive throughout our culture, not uniquely experienced by those who have suffered from intimate violence. But at the time I first read it I thought it provided me with a clearer understanding of the root cause of what had been happening in the relationship between Annette and myself.

More importantly, I became aware during that time that sexual abuse may take a number of forms (Heggen 1993, 22–24), and that none of these forms is necessarily less serious in its aftereffects than another form. For example, though many initially think that abuse involving physical contact, and particularly genital manipulation or penetration, must be the most serious form of abuse, I am becoming increasingly convinced that what is most profoundly at stake is whatever affects our capacity to experience ourselves as sensuous persons who embody passions in the totality of our beings. From this perspective, verbal abuse, involving inappropriate comments, may be just as devastating, or even more devastating, for some victims. Sexual abuse may also be visual, involving exposure to pornography or exhibitionism. Or the abuse may be psychological, such as when a parent behaves in ways that blur appropriate boundaries between the parent and the child (Adams 1991).

A final important piece of my learning involved becoming aware of how widespread sexual abuse is. In addition to the anecdotal evidence I gathered from the stories individuals shared with me, the research I read suggested that sexual abuse has reached epidemic proportions. Though the figures on the prevalence of sexual abuse are constantly changing, particularly with increases reported in the number of males estimated as victims, research estimates suggest that about one in three to four women and one in four to seven men have been victims of sexual abuse as children (see, for example, the studies reported in Finkelhor 1984; Russell 1986; Hunter 1990; Hillman and Solek-Tefft 1988; and Janus and Janus 1993).

While I made these efforts to increase my understanding of sexual abuse, Annette gradually came to a decision that she did not want to remain in an intimate relationship with me, and with great pain I realized I had no choice but to accept that. Everything I had learned up to that point, which has been reinforced in my subsequent research about sexual abuse, made me aware that the healing process would have required hard work, determination, and a significant investment of time, not only for her but for me. If the survivor is not ready to face the abuse and explore the impact it has had on her life, no one can force her to do so.[8] The decision to enter the healing process would have required Annette, and me as her partner, to make an active commitment to heal, to seek professional help and/or support groups, to seek the truth however unpleasant, to face the unknown and give up the comfortable, to make changes, and perhaps most difficult of all, to feel the feelings necessary to resolve the pain (Davis 1991, 29). It was easier for Annette to leave the relationship with me and to connect with a man who, as far as I was able to discern, preferred to remain in a quite distant relationship with her, neither asking for nor offering to provide much intimacy. But it left me without the option of dealing with my own issues within the context of the relationship within which they had emerged.

As I view it in retrospect, Annette and I reached a "crisis of intimacy" in our relationship. In development psychology, the term "crisis" refers to a time of significant change and decision in a person's life, but I have extended the meaning of that term to apply it to our relationship.[9] A crisis is a period of both vulnerability and opportunity, as the old Chinese proverb—"crisis" equals "danger plus opportunity"—suggests, and it involves issues that require decision. The vulnerability is great, because much that is happening makes the individuals feel that their lives are disorganized and in turmoil. They can remain in transition for a long period of time or fall back in defeat and fear. The opportunity is equally great, but it requires risk. A crisis of intimacy can provide the occasion for the couple to go through a transition from one level of development as a couple in intimate relationship to another.

For many people—though I did not experience this, because Annette and I did not stay together as a couple—the recovery process is a way not only of working through such a crisis, but of coming to a greater degree of wholeness than they have ever experienced before.[10] The vulnerability in this crisis lies in the changes that are bound to occur when the survivor of sexual abuse begins to work actively on her recovery, and everything that was familiar is up for review. As her insights, feelings, and behaviors change, so also will all her relationships, and the partner of the abused person may feel that the woman he knew well is acting like a complete stranger. From a Christian perspective, this can be understood as an opportunity to recognize and embrace the brokenness and inadequacy of the relationship as it had existed, in order to be opened to deeper levels of consciousness, insights, and relationship with each other and to God. This crisis can be understood not just as psychological, but as a spiritual crisis that requires both the survivor and the partner of the survivor to confront the emptiness of self and the silence of God, and to do battle with old gods, loyalties, and affirmations that no longer give life coherence and meaning. Letting go of inadequate bases for self-worth and security and trusting in the new and unknown has, finally, to do with accepting the grace of God, with affirming the word that continues to become flesh and dwells among us.

For the sexual healing process to serve as an opportunity, it is necessary for the couple to let the relationship as they have known it die. The myriad of failures and sin, the sense of worth that was dependent on the relationship as it was, the identities they had that made them feel successful because the relationship had seemed to work—all of these have to be let go, to be allowed to die. It is precisely in such an ending of one form of the relationship—which may be accompanied by withdrawal, mood swings, crying jags, irrational anger, regression, resentment, confusion and preoccupation, fear, mistrust, and inconsistency of response—that there may be an opportunity for a new beginning. In the end, both the survivor and the partner can acknowledge the suffering, alienation, frustrated hopes, and false gods they have clung to, and discover a new process of spiritual reconstruction. As denial, anger, guilt, and shame give way to a new sense of self-understanding, they can begin to incorporate what has happened, let go of the way the relationship was, and move into a new chapter of the story of their lives.

Finally, I want to make a brief observation about what we as men, as individuals concerned about the connections between our sexuality and our spirituality, might begin to do to prevent sexual abuse from continuing to be as widespread as it is. In doing so, I am motivated by the same interpretation of the basic theological and ethical meaning of sexual abuse as Marie Fortune, one of the pioneer Christian writers on the topic of sexual abuse and sexual violence, who insists that such intimate violence is a multidimensional sin. By sin she means that it creates "alienation, brokenness and estrangement. . . . Sin is the rupture of relationship and may be experienced psychologically, physically, spiritually, and socially" (Fortune 1983, 76–87). It is a *bodily sin* because it violates the bodily integrity of the abused and may result in lifelong body-related issues for the victim. Child sexual abuse has been identified as one of the initial traumatic causes behind certain illnesses, including multiple personality disorders and eating disorders such as anorexia and bulimia (Redmond 1989, 72). It is a *relational sin* because the perpetrator of such a breach of relations violates trust and destroys the possibility of a healthy relationship between the victim and the abuser. It also makes it difficult for the victim to trust others, and it may impede other current and future relationships. It is a *sexual sin* because it distorts and misuses God's precious gift of sexuality (Fortune 1983, 87). It is a *social sin,* thriving in an environment of sexism that sustains dominant/subordinate relationships and encourages secretive situations; these secretive situations in turn sustain abusive relationships and create a destructive environment.

Sexual abuse as a social sin is illustrated by the story told by Karen, a survivor, who said in a speech:

> When I was four years old I was sexually molested by someone I knew and had learned to trust. That someone was my father. When one is so young it is easy to believe what adults say and do to you is right, even if it is wrong. It is easy to get caught up in promises and special secrets. It is easy to become a victim, again

and again. . . . Incest and rape are not about sex. They are about power and control. It's about big people over little people, superior over subordinate. To heal requires that I gain a sense of control in my life. I've gained enough control to make the transition from victim to survivor. (Poling 1991, 35, 41)

Judith Herman agrees that incestuous abuse is not really about sex but about power and control, and she perceives it as an inevitable result of the patriarchal family structure. She argues, consequently, that what must be done is to make significant and radical efforts to transform the family if we want to prevent abuse from occurring. The idea of "father rule" will have to give way to the cooperative rule of both parents, and the division of labor by gender will have to be altered so that fathers and mothers share equally in the care of children (Herman 1981, 202). I could not agree more. That is where we as men have our work cut out for us, including not just the restructuring of the family and more egalitarian parenting, but the transformation of masculinity more broadly to challenge the ways in which power and control have been so deeply rooted in our understanding of what it means to be a man. In addition, reflecting on this experience moves us to rethink our understanding of God, who has characteristically been viewed in exclusively masculine terms that have legitimated, and even sacralized, the dominance of men and the "othering" of women. Many feminist scholars, and a few profeminist scholars, have written about the resources available in the Christian tradition for developing more inclusive images of the divine (Poling 1991, 153–82; Brown and Parker 1989; Brock 1989; Blomquist 1989; and Bohn 1989). As we move into the twenty-first century, men (and also women) are challenged to create more liberating ways of integrating male sexuality and male spirituality.

Bibliography

Adams, Kenneth M. 1991. *Silently Seduced: When Parents Make Their Children Partners: Understanding Covert Incest.* Deerfield Beach, Fla.: Health Communications.

Bass, Ellen, and Laura Davis. 1993. *Beginning to Heal: A First Book for Survivors of Child Sexual Abuse.* New York: Harper Perennial.

———. 1988. *The Courage to Heal: A Guide for Women Survivors of Child Sexual Abuse.* New York: HarperPerennial.

Bloomquist, Karen L. 1989. "Sexual Violence: Patriarchy's Offense and Defense." *Christianity, Patriarchy, and Abuse: A Feminist Critique.* Ed. Joanne Carlson

Brown and Carol R. Bohn. New York: Pilgrim. 62–69.

Bohn, Carol R. 1989. "Dominion to Rule: The Roots and Consequences of a Theology of Ownership." *Christianity, Patriarchy, and Abuse: A Feminist Critique.* Ed. Joanne Carlson Brown and Carol R. Bohn. New York: Pilgrim. 105–16.

Briere, John N. 1993. *Child Abuse Trauma: Theory and Treatments of the Lasting Effects.* Newbury Park: Sage.

Brock, Rita Nakashima. 1989. "And a Little Child Will Lead Us: Christology and Child Abuse." *Christianity, Patriarchy, and Abuse: A Feminist Critique.* Ed. Joanne Carlson Brown and Carol R. Bohn. New York: Pilgrim. 42–61.

Brown, Joanne Carlson, and Carol R. Bohn, eds. 1989. *Christianity, Patriarchy, and Abuse: A Feminist Critique.* New York: Pilgrim.

Brown, Joanne Carlson, and Rebecca Parker. 1989. "For God So Loved the World?" *Christianity, Patriarchy, and Abuse: A Feminist Critique.* Ed. Joanne Carlson Brown and Carol R. Bohn. New York: Pilgrim. 1–30.

Davis, Laura. 1991. *Allies in Healing: When the Person You Love Was Sexually Abused as a Child.* New York: Harper Perennial.

Davis, Susan E., and Eleanor H. Haney. 1991. *Redefining Sexual Ethics: A Sourcebook of Essays, Stories, and Poems.* Cleveland: Pilgrim.

Evangelical Lutheran Church in America. 1991. *Human Sexuality and the Christian Faith: A Study for the Church's Reflection and Deliberation.* Minneapolis: ELCA Distribution Service.

Finkelhor, David. 1984. *Child Sexual Abuse: New Theory and Research.* New York: Free Press.

Fortune, Marie M. 1983. *Sexual Violence: The Unmentionable Sin: An Ethical and Pastoral Perspective.* New York: Pilgrim.

Gil, Eliana. 1991. *Outgrowing the Pain Together: A Book for Spouses and Partners of Adult Survivors.* New York: Dell.

Heggen, Carolyn Holderread. 1993. *Sexual Abuse in Christian Homes and Churches.* Scottsdale, Pa.: Herald.

Herman, Judith L., with Lisa Hirschman. 1981. *Father-Daughter Incest.* Cambridge: Harvard Univ. Press.

Hillman, Donald, and Janice Solek-Tefft. 1988. *Spiders and Flies: Help for Parents and Teachers of Sexually Abused Children.* Lexington, Mass.: Lexington.

Hunter, Mic. 1990. *Abused Boys: The Neglected Victims of Sexual Abuse.* Lexington, Mass.: Lexington.

Janus, Samuel S., and Cynthia L. Janus. 1993. *The Janus Report on Sexual Behavior.* New York: John Wiley & Sons.

Lew, Mike. 1990. *Victims No Longer: Men Recovering from Incest and Other Sexual*

Abuse. New York: Harper Perennial.

Longwood, Merle. 1984. "Divorce as an Occasion of Moral Reconstruction." *The Annual of the Society of Christian Ethics: 1984*. Ed. Larry L. Rasmussen. Vancouver: Society of Christian Ethics. 229–48.

Maltz, Wendy. 1992. *The Sensual Healing Journey: A Guide for Survivors of Sexual Abuse*. New York: Harper Perennial.

Maltz, Wendy, and Beverly Holman. 1987. *Incest and Sexuality: A Guide to Understanding and Healing*. Lexington, Mass.: Lexington.

Miller, Alice. 1984a. *For Your Own Good: Hidden Cruelty in Child-Rearing and the Roots of Violence*. Trans. Hildegarde and Hunter Hannum. New York: Farrar, Strauss, Giroux.

———. 1984b. *Thou Shalt Not Be Aware: Society's Betrayal of the Child*. Trans. Hildegarde and Hunter Hannum. New York: Farrar Strauss Giroux.

Nelson, James B. 1988. *The Intimate Connection: Male Sexuality, Masculine Spirituality*. Philadelphia: Westminster.

———. 1978. *Embodiment: An Approach to Sexuality and Christian Theology*. Minneapolis: Augsburg.

Poling, James N. 1991. *The Abuse of Power: A Theological Problem*. Nashville: Abingdon.

Raichlen, Steven. September 24, 1989. "Healing a Secret." *The Boston Globe Magazine*, pp. 18–21, 48–53, 62–67.

Redmond, Sheila A. 1989. "Christian 'Virtues' and Recovery from Child Sexual Abuse." *Christianity, Patriarchy, and Abuse: A Feminist Critique*. Ed. Joanne Carlson Brown and Carol R. Bohn. New York: Pilgrim.

Russell, Diana. 1986. *The Secret Trauma: Incest in the Lives of Girls and Women*. New York: Basic.

Spear, Joan. 1988. *Handbook for Husbands/Partners of Women Who Were Sexually Abused as Children*. Long Beach, Calif.: Womontyme Dist. Co.

United Church of Christ. 1977. *Human Sexuality: A Preliminary Study*. New York: United Church.

Warshaw, Robin. 1988. *I Never Called It Rape: The Ms. Report on Recognizing, Fighting and Surviving Date and Acquaintance Rape*. New York: Harper & Row.

Notes

1. In her introduction to the anthology she co-edited with Susan E. Davis, Eleanor H. Haney comments on the frequency with which issues of incest, rape, violence, confusion, and guilt are found in the selections they have chosen (Davis and Haney 1991, xiv).

2. I have adopted this term upon the recommendation of Beverly Wildung

Harrison, who read an earlier draft of this essay and who suggested that it is a better term than sexual abuse, because it does not just focus on genital activity but on body invasion and manipulation of persons. Because of its widespread use in popular discourse and academic literature, however, I have not completely abandoned the use of the term sexual abuse.

3. I acknowledge my indebtedness to James Nelson (1988), not only for borrowing from the subtitle of his book, but for much of what I have come to understand about the complex interrelationships between sexuality and spirituality.

4. I will refer to much of the literature to which my friend Ruth Ann Whitney, MSW, introduced me later, but at this point I want to call attention to Briere's (1993) important recent book on the treatment for sexual abuse.

5. Though they are not limited to a discussion of child sexual abuse, doing this research also allowed me the opportunity to delve into the very significant writings of Alice Miller, particularly *For Your Own Good* (1984a) and *Thou Shalt Not Be Aware* (1984b).

6. "Figures on prevalence of sexual abuse are constantly changing, with increases primarily in the number of males estimated as victims" (Maltz 1992, 5, fn. 1).

7. The individuals who have shared their experiences with me have been in heterosexual relationships, so that is how I have focused this paper. From the reading I have done, however, it seems clear that the issues emerge in a similar fashion in gay and lesbian relationships. Many of the popular books on sexual abuse intersperse accounts of lesbian and heterosexual women or gay men and heterosexual men and their relationship issues, illustrating that the issues are remarkably similar regardless of sexual orientation. See Marvin Ellison's essay in this book.

8. For a good discussion of this, see the section, "What if I'm willing to work through the abuse but he isn't?" in Davis 1991, 54–55.

9. In this section I am drawing upon and adapting a framework I developed in Longwood 1984, 238–39.

10. A discussion of how the healing process affects intimacy is found in Bass and Davis 1988, 223–38.

9

Setting the Captives Free: Same-Sex Domestic Violence and the Justice-Loving Church

Marvin Ellison

If there is a single Christian duty, task, or project, it is not to give to others, but to create and be in community in which people can give, contribute, and feel valuable.

—Gary Comstock

Setting captives free is a basic mandate for faith communities seeking to be loyal to the Jesus tradition. In the Gospel according to Luke, Jesus inaugurates his public ministry within the context of synagogue worship by reading from the Isaiah scroll and proclaiming that God's Spirit "has sent me to proclaim release to the captives, and recovery of sight to the blind, to let the oppressed go free" (Luke 4:18 NRSV). Taking up the task of liberation means enlarging and strengthening community while promoting the well-being of every one of its members. A willingness to pursue justice as communal-right relations means taking up the ongoing, always challenging, and necessarily visionary work of rebuilding community across and in the midst of complex social differences. Under postmodern conditions, justice-makers need ample doses of both moral vision and fortitude, given the interstructuring of oppressions and the often fierce resistance to equitable sharing of economic, political, and cultural power.

Violence between intimates, often referred to as domestic violence, may more aptly be called domestic terrorism. Although battering is sometimes approached as if it is a problem of miscommunication, poor anger management, or mutual conflict run amuck, it is best viewed as analogous to terrorism or hostage-taking, in which one party within an intimate relationship uses a variety of coercive tactics to hold another person hostage

(NiCarthy 1986, 285–304).[1] The abuser may even resort to killing violence in order to ensure the other person's ultimate submission and then, in a defiant act of asserting final control, commit suicide in order to evade accountability. Those who wish to engage in liberating action in response to such injustice within same-sex relationships need courage and insight because of two factors that complicate matters considerably: on the one hand, pervasive societal denial about domestic violence generally and, on the other hand, widespread cultural disrespect for gay and lesbian people, including the devaluing of same-sex relationships.

In speaking of same-sex domestic violence and setting captives free, I have in mind two distinct groups that, because of social oppression, do not keep close company but manage to overlap at certain points. Together they constitute the primary audience for this essay. First of all, as a gay man I write for the gay, lesbian, bisexual, and transgender communities and especially for those directly affected by battering and other forms of intimate violence. Although the gay community[2] must struggle daily for its survival and engage in ongoing resistance to heterosexism and other injustices— including racism, sexism, and economic disenfranchisement—it is also true that silence and denial persist within the community about same-sex battering. While significant attention has been given to bias and hate crimes, that is, to violence *against* sexual minorities, far less attention has been given to violence *within* same-sex relationships, that is, to violence perpetrated by some gay people against other gay people. Specific efforts are needed, therefore, to "make visible the invisible," to protect those harmed, and to hold abusers accountable. On this score, I pray that nothing I write on this topic will undermine the quest for safety by those who have been abused by a same-sex intimate partner, or will give any batterer an easy conscience.

Secondly, as a gay man who is also a Christian educator-activist, I struggle alongside many others, including other gay men and lesbians, to transform patriarchal Christianity into a safe, hospitable, and inclusive faith tradition that is respectful of all people, honors our earth-home, and contributes to justice-making with compassion. I am well aware, however, that Christianity, at least in its white, affluent, and male-dominant configurations, has historically legitimated the oppression of gay people. Therefore, the second group I want to address in this essay is the non-gay majority in churches everywhere, especially those who long to make a difference by becoming advocates for justice and peace in family life and throughout their communities. The truth of the matter, however, is that pastors, counselors, and others will be ineffectual at best and harmful at worst as long as they remain blinded by cultural myths about intimate violence and ideological claims about homosexuality.[3] Because of such cultural captivity, even well-meaning people of faith who wish to be allies of gay men and lesbians will lack sufficient insight about how to name same-sex domestic violence as an ethical problem or how to frame an appropriate pastoral and congregational response. They, too, need to be set free.

Faithful, liberating action depends, to a great extent, on gaining proper perspective about the matter at hand and clarifying a moral vision of non-violent, mutual relations that can protect and enhance our common humanity. As William Sloan Coffin suggests, "The primary religious task these days is to try to think straight. Seeing clearly is more important even than good behavior, for redemptive action is born of vision" (Coffin 1993, 2). Elsewhere I have mapped out three fundamental components of a liberating Christian social ethic of sexuality and intimate relations (Ellison 1996). A justice-focused moral vision—what I call an ethic of erotic justice—stands in contrast to patriarchal Christianity's fearful disparagement of sexuality and bodily life, its devaluing of gay people, and its myopia about sexual violence and exploitation. First, a sex-positive ethic affirms the goodness of sexuality as human embodiment. Sexuality is our remarkable capacity to give and receive pleasure, offer one another comfort, and express mutual respect and intimacy through bodily touch. Second, in contrast to patriarchal Christianity's endorsement of compulsory heterosexuality and its devaluing of non-procreative sexuality, a liberating ethic promotes and takes delight in sexual difference, including the diversity of genders, sexual orientations, body sizes and shapes, and family (and marriage) patterns. Third, a liberating ethic pays special attention to abuse, exploitation, and violence within family life and other social relations. It calls, decisively and consistently, for a fair sharing of power and resources among intimates and explores ways to guarantee the safety, respect, and freedom of all persons, especially the most vulnerable.

As a case study in Christian sexual ethics, this essay analyzes some of the barriers to responding effectively to same-sex domestic violence and, in so doing, underscores the importance of holding together these elements—a sex-positive, graceful appreciation for and ease with difference, along with strong anti-abuse commitment—within a comprehensive Christian moral vision. Although domestic violence is a pervasive problem in this society affecting gay and non-gay couples alike, and although a compelling case can be made that religious communities should be involved in "binding up the wounds" as well as preventing such violence, my wager is that churches will not be helpful to gay people affected by domestic violence—and, in fact, will only compound their suffering—unless and until faith communities recognize and publicly affirm same-sex relationships as morally desirable, fully legitimate ways of expressing intimate love. Entering into solidarity with gay men and lesbians requires religious people to actively resist heterosexist values and practices inside the church (and beyond) and embrace a Christian ethic of sexual justice in the direction outlined above. If people of faith genuinely want peace for those among them who are gay and lesbian, they must seek *justice for* as well as *justice in* same-sex relationships. Simply put, reliable peacemaking in relation to same-sex domestic violence requires justice advocates who are unabashedly positive about *gay* sexuality, respectful of *same-sex* relationships, and at the same time intolerant of abuse whether among *gay or non-gay* intimates.

Male Battering of Female Partners: A Matter of Sexist Power and Control

During the last twenty-five years, feminist activists, along with a wide range of social researchers and community educators, have sought to raise consciousness about domestic violence as a pervasive social problem for heterosexual couples. What is known about male violence against women, including battering, is known first and foremost because of the courage of women who have come forward and told their stories, engaged in self-reflection and theory-building, and developed a broad-based, grassroots social change movement to champion nonviolence within family and other social relations. The domestic violence movement, organized in every state of the union and in many other countries, offers literally life-saving resources to countless numbers of women and their dependent children. Statistics document that each year in the U.S. as many as four million women are battered by their male partners. According to a U.S. Bureau of Justice National Crime Survey, every fifteen seconds a woman is beaten in her home. Further studies indicate that women are six times more likely than men to be victimized by an intimate. In fact, in this society "a woman is more likely to be assaulted, injured, raped, or killed by her male partner than by any other assailant." In addition, "40 percent of all homeless women and children in this country are fleeing domestic violence" (Adams 1994, 12).

Battering is not a matter of one person's "losing control" in a relationship, but rather a pattern of coercive, intimidating behaviors by which one partner seeks to establish and maintain control over the conduct, thoughts, and beliefs of another. As such, battering is purposeful behavior, chosen by the man who batters for a reason, namely, in order to gain something that he desires: power and control over his partner. Although batterers employ diverse tactics to achieve and maintain dominance, including physical, sexual, and psychological abuse, the focus should not be so much on the specifics of what any one batterer does (punching, kicking, yelling, threatening, destroying property or pets, and so forth), as much as on what he gains by what he does. A man receives rewards from his abusive behavior, including compliance, loyalty, and obedience from the one he abuses, as well as reinforcement of his sense of male entitlement to set the rules for his partner and to punish her for resisting his control. No psychological or sociological profile is able to predict which men will batter, but batterers share a common belief system: that intimate relations require someone to be in command, that the man is entitled to exercise control over "his" woman, that violence (or threatening violence) is permissible and effective in maintaining such control, that his abusive behavior will result in few if any negative consequences for himself, and that his abuse will not undermine his sense of himself as a responsible person (Hart 1986, 182–83).

Because it is a man's choice to batter his partner, he alone is responsible for the abuse. At the same time, feminist theorists recognize that battering is a larger, more complex problem than the actions of any single batterer or even the sum total of abuse by all batterers combined. Battering is violent behavior, Susan Schechter observes (1982, 238), that is "individually willed yet socially constructed," which means the problem lies not only within individual batterers (who are therefore accountable for their behavior), but also in the social order itself. On this score, the community bears responsibility for perpetuating, or at least not critiquing, sexist cultural norms and social arrangements that condone and sustain male violence against women and children. Sexism is perhaps less a direct "cause" of battering and more an environmental wellspring that gives rise to men's disproportionate social power and sense of entitlement (Nichols 1999, 3). Addressing domestic violence as a systemic problem requires, therefore, transforming social values and power relations between men and women, including notions of male superiority and a man's right to rule (and discipline) other family members, a right which some men act out violently. Although sexism does not, strictly speaking, cause any man to be violent, it does provide the impetus and cultural legitimation for such choices. If individual interventions are to be effective, they must take place within the context of sustained efforts at social and cultural transformation.

Community silence about these matters only increases men's power to batter and evade accountability. Minimization and denial of domestic abuse give batterers the opportunity to coerce their partners without negative consequences. When institutions, including the church, fail to challenge sexist beliefs, they collude with batterers by tacitly supporting male entitlement and the right to control female partners. Silence and denial allow men's justifications to stand without challenge. Nothing is done to interrupt victim-blaming or stop the tendency to hold women responsible for "provoking" the violence against them. Insofar as sexist oppression lies at the root of male battering, peacemaking requires taking a countercultural stand. Part of the work is more personal, to show respect for women, support their empowerment, and reinforce their right to safety and bodily integrity. Part of the work is more cultural and political, to debunk sexist norms that devalue women and to alter institutionalized power arrangements that grant men unequal social status and privilege. However, not all violence is gender violence, and ending male violence against women, a deeply desirable goal, will not by itself eliminate partner abuse. Another story must be told, listened to, and acted upon.

Making Visible the Invisible: Domestic Violence among Same-Sex Partners

As with heterosexual domestic violence, what is known about same-sex battering is known because of the courage of gay men and lesbians to come forward, tell their stories, and construct both theory and response services by sharing their insights about domestic abuse. In *Men Who Love the Men Who Beat Them*, David Island describes in the third person the experience of his coauthor Patrick Letellier:

> The last two years of [Patrick's] four-year relationship with his lover Stephen had been typified by bruises, humiliation, and psychological abuse. Stephen had kicked, struck, punched, and slapped him. He had shoved and thrown Patrick up against walls and down onto closet floors. From ridicule and harassment, Patrick knew guilt, shame, confusion, and loneliness. Stephen had threatened to kill him more than once. (Island and Letellier 1991, xxi)

Such testimony speaks to a pattern of abuse that is both similar to and different from heterosexual battering. Researchers document, for example, that "domestic violence occurs at approximately the same rate in gay and lesbian relationships as it does in heterosexual unions" (Elliott 1996,

1). Some studies indicate that battering may occur in as many as 47 percent of gay male relationships. Other estimates suggest that between 350,000 and 650,000 gay men are battered each year, a rate comparable to that of heterosexual couples (Hamberger 1996, 84). As one analyst concludes, "Violence between intimate partners is a social epidemic, although we continue to deny the proportions of the epidemic. The problem is probably as large among gay males as it is among heterosexual couples" (Hamberger 1996, 89).

Other similarities exist between same-sex and heterosexual battering. Same-sex victims suffer the same types of abuse, including physical, emotional, psychological, and sexual abuse, as heterosexual women endure at the hands of their batterers. So, too, the abuse often occurs in a cyclical manner in which a tension-building stage is followed by a violent episode, which may be followed in turn by a so-called honeymoon phase in which the batterer relies on sweet talk, gifts, and other indulgences rather than fists, weapons, or threats to control his partner. In addition, victims of same-sex violence often stay for the same reasons that battered heterosexual women frequently stay: not because they like or accept the abuse (so-called female or gay masochism), but because, among other reasons, they love their partner and are invested in making the relationship work, they believe in their ability to change the batterer, they blame themselves for the abuse, and they fear reprisals should they leave. Many victims stay because they lack economic resources and other supports that would make it possible for them to live independently, especially with dependent children. Others stay because it may be safer to remain with a batterer than to leave and thereby risk the danger of escalated violence, including killing violence.

Gay and non-gay victims of domestic violence also remain in abusive relationships because they live complex lives and face difficult choices. Although outsiders may believe that leaving is the best or only option, insiders know that staying may be the safer course. Living as they do under a state of siege, they must constantly strategize in order to handle not only the batterer-generated risks to their safety, but also a range of life-generated risks, including physical and mental health issues, financial limitations, and racism and other discrimination, over which they likewise have little control. This is especially true for socially marginalized persons who must daily confront the additional violence of racial, economic, and other injustices in order to survive.

Typically, a battered person engages in an open-ended process of safety planning, which involves continually weighing risks and options. What Jill Davies observes about battered heterosexual women applies, as well, to victims of same-sex abuse: "Women [as well as gay people] experience battering in the context of their diverse lives." Moreover, "there is much more to a battered [person] than the battering. [They] may be a [parent], a worker, a person with a disability." Furthermore, while violence is a part of their lives, the abuse does not necessarily define their entire life. "For some [people]," Davies acknowledges, "it is almost their whole existence, whereas for others it may be a very small part." In fact, "many battered women [and gay people, as well] do not see physical violence as their primary risk or leaving as their most viable option" (Davies 1998, 4–5). An interpretive framework for intimate violence must, therefore, pay attention to the complex interplay of personal as well as sociocultural sources of endangerment. At the same time, it must not deny the moral agency of people struggling to survive abusive relationships. Yielding to victimism, that is, defining someone exclusively in terms of his or her victimization (Gudorf 1993–94, 19), turns people into passive, helpless objects ("merely" victims) and fails to credit their courage to mount resistance or their creativity to maximize their safety under oppressive conditions.

Although abuse in same-sex relationships reflects many of the characteristics of heterosexual domestic violence, a primary difference is how the social environment of homophobia and heterosexism complicates matters by providing a control mechanism not available to heterosexual batterers. A gay male batterer may exercise the power to "out" (or threaten to out) his partner and thereby extend his control by relying on homophobic prejudice to isolate his partner further from family, their landlord, his partner's employer, and so on. As Pam Elliott, director of a gay and lesbian anti-violence project in Minneapolis, explains, "All battering victims perceive isolation, but gays and lesbians who have no hope of asking for help because of a lack of civil rights protection, and because of having no access to the legal system by definition, are the most isolated victims in society." Because of their stigmatized outsider status and social vulnerability, gay men and lesbians are beaten by their intimate partners and then risk being revictimized if they turn to the state or an outside agency for assistance. For this reason, Elliott continues, "Many gay/lesbian victims tell advocates that they do not complain about the abuse because being victimized by their lover is less frightening than being victimized by the system" (Elliott 1996, 5).

Heterosexism, the social oppression of gays and lesbians, and homophobia, the fear and hostility directed at gay people, provide an unmatched opportunity for gay or lesbian abusers to abuse with impunity. An encompassing, gay-negating cultural environment not only isolates victims, it also lends support to abusive behavior by refusing to recognize it as a serious problem, much less challenge it. In such a social context, without access to support from family, social services, and the criminal justice and legal systems, battered gays and lesbians are not likely to seek outside assistance. If they do, they are not likely to be helped. Gregory Merrill's research supports this conclusion. Three components must be in place, Merrill conjectures, if a batterer is to proceed with carrying out the intention to control a partner: first, a willingness to abuse (and learning how to do so); second, an opportunity to control another; and third, making the choice to control. "Abuse is especially likely to occur," he concludes, "in circumstances in which the potential victim is perceived to be unwilling or unlikely to report, and/or in which the abuser believes reporting will have no effect" (Merrill 1996, 17). For those committed to ending same-sex domestic violence, the change agenda must, therefore, include not only assisting victims and holding batterers accountable, but also changing the larger social context or holding environment. Responding effectively to same-sex battering requires deliberate political efforts to reduce anti-gay oppression and thereby reduce the opportunity and societal support structures that foster the abuse.

A related task requires a clear naming of same-sex battering as wrongful, unethical conduct. However, certain obstacles make such naming difficult. Donna Cecere, a survivor of domestic abuse, offers testimony that illuminates part of the problem:

> We were together for two years. The abuse began early on, though I didn't know enough then to make such a connection. Though a lesbian feminist activist for years at that point, I still thought of battering as, first, a male-against-female act, and second, as being a physically violent act. *I had no concept* of what emotional, psychological, and spiritual abuse was about. (Cecere 1987, 12, emphasis mine)

Without an interpretive framework to name the violence as unacceptable and to assign full responsibility to the batterer, people end up telling a story about the person who is abused rather than engaging in truth telling about how one person has chosen to exercise power and control over another. As Carol Adams contends, "The problem with story telling is that it is most frequently a story" about the victim, who believes that she (or he) "did something wrong, God is punishing me, I provoked the beating." Such explanations "always deflect the focus from the behavior of the [batterer]" and reinforce the tendency not to hold abusers accountable

(Adams 1994, 43). However, justice-making depends entirely upon truth-telling. No liberating action is possible if victims are blamed or their reality discounted by trivializing the abuse, minimizing the danger, or denying that abuse has, in fact, taken place because it has occurred between two partners of the same sex. Rendering same-sex domestic violence invisible is all the more likely if people hold rigidly to the expectation that abuse happens only in those situations in which the recipient has less social power than the abuser, which is typical of heterosexual battering. As the testimony of same-sex survivors conveys, this is not always the case. Abuse also occurs in relationships in which the parties have roughly equal social power and status if one partner is willing to abuse, has the opportunity, and so chooses. The opportunity to abuse is greatly enhanced if the social environment cuts the victim off from social support and if the person lacks credibility as a bona fide victim by virtue of being gay or lesbian.

This last point is especially important because, for victims of same-sex battering, the problem of naming (and gaining a hearing) is compounded by the tendency to interpret domestic violence through an exclusively heterosexual lens. If battering is defined as male battering of female partners, and if intimate violence is argued to be sexist in origin, then these presumptions, which typically guide assessment of heterosexual battering, militate against recognizing men who are victimized or women who are abusive. As Donna Cecere stated above, she "had no concept" of lesbian battering, and without the power to name the abuse as abuse and, therefore, as unacceptable, she "didn't know enough to make a connection." An analytical framework that relies exclusively on gender to assign the roles of perpetrator and victim will not readily clarify for gay men or lesbians their own experience of abuse either as victims or as victimizers, nor help keep the focus on the abusive behavior as the moral problematic. In a homophobic church and society, the moral problem is forever redefined as homosexual identity itself rather than as anti-gay violence and oppression, including the oppression sometimes acted out within intimate partnerships.

Attending to same-sex battering requires developing a theoretical framework that appreciates how violence as social control is generally tolerated in this society, how it can be used by and against anyone, and how grasping what is going on requires keeping the focus on the behavior of the abusing partner rather than on his or her gender or social identity (that is, whether the person abusing is male or female, heterosexual or gay/lesbian, and likewise the person abused). At the same time, the interpretive framework must take into account the social environment, in this case the "holding context" of heterosexist values and power dynamics, which greatly expands the opportunity for the abuse. Heterosexism also gives a cultural pretext for not seeing same-sex abuse as wrongful or significant enough to warrant the majority community's time and attention. As Gregory Merrill sums up the matter, "While these theories should not be identity-based, they also should not be blind to the very real impact of identity-based social oppression" (Merrill 1996, 20).

Another obstacle to naming same-sex battering as unacceptable is the gay/lesbian/bi/transgender (GLBT) community's own inclination toward self-protection in a hostile cultural context. The truth about same-sex battering remains hidden because of the shame experienced by the gay men and lesbians most directly affected by the abuse, but even further because of the reluctance of an oppressed community to make public its problems and grant further ammunition to vilify gay life and culture. Because gays as a group are frequently targeted for violence, including objectification as the stereotyped Other, and because such violence results in few if any legal or social consequences, drawing attention to intimate violence *within* the community may seem unnecessarily provocative and self-incriminating. However, a lack of responsiveness to same-sex battering only perpetuates the problem by not holding abusers accountable and by neglecting the needs of victims for safety and support.

As a social problem, same-sex battering requires a social response. Not only the gay and lesbian communities, but also the heterosexual community at large must be willing to intervene in order to insure the safety of victims and hold batterers responsible for their abusive behavior. In addition, the majority community bears responsibility to convey a compelling message that violence and coercive control, within same-sex as in any other relations, is unacceptable and not to be tolerated. Credibility on this matter depends, to a great extent, on matching rhetoric with policies and programs that offer effective strategies aimed at prevention, as well as crisis response.

From a Theology of Disrespect
to an Ethic of Solidarity and Resistance

The subtitle of Lutheran theologian Joy Bussert's (1986) book on woman battering, "From a Theology of Suffering to an Ethic of Empowerment," suggests how a justice-loving church might respond to the evil of domestic violence in heterosexual relations and, by implication, offers clues about same-sex battering. Becoming conscious of these issues means letting go of one's innocence about injustice (including one's own complicity), recognizing that intimate violence is a pervasive social problem, and owning up to the fact that patriarchal Christianity has long encouraged women to endure rather than protest their victimization, especially at the hands of abusive husbands and controlling male partners. The work of liberation, of setting captives free, begins with listening to and believing women's stories, taking their anger seriously, critiquing the social and religious traditions which legitimate women's subordination, welcoming women's rising power, and reconstructing a Christian theological ethic that truly honors women's humanity while denouncing violence within any and all social relations. Similarly, setting free those who have been held captive in abusive same-sex relationships requires a willingness to listen to and learn from gay and lesbian survivors of domestic abuse, welcome their anger, support their empowerment, engage in a serious critique of socially and religiously sanctioned homophobia, and reconstruct a Christian theological ethic that truly honors gay people and identifies same-sex abuse as a violation of a commonly shared humanity. Lesbian feminist theologian Carter Heyward expresses a theological foundation for a justice ministry this way: "The God whom Jesus knew and loved never calls us to leave ourselves behind or forget our own worth and, at the same time, calls us never to forget that others matter as much as we do. In God, we are called to hold together our own lives and those of others as equally worthy" (Heyward 1999, 122–23).

Marie Fortune, founding director of the Center for the Prevention of Sexual and Domestic Violence in Seattle, acknowledges that the religious community has traditionally responded with silence to violence in the family. At the same time, the church's mandate to advocate justice and peace obligates people of faith to respond proactively to these concerns. "Violence is destroying families," she writes. "If religious institutions and agencies are concerned with saving families, they must place a high priority on the needs of people suffering from such abuse and on the programs that seek to prevent it" (Fortune 1991, 5). To this I would add that it is also imperative that the church recognize, and publicly name, that some of the families being destroyed are gay and lesbian. But is it not legitimate to ask whether traditionally anti-gay religious institutions are, in fact, invested in easing the suffering of gay and lesbian people? In what ways have they shown a willingness to hold themselves accountable for reducing the violence *against* gay people, as well as for responding to the violence *within* same-sex relations?

Fortune is right to insist that "the sum of all efforts to address violence in the family in religious communities must be justice making" (Fortune

1991, 19). Her own work (Fortune 1983, 42–98; 1986, 5–6; 1995) and that of other Christian feminists (Adams 1994, 35) on domestic violence incorporates a principled call for justice for gays and lesbians and for an end to anti-gay violence. Even so, same-sex domestic violence remains, by and large, invisible even within their sophisticated religious feminist (and gay-positive) discourse. The trouble here is that when a problem is not named, a proper response cannot be given. As Fortune herself concludes, "By refusing to acknowledge the problem—by refusing to accept any responsibility for the conditions that condone the battering of spouses and elderly adults and the physical and sexual abuse of children—society allows such abuse to continue" (Fortune 1991, 3). Should we not also name explicitly the wrongness of same-sex battering? Otherwise, church and society, ourselves included, will allow that abuse to continue as well.

James Poling follows Fortune's lead in outlining three guiding principles for a ministry of justice in relation to domestic abuse. The first priority is to promote the safety of those harmed, the second is to call the abuser to accountability (and to transformation), and the third is to restore the relationship if possible. However, if "the harm is too great, the damage too deep, [or] the resistance of the abuser to change [is] too formidable," then it may be necessary to "mourn the loss of that relationship and work to restore the individual (comfort to the grieving)" (Poling 1998, 72; see also Fortune and Poling 1995). These are useful guiding principles for dealing with the *relational* dynamics of battering, but as Poling and Fortune recognize, justice-making requires more than addressing the needs of the individual victim and abuser. The social context that legitimates and reinforces same-sex abuse must be transformed as well, including anti-gay cultural norms and the pervasive societal devaluing of gay people. Moreover, all crisis interventions, as well as efforts aimed at abuse prevention, must be grounded in an explicitly public affirmation of the worth of people's lives *as gay men and lesbians* and of the moral goodness—and the inviolability—of same-sex relationships. As Claire Renzetti argues, "Before you can acknowledge [same-sex] battering, you must first acknowledge [gay and] lesbian relationships" (Renzetti 1996, 66).

Respect for gay people, including respect for and public recognition of their intimate relationships, is an essential component of any credible Christian ethic of non-violence. Philosopher Richard Mohr points out that the phrase "adding insult to injury" speaks to two types of evil that a comprehensive non-violent ethic must name and seek to dismantle. On the one hand, evil-doing refers to the physical harms or injuries that reduce a person's happiness and which typically elicit sympathy from others. On the other hand, evil refers to those indignities, including name-calling and invectives, which a person suffers not because of something he or she has done, but because of who that person is perceived to be. The appropriate response to such insult is not our sympathy, but rather our outrage and our redoubled efforts to communicate respect for that person's dignity. Disrespecting a person does grave harm because insults attack a person as a person in his or her co-humanity. "If our regard for others does not include respect," Mohr writes, "we fail to treat them as persons, and treat them instead as lesser beings" (Mohr 1994, 59). A Christian theology of nonviolence must, therefore, do more than eschew violence in intimate and other social relations. It must also call for deep respect for, and the honoring of, gay people and their full lives, including their loves. Only such a clear and consistent demonstration of respect will grant enough credibility for calling gay and lesbian people to account when they act out abusively.

The role of religious leaders, including pastors and counselors, in responding to same-sex domestic violence is to follow the guidelines outlined above (safety first, accountability second, and then possibly restoration), to listen with respect and care when someone discloses a history of abuse, to make referrals to community resources, including the criminal justice system, and to collaborate with other community leaders and agencies to put appropriate response services in place if they are lacking. The primary work, however, is not preparing for crisis interventions or "putting out fires," but rather to engage in liberating preaching, teaching, and modeling respect in all social interaction, in order to transform the cultural norms that legitimate violence among intimate partners, gay and non-gay alike. A justice ministry must cogently identify and promote culturally-diverse models of community and intimacy based on mutual respect, power-sharing, and partnership rather than possession. Above all, domestic violence must be named as a social injustice that most certainly has personal ramifications but cannot be resolved as an "interpersonal problem." Political change, in the broad sense of the word, is needed to alter the cultural dynamics of power and control that are "writ small" in intimate partner abuse.

A primary difficulty at this juncture is that so many religious people, including pastors, operate with a privatized model of ministry as a "helping profession" that provides support and care for individuals and families in crisis. From this vantage point, doing good means offering services to victims or "needy people" but not empowering people to seek their own liberation and freedom. In contrast, authentic ministries of care are intimately linked to and invested in ministries of justice-making, on the alert for making the connections between caring for the well-being of persons and reforming community through shared empowerment. With respect to professional ethics in ministry, as Karen Lebacqz notes, the norm of beneficence, and especially a paternalistic notion of doing good for others, has unfortunately become the overriding obligation for many clergy. They thereby neglect the centrality of the norm of justice for the Christian moral life and fail to take seriously how freedom requires standing with the oppressed and, in this instance, with the GLBT community (Lebacqz 1985, 126–31).

Standing in solidarity with gay men and lesbians and working to correct distorted power imbalances within families and other social relations will undoubtedly take courage on the part of any faith community. In particular, working to end same-sex domestic violence will require church members to work through their fears that in becoming advocates of justice and non-violence for gays, they risk becoming gay and lesbian-identified (that is, known publicly as gay friendly or even as a "gay church"), and thereby run the risk of losing status as well as possible funding. This fear also affects community organizing among feminists who commit to social change but "put on the brakes" when confronted with lesbian-baiting, that is, by a variety of social control tactics aimed at discrediting and thereby disempowering individuals and entire organizations by associating them with the culturally despised (and highly sexualized) Other. "For my politics," community organizer Suzanne Pharr counters, "if a woman's social change organization has not been labeled lesbian or communist, it is probably not doing significant work; it is only 'making nice'" (Pharr 1988, 25). Churches might take stock about whether they have ever managed to "catch hell" for their justice advocacy, and if they have not experienced such grief, they might well ask if "making nice" has taken precedence for them over making justice.

Advocating justice as mutual respect, care, and power-sharing requires matching rhetoric with action. When a church says "all are welcome" but has no track record of antihomophobia action and no history of explicitly gay-affirmative outreach, the message actually conveyed is a resounding lack of interest in the lives and struggles of gay people and only a begrudging willingness to include them, but only as long as they remain invisible as gay. A ministry of "don't ask, don't tell" is hardly liberating or healing of the violence within and surrounding people's lives. A justice ministry, in contrast, will seek without distinction to "bind up the wounds" of all those who have been harmed. It will also work ceaselessly to alter oppressive social structures and so restore power to those who have been wronged.

The pivotal lesson to be gained from addressing same-sex domestic violence is that a theology of nonviolence must cogently critique not only the violence *in* relationships, but also the violence perpetuated *against* relationships, including gay and lesbian relationships. The church's credibility in offering a liberating and healing word and "setting captives free" depends on whether its call for ending violence is genuinely inclusive and universal in scope, leaving no one out and no one to suffer alone.

I am grateful for the insights on this topic shared by students at Bangor Theological Seminary who were enrolled during spring 2000 in Ethics 1751 (Domestic Violence and Ministry), especially to Margaret Beckman, Kristen Bjorn, Barbara McKusick Liscord, and Andrew Wing, and to my coteacher, Francine Stark, community educator at Spruce Run, the domestic violence project in Bangor, Maine.

Bibliography

Adams, Carol. 1994. *Woman-Battering*. Minneapolis: Fortress Press.

Bussert, Joy. 1986. *Battered Women: From a Theology of Suffering to an Ethic of Empowerment*. New York: Division of Mission in North America, Lutheran Church in America.

Cecere, Donna J. Fall 1987. "The Second Closet: Battered Lesbians." *Open Hands* 3:2, 12–15.

Coffin, William Sloan. 1993. *A Passion for the Possible: A Message to U.S. Churches*. Louisville: Westminster John Knox.

Comstock, Gary. 1993. *Gay Theology Without Apology*. Cleveland: Pilgrim.

Davies, Jill. 1998. *Safety Planning with Battered Women: Complex Lives/Difficult Choices*. Thousand Oaks, Calif.: Sage.

Elliott, Pam. 1996. "Shattering Illusions: Same-Sex Domestic Violence." *Violence in Gay and Lesbian Domestic Partnerships*. Ed. Claire M. Renzetti and Charles Harvey Miley. New York: Harrington Park. 1–8.

Ellison, Marvin M. 1996. *Erotic Justice: A Liberating Ethic of Sexuality*. Louisville: Westminster John Knox.

Fortune, Marie M. 1995. *Love Does No Harm: Sexual Ethics for the Rest of Us*. New York: Continuum.

———. 1991. *Violence in the Family: A Workshop Curriculum for Clergy and Other Helpers*. Cleveland: Pilgrim.

———. Spring/Summer 1986. "Homophobia and Violence: An Unholy Alliance." *Working Together* 6:3, 5–6.

———. 1983. *Sexual Violence: The Unmentionable Sin*. New York: Pilgrim.

Fortune, Marie M., and James N. Poling. 1995. "Calling to Accountability: The Church's Response to Abusers." *Violence against Women and Children: A Christian Theological Sourcebook.* Ed. Carol J. Adams and Marie M. Fortune. New York: Continuum. 451–63.

Gudorf, Christine E. Winter 1993–94. "Embodying Morality." *Conscience*, 16–21.

Hamberger, L. Kevin. 1996. "Intervention in Gay Male Intimate Violence Requires Coordinated Efforts on Multiple Levels." *Violence in Gay and Lesbian Domestic Partnerships.* Ed. Claire M. Renzetti and Charles Harvey Miley. New York: Harrington Park. 83–92.

Hart, Barbara. 1986. "Lesbian Battering: An Examination." *Naming the Violence: Speaking Out about Lesbian Battering.* Ed. Kerry Lobel. Seattle: Seal. 173–89.

Heyward, Carter. 1999. *Saving Jesus from Those Who Are Right: Rethinking What It Means to Be Christian.* Minneapolis: Fortress Press.

Island, David, and Patrick Letellier. 1991. *Men Who Beat the Men Who Love Them: Battered Gay Men and Domestic Violence.* New York: Harrington Park.

Lebacqz, Karen. 1985. *Professional Ethics: Power and Paradox.* Nashville: Abingdon.

Merrill, Gregory S. 1996. "Ruling the Exceptions: Same-Sex Battering and Domestic Violence Theory." *Violence in Gay and Lesbian Domestic Partnerships.* Ed. Claire M. Renzetti and Charles Harvey Miley. New York: Harrington Park. 9–22.

Mohr, Richard D. 1994. *A More Perfect Union: Why Straight America Must Stand Up for Gay Rights.* Boston: Beacon.

NiCarthy, Ginny. 1986. *Getting Free: A Handbook for Women in Abusive Relationships.* Seattle: Seal.

Nichols, Brian. Winter/Spring 1999. "Why Do Men Batter?" *Uptake*, 1–6.

Pharr, Suzanne. 1988. *Homophobia: A Weapon of Sexism.* Inverness, Calif.: Chardon.

Poling, James Newton. 1998. "Preaching to Perpetrators of Violence." *Telling the Truth: Preaching about Sexual and Domestic Violence.* Ed. John S. McClure and Nancy J. Ramsay. Cleveland: United Church Press. 71–82.

Renzetti, Claire M. 1996. "The Poverty of Services for Battered Lesbians." *Violence in Gay and Lesbian Domestic Partnerships.* Ed. Claire M. Renzetti and Charles Harvey Miley. New York: Harrington Park. 61–68.

Schechter, Susan. 1982. *Women and Male Violence: The Visions and Struggles of the Battered Women's Movement.* Boston: South End.

Notes

1. NiCarthy cites Amnesty International's research about prisoners of war and reproduces a "chart of coercion" that depicts the brainwashing tactics used to

control people psychologically as well as physically. As NiCarthy points out, "Most people who brainwash their intimate partners use methods similar to those of prison guards, who recognize their physical control is never easily accomplished without the cooperation of the prisoner" (1986, 286). Emotional and psychological abuse always accompanies and intensifies physical and sexual abuse.

2. I use the term *gay community* to refer to a diverse community of gay men, lesbian women, bisexuals, and transgender persons. Because this collection of essays is written especially for men in faith communities, I am concerned about gay men in battering relationships, but not to the exclusion of lesbians or bisexual persons in same-sex relationships in which violence is present. The reader may discern in context whether the term *gay* refers specifically to gay men or more inclusively to the GLBT community.

3. Studies indicate that while battered women may often turn to their pastors for help, they rank the helpfulness of the assistance they received at the very bottom in comparison to other sources of support and counsel. As Carol J. Adams reports (1994, 5–6), "Women who turned to their clergy for marital guidance stayed longer with their abusers, and the abuse did not subside." Her reading is that clergy by and large are overly confident about their knowledge and skills in assisting people in abusive, dangerous relationships. Clergy too often do not realize the life-threatening nature of battering, the importance of protecting the victim's safety by maintaining strict confidentiality, or how to interpret what is going on when an abuser's and a victim's stories differ dramatically. Without specialized knowledge and skills, pastors and counselors may fail to help and, in fact, may cause more harm.

Part Four

The Physical Body

10

Designing Men:
Reading Male Bodies as Texts

Philip L. Culbertson

*"Why does it always have to be the female body that's presented as
exotic, other, fascinating to scrutinize and imagine?" one woman
asked me. "Why is it never the male body?"*

—Laurence Goldstein

An essay of this type must begin with definitions, in order that the author
and the reader may construct together a line of reasoning. Of particular
consequence between author and reader is a mutual agreement within the
definitional fields of social construction and reader-response. Once these
two fields have been defined and wed, I can proceed to my central argument: that there exists no such reality as a heterosexual male body, for it is
a socially constructed "textless text"[1] that blocks all attempts to read meaning into it.

We know a fair amount about what happens when the heterosexual male
gaze is turned upon women. The victims of that gaze are increasingly finding their own voices and refusing to submit to objectification. But what
happens when the heterosexual male gaze is turned upon another heterosexual male? What happens when a heterosexual male turns his own gaze
upon himself? Writers such as Rosalind Coward (1985, 227) and Maxine
Sheets-Johnstone (1992, 69) have complained about the absence of study
and analysis of these subjects, and indeed it would seem the male body,
already a textless text, has absented itself completely within the past two
decades. I recently suggested that a student do some work on the same
materials this essay addresses, and suggested that he begin by stripping and
studying himself naked in the mirror. Due to his cultural conditioning as a
straight Kiwi male, it took him about six weeks to get up the nerve to look.[2]

Social constructionism argues that human identity, both individual and interpersonal, is the product of the social contexts within which we have spent our lives. A social context teaches us what we are allowed to feel or not feel and how to express our feelings; which relationships are mandatory, preferred, obligatory, optional, or undesirable; what we can dream and what we must never dream; which wishes are within the realm of possibility and which are not; and the common standards of aesthetics, virtue, and common good. Social constructionism creates each of us, in this sense, by teaching us how to see, what to value, and how to respond once we have seen and valued. In other words, whatever characteristics we were born with, what we have become is a product of the various environments in which we have spent our lives, and how we responded to those environments as we tried to make sense of them.

The foundational assumption of reader-response theory is that a text does not have a sole inherent meaning, but has as many possible meanings as its readers bring to it.[3] The idea is long familiar in both Christian and Jewish traditions. Early Judaism spoke of the "seventy faces of the Torah," a metaphor for multiplex meanings (Culbertson 1996, 25–52; 1991a). St. Augustine sought out nine separate meanings for each of the opening verses of the Book of Genesis, and medieval Christianity asserted that every verse of the Bible has at least four meanings: the literal, the allegorical (faith issues behind the text), the tropological (behavior commanded by the text), and the anagogical (the promised rewards in the afterlife) (Culbertson 1991b). While the early writers in both traditions understood the meanings as inherent in the text, today we understand that they are created by the interaction between a text and a reader, placing as much responsibility for meaning-making upon the reader as upon the text itself. In other words, what this essay teaches you will be based on meanings you the reader bring to the text, rather than what I might choose to say to you.

Social constructionism and reader-response theory, then, help us understand that we read meaning into many things other than the printed page. What we are able to see, value, and respond to in a text is socially constructed, and the meaning we draw from whatever we encounter is a priori resident within—generated by—ourselves, and shaped by the complex interaction of culture, life experience, and individual need.

We can now understand a body as a textless text into which outside meanings are read. The study of the human body as a metaphorical vehicle is sometimes called *human social anatomy*. Dutton describes it as follows:

> The human body, in this view, can be understood only in the context of the social construction of reality; indeed, the body itself is seen as a social construct, a means of social expression or performance by which our identity and value—for ourselves and others—are created, tested, and validated (Dutton 1995, 13).

The human body is not simply a blank page upon which words have not yet been written. It is, more aptly, a textless text whose meaning is read by many readers, whether they are invited to read or not. It is a text which is almost always read from the "outside" (the reader introjecting meaning), but which always has the potential to be read from the "inside." The body-bearer may at any point choose to wrest control over the text to interpret it as his or her own, making unique meanings and giving them priority over whatever others read into his or her body.

Objectification, the Male Gaze, and Homosociality

To read indicates "to objectify," to make something an object external to one's self, a "thing" held at a certain distance. We maintain the comfortable fiction that encountering a text is an I-Thou relationship of intimacy, though the history of religious literalism and fundamentalism, for example, indicates it is mostly an I-It relationship. In fact, we can't read into a *subject*, both because it is too close and because it will not sit still for us to do that. We have to objectify in order to interpret and then meaning-make.[4] In the same way, we objectify the body texts around us. At present, the way that men look at women is the most commonly studied form of objectification within the field of gender studies.

The term "the male gaze" seems to have been first used by Laura Mulvey, who argued that within the classical structure of cinema, men possess the gaze and women are its object (Mulvey 1975; see also Lehman 1993, 2–3). A gaze, then, turns a subject into an object. The male gaze values—when turned toward a woman, it desires; when turned toward a gay man, it often despises. In either case, it seizes control from the other. The other may experience the male gaze as a violation, a rape; the object of the gaze is no longer another person, but someone to be possessed or disposed of. Within the world of texts, the male gaze might be described as "one-handed reading," in that its purpose is clearly one of self-stimulation and erotic satisfaction (Schehr 1997, 113), even when, in the course of despising, it becomes sadistic.

One-handed reading, a euphemism for masturbation often attributed to the eighteenth-century philosopher Jean Jacques Rousseau, serves as a commentary to Matthew 5:27-28. There Jesus cautions: "You have heard that it was said 'You shall not commit adultery.' But I say to you that everyone who looks at a woman with lust has already committed adultery with her in his heart." Lust, an overwhelming desire or craving, is the most common synonym in the Christian biblical and theological vocabulary for "objectification," the predictable result of the male gaze. By conflating objectification and adultery, Jesus counsels the nonobjectification of women and others. In turn, both objectification and adultery confirm the power of male desire. When the urge to act out eroticized desire threatens the social fabric, culture then seeks to tame objectification by sanctifying acceptable levels of its expression, particularly in the form of the bartering and brokering of masculine power.

Homosociality is a term coined by Eve Kosofsky Sedgwick to describe the basic structure of patriarchy: men pleasing other men via the medium of women (Sedgwick 1985; Rubin 1975).[5] Sedgwick describes the process whereby men attempt to establish some intimacy with each other (usually in a triangulated relationship with a woman who functions to disguise the gestures between the men) as "homosociality":

> "Homosocial" is a word occasionally used in history and the social
> sciences, where it describes social bonds between persons of the
> same sex; it is a neologism, obviously formed by analogy with
> "homosexual," and just as obviously meant to be distinguished
> from "homosexual." (Sedgwick 1985, 1)

Sedgwick's theory is directly related to family-systems theory, presuming that human beings relate to each other within triangular structures (Bowen 1985; Guerin et al. 1996). In the triangle of two straight men and a woman, the attraction between the two men must be taken at least as seriously as the attraction between each man and the woman. The attraction is heightened when either man realizes that he can accumulate further power and influence by forming an alliance with another of the two members of the triangle. Since women rarely have brokerable power, the obvious choice with whom to form the alliance is the other man. The alliance may take the form of cooperation or competition or even aggression. Whatever its form, the alliance as power-brokering cannot be denied. This desire to unite powers with another man is one possible non-genital form of eros, this desire and attraction creating the exaggerated impulse to homosociality. Sedgwick even describes the attraction as "intense and potent." Most men operate this way on occasion, though few are aware of it.

The male gaze not only objectifies, but *must* objectify for homosociality to work. Ironically, the homosocial system can be maintained only when men avert their gaze from each other; the gaze, however figuratively, must remain focused on a woman. When the male gaze turns toward another man, homosociality threatens to disintegrate into homoeroticism, as the novels of D. H. Lawrence illustrate.[6] Thus patriarchy is built upon the assumption that a male body is a text that will reject all attempts by other men to read it. To accept such an attempt would be to destroy the basis of power and control.

Thinking about writing this essay, I decided to poll a group of men I spend a lot of time with. Sitting in a corner at a party, I asked them, "When a woman walks into the room, what's the first thing you notice about her?" They answered variously: "Her breasts; I'm a tit man." "Her legs." "Her hair." "Her ass." Each man had a quick and clear answer. I continued: "So when a man walks into the room, what's the first thing you notice about him." "The whole package," they seemed to answer in one voice. Not satisfied, I asked my question about men again, and got the same univocal answer again. In fact, the guys wouldn't budge. They would not name a male body part that attracted their attention, would not name any aspect of a male that they read first as an entry point into the larger text. They were willing to engage the text as a whole, but not to do the sort of close reading which is now assumed within the field of textual criticism.

Averting the Gaze, Refusing to Read

Why is it so difficult for men to direct their heterosexual male gaze toward another man? Why is it apparently even more difficult for them to turn the gaze upon their own male bodies? The complexity of the answer may help explain why the subject is almost completely ignored in the exploding literature on masculinity. Let me explore five different reasons, particularly from the point of view of literary criticism and reader-response theory.

Reading Is Dangerous

To read is to risk making one's self vulnerable, to risk encountering what Wayne Booth has called "the otherness that bites."[7] Most people are highly selective about what they read and will avoid texts that threaten their comfort or security. A man may not be consciously aware that to read another man's body is dangerous, but subconsciously he is aware. He is also aware that to read another man's body raises the possibility that another man may attempt to read his, and perhaps in the reading find him deficient.

Reading Repositions the Reader

As I have claimed elsewhere, masculinity as a gender construction in virtually every society is fragile and must be constantly defended (Culbertson 1992, 1994, 2001). Michael Satlow makes the same claim in relation to the Jewish understanding of masculinity: "For the rabbis, therefore, manliness is never secure; it is achieved through the constant exercise of discipline in pursuit of virtue, and vanishes the moment a male ceases to exercise that discipline" (Satlow 1996, 27). To gaze at another man repositions a straight man as a gay man, thereby shattering his fragile masculinity. Reading affects the reader much more deeply than it affects the text; gazing affects the gazer much more deeply than the one toward whom the gaze is directed. Susan Bordo points out that the male gaze has the power not only to objectify, but to feminize:

> What exposure is most feared in the shower? Not the scrutiny of the penis (although this prospect may indeed make a heterosexual man uncomfortable), but the moment when one bends down to pick up the soap which has slipped from one's hands. It is in the imagination of this moment that the orthodox male is most undone by the consciousness that there may be homosexuals in the shower, whose gaze will define him as a passive receptacle of their sexuality, and thus as "woman." There is a certain paradox here. For although it is the imagined effeminacy of homosexual men that makes them objects of heterosexual derision, here it is their imagined masculinity (that is, the consciousness of them as active, evaluating sexual subjects, with a defining and "penetrating" sexual gaze) that makes them the objects of heterosexual fear. (Bordo 1997, 287)

Men's fear of the male gaze, ultimately, is the fear of becoming, feeling, or representing female desire within the phallocentric order. In the shower, the homosexual body is the same as the heterosexual body, the only difference being in the desirer (Schehr 1997, 151).

Reading a Text That Won't Focus

As if the male body were not already a difficult enough text to read, it seems to disappear altogether when a man is unclothed. In a patriarchal system, the penis cues masculinity, and once that occurs, the body, "the being," disappears. The person becomes a function; the form becomes the essence, the masculinity, the "doing." The part overwhelms the whole, so that the whole fades into insignificance, leaving us to attempt to read a part or "member" that is, at best, dissociative. Phillip Lopate writes:

> This part of me, which is so synecdochically identified with the male body (as the term "male member" indicates) has given me both too little, and too much, information about what it means to be a man. It has a personality like a cat. I have prayed to it to behave better, to be less frisky, or more; I have followed its nose in matters of love, ignoring good sense, and paid the price; but I have also come to appreciate that it has its own specialized form of intelligence which must be listened to, or another price will be extracted. (Lopate 1996, 211)

The penis will not behave: now a penis, now a phallus, the one when we wish the other, it is itself a text that we can barely read, even with double-vision. It seems not one thing but two. The phallus is haunted by the penis and vice versa. It has no unified social identity, but is fragmented by ideologies including race and ethnicity. "Rather than exhibiting constancy of form, it is perhaps the most visibly mutable of bodily parts; it evokes the temporal not the eternal. And far from maintaining a steady will and purpose, it is mercurial, temperamental, unpredictable" (Bordo 1997, 265–66). It is this unpredictability that fascinates, frustrates, and ultimately offends many readers of male bodies.

Because it is two and not one, we do not even know how to count the male body parts. Girls are made of indiscrete amounts of stuff: "sugar and spice and everything nice." No quantities are given, nor do they need to be. But boys are made of countable things: "snips and snails and puppy dog tails. . . . Countable, if not to say detachable, things, metonymies of their always castrated penises" (Schehr 1997, 80). But do we count the penis as one and the phallus as another? Or is the penis simply a potential text, a text which seems to self-create at will? In the fifth century, Augustine claimed it was two: the penis, which is the "logical extension" of all rational men, created in the image of the divine logos, and the phallus which, as rationally uncontrollable, must simply be the handiwork of the Not-God, Satan. The phallus for Augustine is the wily serpent in the garden and, as the only body part that refuses to submit to the brain, the constant reminder of our fallenness.[8] Augustine despised the phallus, the conveyer of original sin. And yet even so great a saint could be overcome by his phallically inflated male ego, declaring that in heaven, women will receive their penises back. Perhaps he would have been happier if the penis really had been detachable, to be awarded, or not, like a prize for good behavior.

In a 1986 movie called *Dick Talk,* a group of women are filmed discussing their responses to the male body and to male genitals in particular. In the opening section, "The First," the moderator asks women about the first time they thought about a penis and what they thought about it. One relates how she thought penises were like rockets that detached themselves from men, entered women's bodies, and transformed themselves into babies. She had seen diagrams in a book, and since she had seen her father walking around the house in his shorts without a visible erection like that in the diagram, she assumed that his had become detached. She then relates a dream about men in suits with attaché cases in which they keep their penises (Lehman 1993, 148–49).

A detachable phallus, in the above fantasy, must leave behind only its shadow, the penis. Schehr argues that this is why the penis is hidden so often: "It is my contention that the penis has been the most hidden of male body parts because of the ideological as well as the psychoanalytical temptation to turn the penis into its evil twin brother, the phallus" (Schehr 1997, 16). Note the genitals in the ceiling paintings in the Sistine Chapel: they are all disproportionately small. This makes them safe and aesthetic, an extension of ancient Greek ideals of desirable male nudity. K. J. Dover analyzed the representation of penises on Greek vases within the context of his study of homosexuality in ancient Greece. Attractive penises were particularly small, with no pubic hair: the penis of a preadolescent. Unattractive penises were exaggeratedly large, threatening, and attached to hairy bodies. The cultural index of penile beauty, then, in Dover's reading of vases, is that of modesty and subordination, an abjuration of sexual initiative or sexual rivalry (Dover 1978, 125).

Source of pride, seat of shame, many men cannot figure out how to read their own penises realistically and refuse to read the penises of others. Judaism attempted to resolve the textual dilemma with the cry: "Off with its hat!" Christianity responded more adamantly: "Off with its head," creating a culture of either symbolic or literal castration. The Christian male body was symbolically castrated through body-denial, the circumscription of sexual activity to heterosexual intercourse within marriage for the sole purpose of procreation, and the forbidding of *jouissance,* or "celebratory hedonism" (see, e.g., Ranke-Heinemann 1990). For some of the saints, this was not enough. Origen in the third century, and Peter Abelard in the twelfth century, both Christian saints, are two who excised altogether any genital text from their body, by castrating themselves as an act of bodily mortification (Brown 1988, 117, 168–69).[9]

Reading a Text That Does Not Belong to Us

Those who have the greatest investment in reading interpretive meanings into textless texts are those whose power is most easily promoted by the interpretation. The entire subject of identifying readings, of deconstructing the construction of the heterosexual male body, is so inherently elusive that I had repeatedly to struggle to keep any sense of objectivity while writing this essay.

Those with the greatest investment in reading meaning into the male body are governments and politico-military authorities which, in order to retain their present positions of power, need men to conceive themselves in certain ways. In other words, the primary reader who inserts meaning into the male textless text is the government structure of the society in which these men live. In his essay "Consuming Manhood" (1997), Michael Kimmel points out that in order for a man in nineteenth-century puritan- ical America to become a real man, a "Marketplace Man," governments realized it would be necessary to control the flows of desire and of fluids filling his body. Certain flows of desire would need to be deemed morally repugnant because they were economically counterproductive; undesir- able or counterproductive flows of desire would henceforth be deemed pathological. In *The History of Sexuality* (1978), Michel Foucault stresses the development of such discourses of biopolitics, those official discourses that seek to regulate the individual through a series of proscriptions, admonitions, and recommendations. The discourses of biopolitics involve the identification of the individual with his (and not "his or her") political self as a citizen. The individual was to act so as best to fulfill the functions of a member of society. In order to produce Marketplace Men, bodies would need to be owned, men would have to be read as both heterosexual and "manly," and the siring of children would be understood as mandatory. These were the responsibilities of every good citizen.[10]

Male bodies are textless texts into which governments read self-securing values and expectations, giving the lie to the myth of genuine concern or human rights. Heterosexuality is read onto men's bodies, which is why, in the present debate on the genesis of sexual orientation, gay men can usually chart the development of their sexual self-awareness, while straight men believe they have "always been that way." Heterosexuality is a government-designed and government-controlled process of breeding, of animal husbandry. Masturbation, voluntary celibacy, homosexuality, and any other alternative sexual expressions have to be controlled and even anathematized, for only through heterosexual marriage and the procreation of children can a phallic political power, or patriarchy of privilege, assure its own authority into the future.[11] The heterosexual male gaze is the ultimate sign of capitulation to an imposed external meaning, an abandonment of human *jouissance*.

Reading Unmasks the Divine Ambiguity

An additional difficulty in reading men's bodies confronts Jewish and Christian men, whether gay or straight. Danna Nolan Fewell and David Gunn (1996), and Howard Eilberg-Schwartz (1996; see also 1994), have explored extensively the central gender problem of Scripture: how can men and women understand themselves as created in God's image when God apparently has no body? Eilberg-Schwartz writes:

> Does God have genitals and, if so, of which sex? It is interesting that interpreters have generally avoided this question. This seems a particularly important lacuna for interpreters who understand Genesis 1:26-27 to mean that the human body is made in the image of the deity. By avoiding the question of God's sex, they skirt a fundamental question: how can male and female bodies both resemble the divine form? Since God's sex is veiled, however, any conclusions have to be inferred indirectly from statements about God's gender. But however this question is answered poses a problem for human embodiment generally and sexuality in particular. If God is asexual, as many interpreters would have it, then only part of the human body is made in the image of God. (Eilberg-Schwartz 1996, 47)

The part of a man's body that is obviously not made in God's image is the penis, since we cannot be sure that God has or had one. Nor, on the other hand, can we know whether or not God has a vagina. To read another man's body, therefore, is to read the Divine Ambiguity. And this ambiguity, too, is read into men's penises—into the penises of others, and into one's own.

Given how daunting all this is, it is no wonder that the heterosexual male gaze is never directed toward other heterosexual men. No wonder "the guys" only wanted to look at the whole package, if even that! If a man cannot read the body of another, what then is the effect when he turns his male gaze upon himself, upon his own body with all its strengths and weaknesses? Such questions, at the same time that they identify the continuing invisibility of male bodies in the incarnational tradition, define the future agenda of body theology for adult males, a critical component of male identities in a changing church.

Bibliography

Augustine. 1982. *The Literal Meaning of Genesis*. Trans. John Hammond Taylor, S. J. Ancient Christian Writers series. New York: Newman.

Austin, J. L. 1975. *How to Do Things with Words*. 2d ed. Ed. J. O. Urmson and Marina Sbisa. Cambridge: Harvard Univ. Press.

Bakhtin, Mikhail Mikhailovich. 1981. *The Dialogic Imagination: Four Essays*. Ed. Michael Holquist. Trans. Caryl Emerson and Michael Holquist. Austin: Texas Univ. Press.

Beal, Timothy, and David Gunn, eds. 1996. *Reading Bibles, Writing Bodies: Identity and the Book*. London: Routledge.

Booth, Wayne C. 1990. *The Company We Keep: An Ethics of Fiction*. Berkeley: California Univ. Press.

Bordo, Susan. 1997. "Reading the Male Body." *The Male Body: Features, Destinies, Exposures*. Ed. Laurence Goldstein. Ann Arbor: University of Michigan. 265–306.

Bowen, Murray. 1985. *Family Therapy in Clinical Practice*. Northvale: Jason Aronson.

Browe, Peter. 1936. *Zur Geschichte der Entmannung: Eine religions- und rechtsgeschichtliche Studie*. Breslau: Muller.

Brown, Peter. 1988. *The Body and Society: Men, Women, and Sexual Renunciation in Early Christianity*. New York: Columbia Univ. Press.

Coward, Rosalind. 1985. *Female Desires: How They Are Sought, Bought, and Packaged*. New York: Grove.

Culbertson, Philip. 2001. "Men's Quest for Wholeness: The Changing Counseling Needs of Pakeha Males." Forthcoming in *Theology and Culture*, vol. 1, Auckland.

———. 1996. *A Word Fitly Spoken: Context, Transmission, and Adoption of the Parables of Jesus*. Albany: SUNY.

———. 1994. *Counseling Men*. Minneapolis: Fortress Press.

———. 1992. *New Adam: The Future of Male Spirituality*. Minneapolis: Fortress Press.

———. Spring 1991a. "Multiplexity in Biblical Exegesis: The Introduction to Megillat Qohelet by Moses Mendelssohn." *Cincinnati Journal of Judaica* 2, 10–18.

———. 1991b. "Known, Knower, Knowing: The Authority of Scripture in the Anglican Tradition." *Anglican Theological Review* 74:2, 144–74.

Dane, Perry. 1991. "The Oral Law and the Jurisprudence of a Textless Text." *S'vara* 2:2, 11–24.

Dover, K. J. 1978. *Greek Homosexuality*. Cambridge: Harvard Univ. Press.

Dutton, Kenneth. 1995. *The Perfectible Body: The Western Ideal of Male Physical Development*. New York: Continuum.

Eilberg-Schwartz, Howard. 1996. "The Problem of the Body for the People of the Book." *Reading Bibles, Writing Bodies: Identity and the Book*. Ed. Timothy Beal and David Gunn. London: Routledge. 34–55.

———. 1994. *God's Phallus and Other Problems for Men and Monotheism*. Boston: Beacon.

Fewell, Danna Nolan, and David Gunn. 1996. "Shifting the Blame: God in the Garden." *Reading Bibles, Writing Bodies: Identity and the Book*. Ed. Timothy Beal and David Gunn. London: Routledge. 16–33.

Fish, Stanley. 1980. *Is There a Text in This Class? The Authority of Interpretive Communities*. Cambridge: Harvard Univ. Press.

Foucault, Michel. 1978. *The History of Sexuality*. Trans. Robert Hurley. New York: Pantheon.

Fry, Stephen. 1994. *The Hippopotamus*. London: Arrow.

Gadamer, Hans-Georg Gadamer. 1982. *Truth and Method*. New York: Crossroad.

George, Mark. 1996. "Assuming the Body of the Heir Apparent: David's Lament." *Reading Bibles, Writing Bodies: Identity and the Book*. Ed. Timothy Beal and David Gunn. London: Routledge. 164–74.

Goldstein, Laurence. 1997. *The Male Body: Features, Destinies, Exposures*. Ann Arbor: University of Michigan.

Guerin, Philip, Thomas Fogarty, Leo Fay, and Judith Gilbert Kautto. 1996. *Working with Relationship Triangles: The One-Two-Three of Psychotherapy*. New York: Guilford.

Kimmel, Michael. 1997. "Consuming Manhood: The Feminization of American Culture and the Recreation of the Male Body, 1832–1920." *The Male Body: Features, Destinies, Exposures*. Ed. Laurence Goldstein. Ann Arbor: University of Michigan. 12–41.

Lehman, Peter. 1993. *Running Scared: Masculinity and the Representation of the Male Body*. Philadelphia: Temple Univ. Press.

Lopate, Phillip. 1996. *Portrait of My Body*. New York: Anchor.

Mulvey, Laura. 1975. "Visual Pleasure and the Narrative Cinema." *Screen* 16:3, 6–18.

Ortner, Sherry. 1996. *Making Gender: The Politics and Erotics of Culture*. Boston: Beacon.

Ranke-Heinemann, Uta. 1990. *Eunuchs for the Kingdom of Heaven: Women, Sexuality, and the Catholic Church*. New York: Penguin.

Rashkow, Ilona. 1994. "Daughters and Fathers in Genesis . . . Or, What is Wrong with this Picture?" *A Feminist Companion to Exodus to Deuteronomy*. Ed. Athalya Brenner. Sheffield: Sheffield Academic Press. 22–36.

Rubin, Gayle. 1975. "The Traffic in Women: Notes on the 'Political Economy' of Sex." *Toward an Anthropology of Women*. Ed. Rayna Reiter. New York: Monthly Review.

Satlow, Michael. 1996. "'Try to Be a Man': The Rabbinic Construction of Masculinity." *Harvard Theological Review* 89:1, 19–40.

Schehr, Lawrence. 1997. *Parts of an Andrology: On Representations of Men's Bodies*. Stanford: Stanford Univ. Press.

Sedgwick, Eve Kosofsky. 1985. *Between Men: English Literature and Male Homosocial Desire*. New York: Columbia.

Sheets-Johnstone, Maxine. Summer 1992. "Corporeal Archetypes and Power." *Hypatia* 7:3, 69.

Thompson, Jim. 1988 [1954]. *The Nothing Man*. New York: Mysterious.

Walters, Marianne, Betty Carter, Peggy Papp, and Olga Silverstein. 1988. *The Invisible Web: Gender Patterns in Family Relationships*. New York: Guilford.

Notes

1. Ordinarily a text is defined as a page with words on it. I first encountered the term "textless text" in Dane (1991). He uses the term to describe Oral Torah, but I find the term's usefulness to be much wider.

2. This is not, however, R. Judah the Patriarch, who was referred to as "our holy rabbi" because he never looked at his own penis, or even touched it (b. Shabbat 118b. Nor is it George Eliot's Daniel Deronda, who seems to take three-quarters of this eight-hundred-plus-page novel before he ever notices that he is circumcised. Both serve as examples of men's enormous investment in dissociating from their penises, while simultaneously making them synecdoches of masculine identity.

3. Such a claim is, of course, simplistic, for however passive a text may be, it still has its own syntax, rhetorical structures, and genres. See Gadamer 1982.

4. Many authors develop this idea. Among the foundational texts are Austin 1975, Fish 1980, and Bakhtin 1981.

5. Ortner (1996) describes Polynesian cultures as homosocial, in that powerful men retain their position by bartering young virgins in order to form political alliances. Such a social structure appears to make women important, but in fact their value is only in their agency as "negotiable tender." George (1996) describes

the relation between David and Jonathan as situated at the homosexual end of the homosocial spectrum.

6. See, for example, the relationship between Maurice and Bertie in Lawrence's short story "The Blind Man," or between Gerald Crich and Rupert Birkin in *Women in Love*.

7. "I embrace the pursuit of the Other as among the grandest of hunts we are invited to. . . . But surely no beast that will prove genuinely *other* will fail to bite, and the otherness that bites, the otherness that changes us, must have sufficient definition, sufficient identity, to threaten us where we live" (Booth 1990, 70).

8. See the excellent comments by Rashkow 1994, 32, n.32. For a vivid picture of adolescent revulsion at phallic erection, see Stephen Fry's novel *The Hippopotamus* (1994), 88–89.

9. I believe there are deeper psychological implications of male castration that have not yet been adequately explored. For example, is Christian castration a form of despair masquerading as discipline? Is it an early form of mental illness like the forms of self-mutilation we know today, where a patient will bang her head against a wall repeatedly, creating a controlled external pain that distracts from the uncontrollable internal psychiatric pain? Unfortunately, the subject of voluntary castration in Christian tradition is little written-about; one of the few texts is Browe 1936.

10. In Jim Thompson's novel *The Nothing Man*, protagonist Clint Brown returns from World War II having had his genitals blown off by a landmine. He describes himself as having "given his penis for his country" (Thompson 1988, 3).

11. The *Hite Report on Male Sexuality* (1981) concluded that sexual intercourse for men was satisfying not only because of their attraction to their sexual partner "but also from the deeply engraved cultural meaning of the act. Through intercourse a man participates in the cultural symbolism of patriarchy and gains a sense of belonging to society with status/identity of 'male'." See Walters et al. 1988, 215.

11

Disabled Bodies, Healing Bodies, Christ's Body

Brett Webb-Mitchell

> *Do you not know that your bodies are members of Christ?*
> —1 Corinthians 6:15

Do men with disabilities perceive themselves and their disabling conditions differently in the context of secular (pagan) modern American society than they do in the context of the church, the body of Christ, infused with the Holy Spirit and continually constituted by the narrative of Christ's storied life, revealed in the rich rituals of life together as Christ's people?

This is a question I asked three men, each with what modern America would call a disabled body. In modern America, the descriptive label *disabled body* often connotes that one's body is broken and is no longer "able" or "capable" to do certain things that a healthy, "normal" body can do. It is considered "less than" a healthier body. The disabled body is an "abnormal" body in need of "fixing" or caring attention, of being "cured," and for some, of being "healed" or "made whole."

How do we know that it, the body, is broken or disabled? Usually by comparison with an established normative body. In America, we have an image of what is a healthy body and what is a beautiful body (they are not always synonymous) constantly paraded as the ideal before the American male. We see the ideal in the magazine racks lined with flesh-covered men's fitness magazines jammed with models strutting their six-pack abs, or well-coifed models in *Gentlemen's Quarterly*; in television shows and movies promoting the next sexually potent, young hot bodies; and in the ubiquitous malls with front windows displaying healthy, exuberant twenty-something men, hanging out with the bold, gorgeous, sensual young women (with perhaps a touch of homoerotic flirtation). We are promised by advertisements that if we eat the right food, work out at certain gyms, or have sex in particular positions, we will not only look good, but we'll feel great, combining beauty and health. Furthermore, we are promised that if we work out daily while we are young, swallow the right combinations of vitamins later on in life, and take a Viagra pill daily, we will live to a good old age in an acceptable rate of decline, with the promise of sex until we die.

The one who disturbs our dreamy slumber from this great American mythic-poetic narrative is the person who is, in all actuality, no longer a person, but a "body with an illness," a disability, the "disabled one," an "it"; an object of sympathy or pity, or what Arthur Frank (1995) calls the "wounded storyteller." In America, to be disabled is equivalent to being "strangely different" at best, and a gross, misbegotten deviant at worse. I have heard Christian congregations pray for a person with a disability to be made whole while also praying that no one else will become disabled like "the one we just prayed for."

In general, a disabling condition of the body is a stigma in American society. Being disabled is a fleshly, visible sign of being marked as weak, crippled, and imperfect.

Erving Goffman (1963) wrote that a stigma shows that society demands a considerable level of body control from its members in order to be considered "normal." Any loss of control is stigmatizing, and special work is required to manage the lack of control. Goffman points out that a stigma is embarrassing, not just for the one who is stigmatized, but for those who are facing the one with the stigma and have to react to it. There is much energy expended as the one with a disabling condition tries to make life easier on the one without a noticeable disabling condition, all while living with the disabling condition itself.

A person with a disability in America becomes part of a group of others who share the same kind of disabling condition. Suddenly, one is no longer "Jordan" or "Lacey," but one is lumped into the generalized category of the "Disabled Ones." For some disabling conditions, there are group support networks, a national office, a Web site, a 1-800 phone line for crisis intervention, a list of professional speakers and annual conferences with fine banquets, literature and rhetoric that is specific to the disabling condition, a liaison in Washington, D.C., who is working for governmental funding for people with "your" disabling condition, and a pharmaceutical corporation that can make and sell drugs to help the disabled one cope with the world. It has almost come to the point that one wouldn't know how to live *without* the disabling condition. One's primary social context determines what is considered disabled or "temporarily able-bodied." In the case of most industrial societies, a disability is defined by professionals and elected representatives. Simply put, the body politic decides what is or isn't a disabling condition.

For example, in the 1960s, there was no one in America with a learning disability. It wasn't until the federal and state governments started to sponsor bills and support legislation for funding of programs for people with a learning disability, beginning in the 1970s, that there was the categorization and diagnosis of a learning disability. Furthermore, the term and definition of *mental retardation* changed numerous times through the twentieth century, thanks to acts of the U.S. Congress.

Being disabled or having an illness in modern America is a challenge, to say the least. Arthur Frank observes rightly that the body that is ill or disabled is not silent, but does not use speech per se; yet it begets speech, often from others: "It speaks eloquently in pains and symptoms—but is inarticulate. We must speak for the body, and such speech is quickly frustrated; speech presents itself as being *about* the body rather than *of* it. The body is often alienated, literally 'made strange' as it is told in stories that are instigated by a need to make it familiar" (Frank 1995, 2).

Furthermore, in the American narrative, one's body is not connected to any other bodies. You, the individual, are in control of your own body, both in good *and* bad times. Each person is an island by itself in the rushing stream of American life. The implication is obvious in light of the American male who is disabled: because each person owns his body; one's neighbor is not responsible for what another person does with his or her own body. The disabled male has to take care of his own bodily needs. It is each person for himself: a social Darwinist "survival of the fittest." Such a narrative, and the practices it generates, determines, and nurtures, makes being a male with a disability an adventure at best, and makes him a recluse or homeless at worse.

I am interested in how our understanding of a disabling condition is shaped and nurtured by the myriad of larger stories in which we attach or embed our own stories. This includes the narratives we inherit that are already present and articulated in the community into which we are born and raised: a narrative we have no choice but to inherit. In other words, because all disabling conditions are political, in that a certain body politic determines what is or isn't a disabling condition, I will argue that the context of the body (writ large) politics in which we learn our inherited narrative, and the narratives that constitute that community or social group we are part of, determine how we understand and live with ourselves, regardless of how capable or disabled we are. My very understanding of my body and what is a body, as well as what it is to be disabled, is defined and given merit or worth by myself and others who have lived prior to my presence, or are living with me in the context where I live.

In this project, I endeavored to find out if there was a difference between understanding one's disability in the American narrative or in the Church's narrative by interviewing three men with different kinds of disabling conditions. There is Rick, whose body is obviously disabled due to cerebral palsy. Scoliosis of the spine has caused his back to be twisted in an odd shape. As he stands at the church's front door, greeting you as the pastor of a Lutheran church, your eyes quickly notice his Canadian crutches supporting his crooked frame. Tony is a man living with AIDS. His disability is easy to see sometimes; for example, he had a goiter that I noticed when we first met. Other times, his disability is well hidden, and all you see is his mischievous smile. Finally, there is Kevin, a man whose body is engaged in a tireless act of obsessive-compulsive behavior, though Kevin tries hard to hide his disability from anyone else's gaze. All three men are devout, faithful Christians. And all three understand the persuasive, oftentimes subtle, yet constantly bombarding vision of being an American male. Yet all three have a different interpretation of how they understand their disabling condition within the Church, as constituted by the narrative of the Christian story.

Rick's Story

Rick is a white, forty-two-year-old man with two rambunctious and "bright-as-a-whip" children, married to a spouse who understands herself as his equal in most matters of life. Rick is an ordained minister in the Evangelical Lutheran Church in America, and he is the solo pastor of a good-sized congregation in Vermont. Rick also has lived with cerebral palsy from birth. The diagnosis was initially spastic paraplegic, then diaplegic, and then in one week, they took that label away as well, leaving him quadriplegic.

When he was young, Rick wanted another body that would let him do what he wanted to do: "I'd be playing baseball, or I would be an astronaut. I dreamt about flying a fighter jet, and doing all that stuff."

In the context of modern America, Rick does not understand and perceive himself as attractive. For example, Rick told me that he doesn't like to look at himself in full-length mirrors because, "I don't like what I see there. In stores where there are plenty of full-length mirrors, all I see is a broken body. It doesn't mesh with my internal vision of who I am, which has been pretty constant for forty-two years. I don't see myself as attractive." In other words, said Rick, "Commercials aren't directed to me."

Yet Rick understands and perceives himself differently within the body of Christ: "My disability is not as big a deal in the body of Christ as it is in America, because there is a willingness to be vulnerable and weak in the body of Christ, whereas we have to be very strong out in the world."

With his body that is considered "disabled" in the world, Rick knew that he was going to be a pastor, "because God knew what he was doing." Rick continued:

> I'm doing what I'm doing because my body is not an issue, at this particular time, especially in this parish, being accessible with accessible people. In the body of Christ I don't think folks see me and my disability in the same way I see me and my disability. My disability has very little importance to them. I feel that the congregation expects that because of my experience, I'll be able to relate to their aches and pains, to the point of where they feel I can handle their pain better because I'm disabled.

From twelve years old, Rick knew that he was accepted just as he is: "[my life and] my gifts were valued in the Church."

Tony's Story

Tony is a dancer. His body is taut, with little signs of fat anywhere on his slender physique. Though there is some grey in his slight beard, Tony's eyes sparkle, revealing the youngster, if not the jester, within. He stands almost six feet tall, and when he hugs, he embraces the other person totally, yet gently. When he is feeling enthusiastic, or serious about one matter or another, his eyes grow large, pushing out the wrinkles on his otherwise smooth forehead, and he snaps his fingers and waves his arms.

Tony is living with AIDS.

He learned he was HIV positive after he went to get tested anonymously because of a persistent pain that wouldn't go away in his body. "I think it's about four to six weeks before they have the results. So I called them up . . . there was a pause . . . and the nurse said, in a solemn tone of voice, 'Why don't you come down [to the office].'"

Scared, Tony started to think through the anatomy and physiology of the body:

> We have all these kinds of bodies, and I partied a lot . . . no won-
> der other people have bodies where they just say, "Okay, I've had
> enough." You know, understanding these things, how, you know, I
> just look at the times I drank and partied and smoked tons of cig-
> arettes, all-night parties and going to studio, no sleep . . . and that
> was the attitude that I kind of took when I looked at everybody
> else, all of these people that were dying of AIDS. I was like, jeez,
> mine, my body, will grow up and, you know, see you later. And so
> I was thinking of it like that.
>
> On the way down, I was beginning to pray about it, that if I was
> positive, I would ask God to be with me, and if I wasn't, he would
> be with me also and I would change my lifestyle. So I remember
> walking in, and there was always this solemn look. I'll never forget
> the lady. I looked at the lady, and she calls me in and closes the
> door, and it's like I've been convicted of a crime, and my punish-
> ment is death. And she says, "Well, your results came back, and
> they came back positive. I'm really sorry." I felt as if I was really
> kind of scared. And she said, "What do you want me to do?" And
> I said, "I'd like to start working on that now." So she decided all
> about the AZT and that stuff. . . . They gave me a shot, and then
> she said to me, "Well, I think you should get your life in order," and
> I said, "Okay, I'll get back with you," and she wanted me to see this
> doctor and get a physical and all these things, and stuff like that,
> and so I scheduled an appointment to come back.

When he left the nurse's office, he went to his boss at a bookstore where he was working at the time—"She was the first person I told"—who said that she would take care of him. The next person he told was his dance instructor, who automatically knew Tony was coming with such news. "I think he knew because a lot of his friends died of AIDS, so when I walked in he asked if I was okay, and he suggested that we go to a health project office."

At the health project office, the nurse pulled out forms and started to quiz Tony: Do you have Medicare, Medicaid? Do you have a will? Tony said, "I looked at her and said, 'I'm not dead yet. I'm not ready to be set up for death yet.'" The nurse, surprised by his response, then asked if he wanted an assigned "buddy" as part of the buddy system program. Being in the world of dance and theater, Tony was friends with someone who lived in Pittsburgh who was also living with AIDS, and had not taken any standard medication for AIDS: "He's a long-term survivor, and he was doing all that alternative stuff, and I told him I was interested in alternative medicine, because I was watching these people take AZT and continually dying right and left."

Tony's friendship with another man living with AIDS brought both a sense of humor about living with the illness, as well as release from despair and depression. Tony remembers walking with his friend across the street when he almost walked in front of a moving car, and he was pulled back by his friend. They laughed uproariously: "We both almost died from getting hit by a car, not from complications from AIDS." Tony and his friend continue to go to some small-group meetings for people living with AIDS. Tony remembers distinctly the depression that hovered over many in these group meetings, in which he caught himself smiling. "They asked me how long I had AIDS, and I said it was my third day. And they said, 'and you're laughing?' I answered, 'Yeah . . . why? Should I cry?'"

Along with learning about new herbs in the treatment of complications from AIDS, Tony came to see again what he calls "the spiritual connection." Tony remembers from an early age that he was in the hospital because of meningitis, "and everybody came and prayed for me, and at that age, nobody was supposed to survive, and I did. I think it had a lot to do with prayer, and family." Tony comes from a family who believed in what some would call "the power of prayer" and were believers in miracles. "I remember my great-great grandfather started a church, and he and his family used to sit around and talk about these miracles that went on. My great-great grandfather would go sometimes to pray for people . . . watched people at death who then became well."

In light of the medical community's telling Tony that he is ill, and America telling him that he is going to die of AIDS because of the kind of person he is or because of the "lifestyle choices" he has made, Tony doesn't necessarily see himself living with a disability in the context of the Church:

> Because, for number one, my spirit is alive. Bringing both the body and the spirit together in harmony—that's life. When I see many people in the church that are so Christian, they talk about the Holy Spirit, but you don't see anything. They say they believe in God, but they don't believe in the miracles of Jesus Christ. As I go into churches, I go in there with the presence of Christ. What does that mean to me? The joy of coming into his house and worshiping and sharing that [good news].

What fills Tony with joy is the attitude that his life isn't in his hands any-more, but in God's hands. That gives him not only joy, but a way of living that baffles most people: "They see me dance, [and they] think [I'm] in denial of being HIV positive." People in the medical profession also have a hard time when Tony walks in and doesn't look ill, doesn't need anything from them, or is not near death, because then it is hard for them to help him. The world around him wants him to be a poster boy of a man living, surviving AIDS. It is one poster Tony refuses to lend his image to.

Tony does have some regrets. There are difficult times: "I see a nice-built guy, and I want to go and make my body look like his," but it is harder to do, the older and sicker he becomes. He is starting to feel some excruciat-ing pain that is difficult to endure: "[it is as] if my feet were being pierced." When I asked Tony if he was going to be healed by God of such pain caused by living with AIDS, Tony thought for a moment, and then said in hushed tones, "I'd like to be close to God."

Kevin's Story

Kevin is a tall, attractive young man in his twenties. Physically, he is a handsome man, with a dark head of hair, a carefully cut, lithesome body, and a sweet all-American–Colgate smile. He still considers himself a newly-wed after three years of marriage and is currently living in the Midwest, serving a small church as a lay preacher, while quietly starting his career as a writer. Kevin has the mind and imagination of a writer.

Kevin is also disabled, though his disability is quite hidden from our view (which takes tremendous work on his part): he has obsessive-compulsive disorder, otherwise known as OCD.

Kevin first noticed it when he was four years old:

> I have a particular memory of my mom not paying attention to me. So I threatened her that I was going to leave, and she said, "That'd be fine." Since that didn't work, I thought, "well, she really liked the Christmas gift I gave her. So I'll go get that; I'll bring it down to the basement (where his mother is) and show her while I tell her, 'When I leave, I'm taking this with me,' and see if that gets a reaction out of her." So I went upstairs and got this little Christian thing I made her that said "Noel" on it—it had a little boot or some bell or something—and I took it downstairs and I told her, "Not only am I leaving, I'm taking this with me." And

again she said, "Well, that'd be fine," and made some smart comment about packing a toothbrush or something like that. Frustrated, I started to walk up the stairs. And as I was going up the stairs I had my hand on the handrail, and I was just sort of patting it along the handrail as I went along. About halfway up the stairs I patted it and I kept on going, and I thought to myself, or something came over me, that I needed to pat that handrail again, and I thought at first—and this is what I thought probably for about the next six or seven years—that it must be because the handrail is animated, it has life, and it will feel left out if I don't touch it again. And so I touched it again. It felt like everything was okay with it, and then continued on up the stairs.

Kevin often thought that inanimate objects had life, and that if he didn't touch them again, they'd feel sad at best, or worse, he'd feel a sense of doom and dread if he didn't pay attention to the inanimate object. For example, he would pick up the phone, hang it up, pick it up again, hang it up, all with no thought of telling people what he was doing. He rationalized it: some kids played football with certain superstitions, and he had some novel superstitions to make it through life. At first, his OCD was his very own brand of superstitious rituals.

When Kevin was eleven years old, he came to associate the ritualistic behaviors of OCD with friendships: "I associated it with . . . touching things multiple times, or whatever else my OCD was telling me to do, [or] it would be worse with this kid who was picking on me." Notice that the OCD was now an authoritarian presence in his life, and one that he must obey . . . or else.

Afraid of those who would bully him, Kevin would ward off the others by standing in front of a mirror by himself. If anyone else's image was in the mirror, especially another child who picked on him, Kevin would get out of his desk and stand in front of the mirror "in such a way that no one else behind me could be seen, and so that mirror only had me in it, and then I would go sit down. And then if I happened to see someone else (in the mirror) I would get back up and do it, you know, constantly, and obsessions and compulsions like that dramatically increased during those years."

The first time he told a friend about his disability was when he was fifteen years old. Kevin was about to leave the house to go outside with his friend Russ. But before he could leave, Kevin had to put on a particular pair of shoes, or else there was going to be some kind of doom on the trip.

He couldn't leave the house without those pair of shoes, which he couldn't find, so he told Russ that he couldn't go with him. Russ stormed out of the house, mad at Kevin. It was then that Kevin realized that he was about to lose his best friend, so he had to tell Russ about his compulsive behavior.

Before he called Russ to apologize, Kevin called a member of the church who was a psychologist. Upset and crying, Kevin told the psychologist his story. The psychologist went with Kevin to Russ's house, and together they talked to Russ about Kevin's disorder. Russ was relieved that Kevin's behaviors had nothing to do with him per se, but were about his compulsive disorder.

By the time that Kevin had come to graduate school, he had told only nine people in his life, including his wife and me, though his mother still does not know.

In talking with a counselor during his undergraduate days, Kevin was given the following therapeutic program: first, he is to keep a journal, and every single time he desires to follow through with an obsessive behavior, he is to write it down right away. If Kevin follows through with a compulsion, he is to write that down as well.

Second, Kevin is to begin stopping the compulsive behavior by focusing on the small ways he obsesses, and he is to go for as long as possible without acting on the impulse to be obsessive, without "doing the compulsion, and then if I eventually have to do it, fine, consider that a victory. Next time, try and go longer, and if you have to do a compulsion eventually, do it, but then go longer the next time without doing it."

Yet for Kevin, part of the problem with the second process is that it is hard to write down the compulsion:

> I mean, [it is] similar to looking at someone else's reflection in the mirror. . . . It's the same for me with saying someone's name out loud, writing down their first name, even at times thinking their name, depending on what I'm touching or doing. So it was next-to-impossible for me to write down what was going on, because writing it down was just as hard as whatever the thing I was doing was . . . Because I didn't want to write their name—it was hard enough just to think their name, for fear I would take on their characteristics.

Kevin's obsessive behaviors are often a mirror action of another person he admires or dislikes. For example, as a goalkeeper for soccer (and he understands himself to be a fine goalkeeper), if he gets "scored on," he associates the error with the "fact that I had looked at [the other goalkeeper], and played poorly because [the other goalkeeper is poor at his job], and I had taken on his characteristics. It's that simple."

Kevin's obsessions continued, without my being aware of it, even during the interview. He told me that when the cord attaching the tape recorder to the outlet hit the window we were sitting by at the same time he saw a bald man walk by, he tapped the window with the cord purposely so that he wouldn't become bald. Or, when Kevin went into the bathroom, he went by the mirror three times to be sure to leave his image there for fear that he would either inherit the image of the person who had been in the bathroom before him, or the one who came in after he left.

It is obvious that Kevin is wrestling with OCD. He doesn't wish to be a person who needs help, or a person to whom the world says, "You need help." He doesn't want to admit he has a problem, because he is so well-narrated by the mythic-American dream for white Anglo-Saxon Protestant males. Kevin admits that he's already accepted the American narrative over what he wants to be the primary narrative of his life: a Christian narrative. Why? "Because I just haven't been trained in a community who believes it. And so, that's a struggle for me. But I know the Christian narrative teaches me whose I am, and that's most important," said Kevin.

What kind of Christian community would Kevin find healing? "[One] where dependence upon one another was realistic, where there . . . didn't have to be heroes who never needed help, but everyone needed help . . . there was no separation between needing help and being a hero . . . if I were in a community where it's a virtue to accept the support of other people." Yet Kevin doesn't see his OCD as a "damning vice," but as almost a "hyper-way of being a Wesleyan."

In the church, Kevin understands that being vulnerable, which is the way to living Christian community, is a problem, "because of how I understand the way the church works [today]. I understand that vulnerability is necessary for the church to work, but I have to be not only someone who helps, but someone who is helped, for the community to work well. I have to be [the one confessing] to find my identity in the Church." While Kevin believes all people in the church need help and are capable of giving help, Kevin can't get over the divide between those who need help and those who give help. Kevin feels that he is stuck being a helper.

When I asked Kevin if he was courageous enough to share his vulnerability of being OCD with others in a congregation, Kevin was silent. In low, hushed tones, Kevin admitted that he didn't, for that would put him in the role of needing help. Even though he believes that the church is a place where everyone needs help from one another, he isn't able to confess it.

He is frozen, scared that he is the only one with anything to confess. Even though he might give permission to others with OCD to tell their stories in the context of Christ's story, in Christ's community, Kevin is terrified of sharing his own story, afraid that others will write him off as "the disabled one" or the one with OCD and no name, or that he will be introduced as: "Obsessive-Compulsive Disorder, who happens to be Kevin." Even though Kevin is bright, articulate, and an amazing graduate student, he has never put together his intellectual gift with his disability, or realized how his intellectual abilities give him the capacity to talk about, if not reform, how people in a congregation understand a person with a disabling condition. Yet for the time being, Kevin chooses to remain what he calls a "secret OCD, a closet OCD, a basement OCD" because, like Tony, he refuses to be a poster boy for his disability.

Dependent upon Christ

The unnamed general theme of these narratives is of men struggling against aspects of the status quo of the American narrative while discovering their own place within the body of Christ, in which they know their hope resides. This theme has three characteristics that are instructive for understanding the power of social narratives. First, each man struggles with his identity in being a person with a disabling condition in the context of American society. While Rick wanted to be an astronaut or baseball player, Tony a professional dancer, and Kevin a scholar extraordinaire, they have come to understand that they are made whole and healed only in the context of Christ's body. There is a resistance, a story of struggle against, yet a tale of survival in each man's narrative as they cast aside the American victim narrative. None of them is willing to be labeled "the disabled one" by America's medical community or political system.

Second, each person's disability narrative changes or develops as they resist the imposing silence of suffering that American society forces them to make a habit. In other words, they begin to tell their stories of suffering injustice and ignorance, and in telling the story, they gain power: power to tell their stories honestly, to be courageous in living in the humility of their broken-life story, while at the same time being faithful to God. Rick, Tony, and Kevin understand, in different ways, that temporarily-able-bodied people are people uncomfortable with our stories, our bodies; we are uncomfortable with the strangeness or the mortality of our own beings. While Rick, Tony, and Kevin live in the daily tension of knowing they are mortals, dependent upon others and God's good grace performed in the action of others, other people are not at home or have never met their mortality.

Finally, Rick, Tony, and Kevin remind us, in their dependency, that we are all, in Christ's body, created to be dependent upon Christ. While we all have some real, tangible limits on what our bodies can or cannot do—with the good chance that the older we get, the less our bodies will perform at will—these three men have already met and are well-acquainted with their limitations. Because of such knowledge, their obvious sense of vulnerability and their learning to embrace the boundaries of what they can't do, each man has made the reluctant discovery while reaching out for help that his body *is*, as St. Paul reminds us, a member of Christ's resurrected and living body.

This is perhaps one of the greatest differences between the modern American narrative on disability and the Church's narrative about men with what America considers a "disabling condition." Our connection and unity are found in no longer owning "our" bodies, but in our bodies being connected with a body *greater* than our individual selves. Furthermore, with our bodies united with one another in Christ's body, "anyone united to the Lord becomes one spirit with him," as Paul writes (1 Corinthians 6:17).

The implication is this: those things that I cannot do with my body, others can do for me "in the name of Christ," and it is *as if* I were doing the very thing. For others can now be my body. I can be Rick's arms and legs, either taking him to certain events that he could not get to without assistance, or going in his name and regaling him with stories of the event. As Tony's body slowly deteriorates from complications of AIDS, I, as his brother in Christ, need to learn to both rejoice *and* weep with him (Romans 12:15). With Kevin, I need to stand with him as he practices the virtue of courage in love in sharing with others his shortcomings as a man living with OCD.

And what these three narratives point out is the beautiful truth that reveals the hollowness of the American narrative: out of these stories of broken bodies, there is healing of our bodies, minds, and spirits, as these men create for others in Christ's body the opportunity of being community, being Christ, one with another, in the Spirit of God.

Bibliography

Frank, Arthur. 1995. *The Wounded Storyteller*. Chicago: Chicago Univ. Press.

Goffman, Erving. 1963. *Stigma: Notes on the Management of Spoiled Identity*. Englewood Cliffs: Prentice Hall.

12

Can Men Learn to Float?
Spirituality and Health Crises

Jerrald Townsend and Robert Bennett

Health crises change men's spirituality, often enhancing it, but certainly challenging it. Whether men are in crisis themselves or are serving as care-givers, any crisis in one's physical health provides an opportunity to pay attention to spiritual issues as well—perhaps deepening spirituality, perhaps redirecting it, or perhaps just noticing it.

We ought to know. Jerry had an automobile accident in July 1987 that nearly killed him, dislocated his hip and seriously scarred his face, and hos-pitalized him for over a month. In December 1998 he went through quadruple arterial bypass surgery. In the Cardiac Intensive Care Unit in his hospital—Riverside in Columbus, Ohio—just after his surgery, the twelve bays of the unit all contained male patients, eleven of them in their fifties and the last in his seventies—a vivid illustration of the importance of health care for men "of a certain age." In addition to our own experiences, we have also, as faithful Episcopalians and concerned human beings, been involved with many other health crises, some of them involving men in parishes where we have been members, or in Jerry's case, worked as a pastor.

The spiritual growth that arises from health crises is important for practical reasons. Without serious attention to spiritual issues, men's health crises produce so much anxiety that the crisis is amplified. Deepak Chopra and others have been teaching us recently that deeper spirituality increases—or at least accompanies—physical health and longevity. Meditation lowers blood pressure. But more importantly, we live in spiri-tuality as the children of God, and health crises prompt us to realize that relationship more immediately and fully.

As a gender group, men tend to "translate" anxiety into health crises. Our anxious, success-focused approach to life, work, family, and even leisure destroys our bodies. In general, men tend to pay much more attention to issues of success or winning than they do to spiritual health, to maintaining a healthy relationship with God and with the spiritual community. Even if they happen to be involved in a faithful congregation, many men continue to focus on their physical and financial health and to neglect their spiritual growth until some crisis interferes. Even then, the actual crisis obscures the spiritual opportunities, and it is only upon thinking back that people recognize the spiritual dimensions of the crisis.

Pastors, therefore, are more likely to deal with their parishioners' health crises than they are, directly, with their spiritual lives, and in Jerry's nineteen years as an ordained Christian, he has spent much more time dealing with health crises than with spiritual ones. But pastors deal with spirituality in two principal ways: first, when parishioners ask them questions or need to talk about the spiritual journey, a spiritual crisis, or their prayer life; and second, in sermons, bible study, workshops, and other forums that encourage parishioners to develop their spiritual lives.

Health crises come to the attention of pastors in two ways as well: indirectly, or through direct information from the patient. Many parishioners, particularly men, hide them, either because they consider them private and thus to be protected carefully, or because they believe the crisis results from their own misbehavior, and consequently want it kept secret, especially from their pastor. Pastors learn about health crises through regular hospital-calling, in the course of which parishioners may turn up as patients, or when family members notify them. Sometimes parishioners who are particularly frightened by a health crisis will reveal it to the pastor when ordinarily they would not. On the other hand, those who see a connection between their spirituality and their health, whether or not they are in crisis, are more likely to want the pastor to know and to inform him or her directly. In either case, health crises can provide an unexpected "teachable moment" or "an occasion for grace." People involved in them are more likely than others to change their attitudes toward spirituality, let alone toward privacy and shame.

Men tend to react to health crises, as to most events in their lives, in terms of what they need to do, either to get through the crisis or to avoid or prevent it. They are concerned with changing their behavior, and their spirituality tends to focus on petitionary prayer, such as: "Oh Lord, change my cholesterol level." "Dear God, please clean out my arteries." "Father, get me through this chemotherapy." These prayers ask God to fix the situation before the situation becomes a crisis, or to end the crisis itself. During the crisis, such prayer may well focus on simple survival: "God, get me through this alive, or at least calmer."

After a health crisis, spirituality may focus on support for practical methods of avoiding recurrence or dealing with the consequences of the crisis. Thus, it is something like a spiritual version of cardiac rehab: go in, strengthen the heart/spiritual life, and regulate the heart rate/spiritual life. Type A spirituality, stemming from the Type A personality common to men, is practical, active, and often anxiety-ridden. Their approach to meditation, for example, is pragmatic—it is "useful."

For many men, experience in a health crisis has no spiritual content at all, not even this petitionary, practical one. For such men without a spiritual component, life goes on with no reference to God. The only thing that makes a difference to them is human behavior—their own or that of others, who in health crises are companions and health professionals. Such men are likely to believe that it's the doctor's job to fix the situation and their own to make enough money to hire a doctor competent to fix it. "Fixing the situation" is the main point. This approach ignores the fact that sometimes death is the best form of healing. Men find this hard to accept, since they view death as "failure" on the part of one's self, health professionals, and God. Failure is unacceptable, especially when viewed through the masculine stereotype and through male behavior.

Three of our parents have died in the last six years; Robert's father is living in a retirement home and is very healthy for someone in his eighties. When Jerry's father died, it was clear that for him, as for many people, death was the best alternative, the most grace-filled form of healing. The continued physical existence that we often equate with life would have been lacking in human dignity and more painful than death itself. His father had struggled to extend his physical existence, despite lung cancer, in order to care for his wife, but finally realized that his physical existence was so painful and difficult that he needed to let go and die. In his death, he therefore escaped the pain and humiliation of his disease. Still, he did not finally let go until he had been hospitalized, a few days before his death. Jerry's mother could not visit her husband after he left their home for hospitalization, which helped him to let go, and meant that she never quite believed that he was dead: for the rest of her life, her fantasies included his walking into the room.

The juxtaposition of families, parishes, other groups of caregiving friends, and health crises can be very difficult both for the patient and for the family. Family members coming from another city might not allow friends to care for the patient, although friends have been the primary support network for years; they may insist on a private funeral for only the family, preserving privacy and ignoring the needs of the community and sometimes the wishes of the deceased. In the last year of Jerry's mother's illness, a woman from his father's church came for her regular visit and was told by the caregiver, "I'd prefer you not come in." The caregiver was minimizing the value of the system of care that had sustained Jerry's mother. In this case, fortunately, the visitor asserted that nothing was going to prevent her from seeing her friend, and she did have her visit.

In some cases, excessive visitors can be damaging, of course. But when Robert's mother was in her final illness, as has been the case with various parishioners, family members assumed that someone from the family always had to be present, because "she didn't have anybody else, did she?" Recently, in another example, the children of a dying parishioner arrived from out of state and gathered around her in a protective circle that provided her with the support and care she needed but which prevented her pastor and several long-term friends from offering their support.

The church ought to be a defense against the sense that in times of health crisis, only family is important. The attitude that only family counts adds to society's sense that men can't take care of people, since the various forms of the church are still primarily organized by men and are male-oriented, and the majority of clergy are now still male. Laboring under the assumption that men can't care for people in crisis, families may expect to find pastoral care less effective than familial care. This is misanthropy in the original sense of the word: "disliking men." The AIDS crisis has made clear to a great many people that men *can* care for other men in crisis, sometimes even better than their families might. Caretakers don't have to be family, we have learned, or the definition of "family" has changed (Culbertson 2000, 12–13). The AIDS crisis has taught us the value of "floating," and the clear lesson that "fixing" is not what is basically at issue in a health crisis. For many years, with no cure for AIDS, the crisis has shown us that spirituality is more important than cure.

Larry and Kevin, for example, were a male couple we knew in a parish. Larry was so ill with pneumocystis pneumonia that he could barely care for Kevin in his dementia and pneumonia. Therefore he postponed going into a hospital longer than he should have, until after he had arranged for Kevin's family to care, temporarily he believed, for Kevin at home in a distant part of the state. Shortly after Larry entered a hospital, Kevin died at his parents' home. Larry left the hospital to attend the funeral and returned, three days later, much more ill; he died three days after that—clearly exhausted but also liberated from his sacrificial responsibility.

In another parish, the husband of a dying woman was able to achieve a closer relationship with his oldest daughter because the dying process allowed her to tell her children and other family members the great secret of her life and their family: her oldest daughter was not her husband's biological child, as they had pretended for years. Her romance with a soldier during World War II had left her pregnant, which she realized only after learning of the soldier's death. Her husband and her daughter, because of the honesty now afforded them, were able to acknowledge the depth of her love and to respect their relationship with each other more.

In another parish, for two men in relatively minor health crises, Jerry was the first man who had ever paid consistent attention to them as people. Both middle-aged men had many men they considered friends—golfing and fishing buddies, business associates—but these relationships were always about the activity or the business rather than about their personal lives (Culbertson 1992). When each was in the hospital for an extended stay, Jerry as pastor visited daily, talked about prayer and community, and paid attention to each man's fears and worries. For one, the principal worry was the common one that he was the same age his father had been at his death. The other's fear was, "I'm losing control of my body." Due to differing views in some parish conflicts, the two men had become so estranged that they did not speak to one another for many years, but finally they came to a reconciliation, perhaps through the realization that they shared the bonds of having survived a health crisis and of a close pastoral, and spiritual, relationship with their former pastor.

Another parish experience is memorable for a layman who was an excellent caregiver, notable for his dedication, fidelity, and loyalty. Met out of context, he would never seem to be a caretaker, since he was a nonstop talker who dwelt mostly on himself. But he had the capacity to be able to hear others, and people responded to him for that. At his funeral, many remembered his attention to them in times of crisis and spoke glowingly of how his attention had deepened their faith.

When Jerry suffered his accident, and again when he had open-heart surgery, he developed the practice of "floating." But the spirituality that manifested itself in him during these crises was not something developed at the time of the crisis. It had always been there. As he remembers it, the way he survived the difficulties and discomfort of his years in a small, rural, North Carolina high school was to keep reminding himself that he only needed to survive for a specific period of time. One of his teachers had initiated this concept by saying, "Wait until you get to college and you will realize that 'they' are the strange ones, not you."

Simply waiting, however, is not sufficient for survival. There must also be some element of consciousness or awareness of the process. Jerry reports, "I remember being very aware of this in a few instances of 'tubing' (floating down a small river on an inner tube—a popular recreation in Central Ohio). It suddenly struck me that 'going with the flow' was a perfect model for faith, for the trust in God's grace that enables us to live faithfully. If I could just let go of my worries about direction and timing then I could lie back and enjoy the process without interrupting or worsening it." Floating, therefore, is a doubly active process. First, there is the difficult task of letting go of expectations and worries about outside matters—all of the Type A concerns that fill the lives of many men. When we do this poorly, then our anxieties make any process or experience seem more strenuous and sometimes painful. Second, there is the less familiar but easier task of paying attention to what is going on "in the process"—being aware of what changes and of what one experiences. This second activity seems to be very particularly important and meaningful in the realm of spirituality. When we are caught up in experiences of spiritual growth, it is so easy for us to focus on the crisis itself rather than on the growth and the events of change.

During his recovery from the automobile accident, and again after the cardiac surgery, Jerry found himself actively practicing this floating through long periods of pain and frustration, through difficult stages of rehabilitative treatment, and through the interminable waiting associated with living in hospitals or nursing homes and with physical recovery. Often, he heard himself saying, "All I need is to survive this. Keep breathing and float." This practice has also proven quite helpful in such regular events as dentist chairs, traffic lights and pointless meetings.

After the automobile accident, he very vividly realized the value of many people praying for him, individually and in groups, not only throughout the diocese but throughout the country and the world, both church-centered and not churched. Prayer from many not-perfectly-corporate groups strengthened him by reminding him of the "flow" that surrounded and supported him through the process. "The river of God's healing and redemption kept me afloat!"

Robert is part of the prayer group of one local parish, and appreciates receiving calls, usually on his voice mail, requesting prayer—often for someone unknown and identified only by a first name. The process of praying for these people over months and years extends the sense of the universal, living body of Christ.

As the male partner in a health crisis situation, Robert learned a good deal about letting others care for him. He learned to respond clearly and honestly to people who said, "Please let us know what I can do," with a blunt statement like, "I'd really appreciate your inviting me for dinner. I'm free Wednesday and Thursday." In both cases, he realized that after a day spent largely in the hospital or nursing home, he needed company, a meal, and a chance to talk not only about the crisis, but about something else of interest to the friend. Sitting in waiting rooms for days on end is itself a spiritual experience, of course. A few weeks after each of these crises, Robert realized that he had not recognized the situation as a life-threatening one, although each one was; he had also not predicted the extent and difficulty of recovery. He dealt with the possibility of Jerry's death only after dealing with the details of caretaking and recovery.

After Jerry's accident, Robert spent five weeks in Cleveland, away from home, staying with friends and visiting the hospital for most of each day. He had a much stronger sense than at any other time in his life that what he was doing was important and that he was exactly where he needed to be. Women were very important in their support group. For three of the five weeks, Robert stayed with a close spiritual friend and her husband. The first time Jerry took communion in the hospital, the Eucharist was celebrated around his bed by two female priests, with Robert and several laywomen present. Jerry and Robert were struck by the loyalty and dependability of the women who were their spiritual friends and community, with whom they had participated in many retreats and activities.

Nevertheless, at the beginning of this period, Robert depended on a male friend. He had called a couple asking for a place to stay, and these friends invited him there for as long as he wished, although the wife was out of town. The husband was a wonderful sense of support. Each night, he handed Robert a list of his messages, cooked dinner while Robert dealt with them, and took a walk after dinner to discuss Jerry's situation and life in general. Robert will never forget his compassion.

For Jerry, during his health crises, important issues became spiritual issues. He dealt with losing control of his body, realizing that he needed to pay attention to it if he were to survive; he had always refused to consider himself as a body and had refused to pay much attention to his physical health. Taking responsibility for one's situation and "floating" can paradoxically sometimes be mutually exclusive. He also dealt with the delusions brought on by medication and, after his heart surgery, with the lack of quiet and privacy endured during two weeks in a nursing home—while learning to walk "for the third time in my life."

What are the lessons or morals that we hope to offer in this ramble through our experience with health crises in our own and other men's lives? What do these stories tell us about spirituality for men? It may seem obvious that health crises, especially the sudden shattering events in many men's lives, do provoke spiritual challenges and crises. Physical break-downs cause us to reevaluate our patterns of behavior, often including the way we conduct our spiritual relationships with God and with other peo-ple and with ourselves. The male focus on success or failure forces us to deal with shame (our sense of responsibility) and thus calls us to examine our status in God's redemption of the world. Health crises often bring great spiritual benefits:

- awareness of one's body as God's creation
- the value of acknowledging and sharing one's fears and worries
- deeper recognition of the love and support available from other people
- acceptance of the care available from strangers and friends
- our common experiences of survival and danger
- changing our stereotypes of men, in our own behavior and attitudes toward others
- understanding new levels and depths of spiritual connection even the healing power of death

Perhaps the simplest thing we learn is that anxiety—the spiritual dis-ease of not trusting in God's caring oversight—is destructive of our bod-ies, our lives, and our spirits. Lying in a bed unable to walk has taught us that the best cure for this anxiety is learning to "float": saying one's prayers, handing the process over to God, and just floating on the river as it "goes rolling along" in grace. Amen.

Bibliography

Chopra, Deepak. 1990. *Quantum Healing*. New York: Bantam.

Countryman, L. William. 1999. *Living on the Border of the Holy: Renewing the Priesthood of All*. Harrisburg, Pa.: Morehouse.

Culbertson, Philip. 2000. *Caring for God's People: Counseling and Christian Wholeness*. Minneapolis: Fortress.

———. 1992. *New Adam: The Future of Male Spirituality*. Minneapolis: Fortress.

DelBene, Ron. 1996. *The Breath of Life: A Simple Way to Pray*. Nashville: Upper Room.

Howatch, Susan. 1996. *Glittering Images*. New York: Crest.

13

The Integration of Sexuality and Spirituality: Gay Sexual Prophets within the UFMCC

Robert E. Goss

> *We must be prophets of a sex-positive truth.*
> —Rev. Larry J. Uhrig

The Catholic Church has named homosexuality as "intrinsically evil" and "objectively disordered," while other churches have labeled homosexuality with equally hideous epithets (Ratzinger 1986, 2). "Thou shalt be heterosexual" has become the eleventh commandment of many churches in their campaigns to prevent civil recognition of same-sex unions, the implementation of the Employment Nondiscrimination Act (ENDA), a comprehensive federal hate crimes law including sexual orientation, and the many local and state ordinances designed to protect sexual minorities. Some gay men have chosen to remain closeted in such abusive churches, while others have decided to be open about their homosexuality and fight for acceptance within their church. Others have left the hostile climate of their church for safer havens to integrate their sexuality with their spirituality.

Many gay Christians have found the Universal Fellowship of the Metropolitan Community Churches (UFMCC or MCC) to be a safe community in which to practice their Christianity without sacrificing their sexual lives. The Metropolitan Community Church was founded by Troy Perry in 1968 when he was expelled from ministry in his denomination for being gay (Perry and Swicegood 1992). Although UFMCC includes men and women of all sexual orientations, the focus of this essay is on gay men's spirituality and the challenges to integrate their sexuality and spirituality. Due to the constraints of this essay, I will not explore all issues and challenges, such as HIV status, open versus closed relationships, and the emergence of leather spirituality.

The epigraph at the beginning of this essay was written by UFMCC minister Larry Uhrig, one of the many saints who have died from the ravages of HIV. UFMCC attempts to be a sex-positive church, teaching a sexual theology where sexuality becomes the paradigm for creating and doing Christian theologies, and which aims at the integration of sexuality and spirituality.[1] The MCC vision of justice involves healing the split between sexuality and spirituality within the Christian churches and assists queer Christians in rediscovering God's gift of diverse sexualities and genders.[2]

My own social location is that of a queer theologian, a MCC clergy and spiritual mentor, and an instructor in the sexual theology class for MCC clergy.[3] The explorations in this essay arise from facilitating a number of gay men's groups, spiritual direction, and general conversations with a wide range of gay men within UFMCC. Two prefatory remarks are necessary. First, gay men speak differently with other gay men than with mixed-gender groups. They are willing to speak candidly about their sexual experiences and their spiritualities. Many of the men's group sessions have been emotionally intense and thoroughly erotic, generating friendships as men shared their narrative histories of struggle, coming out, the challenges experienced, and how they find God and Christ within their sexual lives. These sessions created an environment in which men could speak the truth about good sex, healthy spirituality, and their intersection. The texts of their lives, along with my own, form the basis of the reflections here. Secondly, sexuality implies a relationship—whether it is a transient encounter or a long-term, monogamous coupling. Gay men craft their sexual lives as Christians in diverse patterns of relationship. Some are single; some are in coupled relationships. Others are in polyamorous or multipartnered relationships. I find nothing theologically incorrect with a variety of consciously chosen ways to relate sexually with other human beings.

In my book *Jesus ACTED UP*, I explored some ways in which gay men can retain their integrity and a healthy connectedness to Christianity (Goss 1993, 35–37, 123–41). First, I encouraged gay men to come out. This is not only important from a mental health perspective but also from a healthy spirituality perspective. To be out confronts your own internalized homophobia and ecclesial homophobia. For many gays, remaining in a homophobic church is an isolating experience. The refusal of many churches to even listen to and dialogue with gay men creates a toxic environment for their mental health and often impedes faith development.

When gay men come out, ecclesial rejection and hostility force them to embrace exile to find safety. Many gay men find solidarity in affiliating with translesbigay people of faith.[4] In this essay, I will explore the coming out of gay men and their embrace of an exile community of faith such as UFMCC where they can come out spiritually and work to integrate their sexuality and spirituality.

Coming Out

"Coming out" has many definitional features in common with what William James described as a "conversion." It is a process—gradual or sometimes sudden—by which a divided self and a sick soul become unified and consciously right.[5] The closet represents a wrestling between divided selves, between the repression of homoerotic desires and being true to your sexual desires. Coming out expresses a type of conversion process, a breakthrough experience in which a gay man publicly confesses his own erotic desires toward men. It is a type of conversion process whereby a gay man turns away from the norms of compulsory heterosexuality to embrace an openly homosexual identity.

Gay men embody social injustice within their bodies and their sexual practices. They pass as heterosexual while their sexual desire directed toward men is repressed or expressed secretly in fragmentary encounters. Reporter Judy Thomas, of *The Kansas City Star*, wrote a sensitive series of articles on Catholic priests who died of AIDS or who were living with HIV. From this series, it is apparent that the suppression of sexuality does damage to the person, fragments sexuality from spirituality, and subverts a capacity to express sexuality in mutually loving relationships. Sexuality is at the heart of our personhood. Closeting and repressing sexuality damages the person in his development and, I would add, in his spiritual development.

Cultural and religious homophobia have damaged the spirituality of many gay men through their abusive messages about same-gendered sexuality. Gay men have been socialized as males within cultural heterosexism. Psychologist Gregory Herek defines heterosexism "as the ideological system that denies, denigrates, and stigmatizes any nonheterosexual behavior, identity, relationship, or community" (Herek 1999, 321). Gays have suffered homophobic reactions to their sexuality, ranging from verbal abuse and mocking to murderous rage and assault.[6] Gay children grow up with a sense of difference and isolation. As they reach adolescence, they learn protective concealment of their feelings, pretending, and the development of a false public persona. The closet is a complex network of power relations that reinforce the above social mechanism of "passing" as heterosexual and concealing same-sex desire. Closets differ in size, style, power, and lethalness. Concealing one's authentic sexual identity often exacts a heavy toll, inducing anxiety, low self-esteem, and depression. Ecclesial closets are, in particular, spiritually lethal because they use religious practices and preaching to isolate gay men with messages of self-contempt, internalized self-hatred, and loathing. The impact of closets is stultifying to personal development and is stifling of spiritual growth.

Most gay men come into UFMCC from other denominations where sex has been equated with "God-denying lust"(Stuart 1997, 199). Many gays have experienced damaging messages about sexuality in general, as well as their own sexuality. Ecclesial homophobia has shamed many gay men into remaining silent about the erotic truth of their lives. Guilt and shame have led many gays to reject themselves rather than their churches. Some have suffered religious abuse, driven from communities and families because they dared to be who they are. Chris Glaser writes:

> Spiritual abuse is the wounding, shaming, and degrading of some-one's spiritual worth by a perpetrator intent on taking control. Spiritual abuse is any attack (subtle or blatant, unintended or intentional) on our belovedness and sacred worth as children of God. This spiritual abuse is particularly keenly felt among gays and lesbians. Spiritual abuse is far more pervasive and permissible than other forms of abuse because it is perceived as ordained by God. (Glaser 1998, 39)

Glaser is correct to label this spiritual abuse. For example, there have been a number of gay men within my own congregation who, in desperation to fit into their churches and be accepted, have tried all sorts of methods to become heterosexual. They have prayed for change; communities have prayed over them to deliver them from the sin of homosexuality. They have turned to ex-gay ministries or sought out reparative therapy.[7] Many gays have tortured themselves with valiant attempts to change sexual orientation, while many professional therapeutic associations have claimed that sexual behaviors can be changed but sexual orientation cannot. For myself and other gay men, to remain in the closet is ultimately to refuse that God loves us as we are.

Churches, and frequently families, exert tremendous pressure upon gay men to remain closeted and conform to compulsory heterosexuality. One gay man recounted how his Catholic mother refused to sit at Mass with him and his lover. He had to separate from both his mother and Holy Mother Church to become healthy. He came to MCC to find a safe space, a community where he could be open about his sexual identity, touch his lover tenderly during service, integrate his sexuality and spirituality, and deepen a relation to the risen Christ. This former Catholic said, "When I walked through the doors of MCC of Greater St. Louis, I knew that I was home." I have heard this response many times over from gay men journeying into exile and discovering UFMCC as a place of safety.

The split of sexuality from spirituality is painful and destructive to the spirit because it requires the suppression of the erotic, and because the erotic provides a source of power, self-knowledge, and spirituality. The erotic plays a central part in many gay lives and much gay spirituality. To closet oneself is to closet God and the full potential of one's spirituality, for such closeting is destructive to the human spirit and its potential for faith development. In an autobiographical essay, I wrote:

> In coming out, my life was forever changed. I realized that eroto-phobia and homophobia alienated me from the most creative and loving power of the universe. God was at the root of my deep sexual longings. I made authentic connection with the source of my erotic power and my vocation to priesthood. I moved from fear towards joy, a desire to authentically connect with other men, love women, humanity, and the world. The closet controls homoerotic desire; it restricts sexual desire to the furtive and the secretive. Following Christ meant becoming who I am in erotic connection with other men and humanity. (Goss 2000, 301)

A number of queer authors have described coming out as a sacrament (Goss 1993, 127–31; Glaser 1998; Hunt 1991; Heyward 1989, 82). It is a coming out of oppression, coming out to love. It is a coming out to ourselves, God, family, friends, and community. Many men have risked coming out and found acceptance with families and friends, while others have taken the risk, found rejection, and created "families of choice."[8]

Coming out becomes an intensification of identity whereby gay men give public expression to desires formerly hidden or closeted. Gary Comstock suggests that in the process of coming out, gay men relive the Stonewall Rebellion:[9] "Stonewall is our sense of encouragement and possibility; and Stonewall is repeated as we continue to face down threats, solve problems, and move beyond barriers" (Comstock 1993, 125). The act of coming out is a rejection of salient values of heterosexist culture. It is coming out of traditional family values into new values that affirm gay sexuality, relationships, and values. Psychiatrist Richard Isay comprehends coming out as an emotional transition from inauthenticity to authenticity:

> Coming out alleviates the anxiety and depression caused by the sense of inauthenticity that arises from hiding or disguising oneself. Closeted gay men are usually cautious and circumspect in their social discourse and relationships. After coming out, they inevitably affirm that they are now more self-assured and that all relationships, including those with straight people, are more authentic and, therefore, more gratifying. (Isay 1998, 8)

In coming out, gay men enjoy a hard-earned freedom while relishing a new, authentic public self.

For many gay men, coming out is an event that they remember in vivid detail. It remains as significant as the meeting of a lover or life-partner. In the five-week Gay Men Talking Spirituality and Sexuality group, each of the eight men could narrate the exact moment of their coming out and elaborate in detail the process of coming out, who they came out to, and who accepted them and who did not.[10] They could tell you about the pain of concealing their sexual identity from others and the toll that concealment exacted on their emotional health and spiritual development. For many, coming out is coming out of self-hatred; it is synonymous with the process of self-acceptance.

Coming out begins an important developmental trajectory along which gays experience a type of death of their past closeted life and a new life fraught with possibilities and with dangers. Many gays pay a price for their affirmation of a gay sexual identity—often losing families and friends, facing economic danger and housing discrimination, becoming targets of harassment and violence, and confronting ostracism from their churches (see People for the American Way 1999). For many gays, it means the abandonment of church and even Christianity; for others it means embarking upon a journey toward spiritual integration of their sexual lives. As gay men come to terms with the exile of coming out, they search out communities where they can experience faith in God (or the equivalent) and where they can be open about their sexual lives.

Coming into MCC and Coming Out to God

The late queer theologian Robert Williams noted: "Coming out is a process with a beginning, but no end. It is nothing more or less than making a commitment to tell the truth, to live the truth, to do the truth" (Williams 1992, 171). Some gay men enter an exile Christian community such as MCC, either to make peace with Christianity or to affiliate with a translesbigay community of faith where they can safely explore their sexual identity as Christians. MCC churches have become a place of sanctuary and welcome for gay people at risk. For many, MCC becomes a community of healing where they can experience their sexual lives without shame and guilt, break down the sense of isolation, end the pretending and the hiding, and be themselves. Within MCC, gay men can relax and can find a sense of solidarity with people like themselves; they also find pride in themselves, role models, new models of relationship and families, and healing.

The internalization of coming out requires men to relearn behaviors that edited out their sexuality from their religious practice. Their struggle with sexuality, however, is not completely over, for the abusive messages from their previous denomination remain ever below the surface. It is often a difficult struggle for many gay men to reach the point where they can move beyond the years of negative messages about homosexuality from their churches and understand same-gendered sex as a gift from God. Some folks are better able than others to escape the religious abuse. One gay man noted, "Jesus' resurrection is a coming back from the torture of the closet to a promise of hope."

The promise of hope means learning to integrate embodied sexuality within Christian practice. Gays learn to live incarnationally. They previously learned to edit embodied living within the closets of the church and need now to discover the original blessing of their sexuality. Within MCC, gay men work at repairing the psychic wounds of abuse and low self-esteem inflicted by society and church. They work at integrating their self-acceptance as gay with religious values less oppressive and more affirmative of the grace of their sexuality. After many years of being out, one couple wrote, "Sexuality and spirituality are gifts from God to use and share. As gifts, there are certain responsibilities included in these gifts: never harm, joyfully pleasure one another, and mutually share power over one another." These were hard-earned insights that came from much personal wrestling with the negative, homophobic culture of their previous churches, abandoning sexual fear, and finding an experience of grace within their love-making and acceptance within a faith community. These insights are discovered in a journey within a community of faith that accepts the embodiment of God in Jesus and preaches incarnational living inclusive of their sexual orientation.

Most MCC churches offer "Homosexuality and the Bible" courses to assist men coming from evangelical and fundamentalist traditions and to combat the religious abuse of those churches that use biblical passages to condemn homosexual behaviors. At MCC of Greater St. Louis, my own faith community numbering four hundred, I offer a four-week course, meeting one evening a week for an hour and a half. The first two sessions cover the texts most often applied to homosexuality from the Hebrew and Christian scriptures. My intent is to demonstrate that God is not homophobic. Only churches are homophobic, when they choose to misread the scriptural texts. During the third session, we review a tape of biblical experts from the 1998 annual meeting, in Orlando, of the American Academy of Religion/Society of Biblical Literature.[11] These three sessions aim to deconstruct the textual violence of churches by explaining the context of the six biblical texts applied to homosexuals as one of gender transgression. My pedagogical purpose for a historical examination of those biblical passages within their sociocultural context is to undermine the years of fundamentalist interpretations of the Bible and the negative messages that God condemns homosexuality. For many (not all) gay men, such historical explanations assist them to realign their lives with a more sophisticated approach to the Bible. The fourth session moves from biblical text as enemy to biblical text as "friend" (Goss and West 2000). Frankly, the hardest class with gay men is the exploration of the biblical text as "friend," where they can find empowerment for their lives and then realize the original blessing of their sexual lives, for they have experienced the Bible as an instrument of terror and repression of their sexuality for years. They need to come to see the text anew as a locus for empowered love and grace.

Gay men have cultivated their sexuality and spirituality, often as parallel tracts, sometimes as converging courses of personal development. Sexuality thus becomes a personal and communal resource for spiritual integration. Completing the coming out process may lead to a further process, what I call "coming out to God" or "coming out spiritually." It is no less courageous than coming out to family, friends, and coworkers, for coming out to God means facing all the negative, erotophobic messages associated with Christianity. Churches have been excellent conduits of erotophobia, let alone homophobia. Within this new perspective, gay men no longer view God as judge or parent. God becomes friend or lover. The gay reintegration of spirituality and sexuality means first finding acceptance with God, envisioning body and sexuality as gifts from God, and finding God within sexual experience.

Coming out deepens the relationship with God. Gay men try to integrate their sexual lives with their spiritual lives. One MCC clergy spoke of his coming out and coming into MCC; he brought God into cruising:

> When I was first coming out in MCC of San Francisco in 1972, the late Jim Sandmire was pastor. He was, for that early time in our history, quite bold in exploring sexuality as part of spirituality in his sermons. One of the things he said in a sermon early in my experience was a warning: he said that we must learn to take God with us in every moment of life, to devote every part of life to God. He said that if we thought we needed to exclude God from our cruising and tricking, we were about to walk right into sin. He advised us to learn to invite God right into that bar with us. For a Southern Baptist seminary student, that was powerful (not to say shocking) stuff, but it immediately resonated in my soul as the Word of God. Almost from the beginning of my gay life, then, I actually did stop and pray before going out to cruise. It usually was for God's guidance in opening me to whatever God might have in store for me, and for self-awareness so that I would move away from sinful behavior such as using another person as an object. I believe that attitude of prayer cruising, if you will, has been basic and essential and wonderful in my life.[12]

Coming out allows many gays to reframe their sexuality within a spiritual context. For some readers, the above quote may be shocking, but many gay men begin to integrate their sexual lives with Christian practice.[13] To live a healthy spirituality, many gay men within UFMCC allow themselves to experience their erotic desires as gateways to the sacred.

Wholeness:
The Convergence of Sexuality and Spirituality

If Origen and other early Christian writers were correct in their contemplative insights that "God is Eros," then the mystery of the Incarnation is the physical unfolding of God's erotic love for us.[14] The Incarnation of God is thoroughly enfleshed in human sexuality, and our experience of the risen Christ is thoroughly enfleshed in our physical knowing and loving. There is certainly a convergence of deep spirituality and deep sexuality (MacKnee 1996; Helminiak 1996, 233–67). If this is the case, then there is no place for body-loathing or the despising of human sexuality within our

Christian spiritualities. Body-negative and sexually-negative theologies need to be corrected to once again affirm the mystery of the Incarnation. For some gay men, the power of sexuality and spirituality joined are too frightening to contemplate, while others within MCC have reached a level of growth where they no longer separate sexuality and spirituality.

In her relational theology, Carter Heyward speaks of coming out of aloneness and into erotic relation:

> Coming out of the chilly delusion that personhood is autonomous, breaking free of the notion that self-possession should be our personal and professional goal, we come into our power to call forth the YES that connects us—our erotic energy: our sensual and sexual yearnings, our openness to sacred movement between and among ourselves. Coming out, we invite each other through veils of fear set between us for generations. Learning how to love one another, we find our bodyselves opening to a realm of life, confidence, and power we had not dared, alone, to believe in. And this opening is prayer. (Heyward 1989, 22)

God is incarnate in our sexuality and in the development of our erotic spiritualities. In sexuality, God exists vividly and relationally. According to Heyward, healthy sexuality and spirituality lead to life-affirming and life-giving connections. Our spiritualities affirm the erotic as essential to the love of God and the love of humanity. One MCC gay clergy echoes the sentiments of Heyward's relational, erotic theology:

> I'm a little abnormal for a gay man, in that there is still a link between sex and love for me. Comparatively, I've had very few sexual partners and most of those encounters have been in a relational context. I've only had a few casual, anonymous sexual encounters . . . therefore the act of love-making for me has always been in the context of making a connection with that other person. What I have come to realize is that connection is a connection between the divine in my partner and the divine in me.

For many gay men, living incarnationally includes a healthy sexual life and spirituality. Gay sex leads to profound levels of wholeness, expelling the residues of internalized homophobia and realizing the grace of sexuality.

But not all sex is spiritual; neither is gay sex always spiritual. Another gay clergy correctly spoke about the need of discernment as part of the process of integrating sexuality and spirituality:

> My basic opinion is that once we've come to the point where we accept all kinds of sexual experiences as spiritual, we just need to discern which ones of those experiences feel healthy or the best for us, and to integrate those into our lives. If a person finds himself repeatedly engaged in sexual activity that does not feel healthy for him then there may be other issues to deal with before integration can even occur.

Not all sex is right or appropriate for particular gay males. Discernment is a necessary art in prayer that I try to teach gay men in spiritual mentoring or direction. Such discernment is also necessary in sexual encounters and relationships. Discernment of the consequences of particular gay sexual encounters becomes also a means for judging their spiritual validity. Is it connected to a celebration of our sexual selves? Does it express our need for connecting physically and spiritually? Does the sexual encounter embody mutuality? Love? Justice? Does the encounter bring us closer to God? Do I find the God in the person(s) with me? These are some of the questions that gay men might ask in discerning whether their sexual encounters are spiritual.

Some MCC clergy surveyed found Jesus as a template for integrating sexuality and spirituality. For example, one MCC clergy found that any male fantasy could include Christ:

> It occurs to me that any male image I may employ during a fantasy could be that of Jesus the Christ. However, you are aware that I have considered a sexual relationship with Jesus evidenced by my sermon . . . but the story was more about "falling in love" with Jesus, than about having sex with Jesus.[15]

Erotic undercurrents have always been present within the mystical traditions of Christianity. There are a number of mystics who speak of sexual rapture in their relationship with Christ. Theirs is an embodied, contemplative experience of love. In a sixteenth-century devotion manual, Francis Rous writes, "If [Christ] comes not yet into thee, stirre up thy spiritual concupiscence" (Rambuss 1998, 1). In an autobiographical essay, I focused on my own journey from guilt and self-hatred to learning to love myself as God erotically and physically loves me. I found within my own lovemaking with my partner that Matthew Fox's words bear some truth: "Every time humans truly make love, truly express their love by the art of sexual lovemaking, the Cosmic Christ is making love" (Fox 1988, 172). Lovemaking becomes an intensely erotic, spiritual connecting with Christ.

But the image of Christ in lovemaking was not a universal template for the integration of spirituality for all respondents. A gay transmale clergy writes about his open relationship with his lover and the spiritual dimensions of his sexuality:

> My lover and I have been together eleven years and are non-monogamous. We believe that love multiplies and that when we act in loving ways, in ways that respect ourselves and others, that that adds strength to our relationships. Sex with other people isn't something that pulls us apart, but rather something that adds goodness to our lives and to our relationship. This has come from our spiritual practice and our commitment to healthy spirituality and sexuality.

I have had the honor of learning from two gay men with thirty-some years of experience each in leather/SM sex (both seeing this explicitly as a spiritual practice as well as a sexual one). One of them taught me to approach each man with two things in mind: (1) that this person in front of me is the most beautiful thing that I had ever seen, and (2) that this was the first (hu)man I had ever laid eyes on. I would add a third thing that I do in my practice of this, which is to see the presence of God within that person.

Realizing the God within the person becomes a central practice of spiritual sex. Gay sex, thus, can become a locus of truth and likewise a means of grace.

Integrating the Sacred and the Erotic

Many chaplains will readily admit, from their experience at the bedsides of gay men dying from AIDS, the depths of gay spirituality. There is no question of heroic spirituality among gay men. The evolving integration of sexuality and spirituality among gay men within UFMCC is not so unusual when we investigate how gay men are culturally handling the conflict between sexuality and spirituality. Over the last decade, a number of popular books and videotapes have emerged detailing attempts to locate gay spirituality within gay sexuality (Barzan 1995; LaHuerta 1999; Thompson 1998). Tibetan Buddhist scholar Jeffrey Hopkins has just published a gay tantric manual of sexual practices to harness orgasmic energy for enlightenment. Former Franciscan Michael Kelly has a six-part video series entitled *The Erotic Contemplative* aiming at the integration of gay sexuality with the Christian biblical and mystical traditions. Kelly maintains that deep sexuality and deep spirituality converge, finding their source in God.

Gay men are not only coming out to the stirrings of their hearts and the longings of their loins, but they are "coming out spiritually," integrating the eros of their hearts and their loins. Gay men within UFMCC are, likewise, part of this cultural gay trend to recover their sexuality as one of the primary sources of grace.

Robert Barzan details what such an integration of gay sexuality with spirituality might look like: "A healthy eroticism and spirituality . . . encourages love, compassion, truth, tolerance, forgiveness, generosity, trust in our physical selves, respect for the land and other forms of life, peace, social justice, and community based on these spiritual values" (Barzan 1995, 17). From my personal experience and observations, I believe that gay men within UFMCC have embarked upon a spiritual path where the sacred and the erotic converge and where these criteria will flourish and blossom, contributing to an eventual sexual reformation of Christianity (Goss 1999).

Bibliography

American Psychoanalytic Association. 1998. "Psychoanalytic Reflections on Homophobia." APA New York. <http://www.apsa.org/pubinfo/hreflections.htm>.

Avis, Paul. 1989. *Eros and the Sacred*. Wilton, Conn.: Morehouse.

Barzan, Robert. 1995. *Sex and Spirit: Exploring Gay Men's Spirituality*. San Francisco: White Crane.

Comstock, Gary. 1993. *Gay Theology without Apology*. Cleveland: Pilgrim.

Duberman, Martin. 1994. *Stonewall*. New York: Plume.

Fox, Matthew. 1988. *The Coming of the Cosmic Christ: The Healing of Mother Earth and the Birth of a Global Renaissance*. San Francisco: Harper & Row.

Glaser, Chris. 1998. *Coming Out as Sacrament*. Louisville: Westminster John Knox.

Goss, Robert E. 2002. "The Practice of Safe Texts." In *Sex with God: A Queer Christian Sexual Theology*. Ed. Robert E. Goss. Cleveland: Pilgrim.

————. 2000. "Passionate for Christ: Out of the Closet into the Streets." *Male Lust: Pleasure, Power, and Transformation*. Ed. Kerwin Kay, Jill Naigle, and Baruch Gould. New York: Haworth.

————. 1999. "Sexual Visionaries and Freedom Fighters for a Sexual Reformation: From Gay Theology to Queer Sexual Theologies." *The Lesbian and Gay Christian Movement: Campaigning for Justice, Truth, and Love*. Ed. Sean Gill. London: Cassell. 187–202.

————. 1997a. "Queering Procreative Privilege: Coming Out as Families." *Our Families, Our Values: Snapshots of Queer Kinship*. Ed. Robert E. Goss and Amy Adams Squires. New York: Haworth.

————. 1997b. "Recovering Jesus' Sexuality." *Toward a Theology of Sexuality*. Los

Angeles: UFMCC Commission on Spirituality, Faith, Fellowship, and Order. 1–14.

————. 1996. "Erotic Contemplatives and Freedom Fighters." *The Journal of Men Studies* 4:3, 249–51.

————. 1993. *Jesus ACTED UP: A Gay and Lesbian Manifesto.* HarperSan Francisco.

Goss, Robert E., and Amy Adams Squires Strongheart, eds. 1997. *Our Families, Our Values: Snapshots of Queer Kinship.* New York: Harrington.

Goss, Robert E., and Mona West, eds. 2000. *Take Back the Word.* Cleveland: Pilgrim.

Guy, David. 1999. *The Red Thread of Passion: Spirituality and the Paradox of Sex.* Boston: Shambhala.

Haldeman, Scott. 1996. "Bringing Good News to the Body: Masturbation and Male Identity." *Men's Bodies, Men's Gods: Male Identities in a (Post-)Christian Culture.* Ed. Bjorn Krondorfer. New York: New York Univ. Press. 111–24.

Harvey, Andrew. 1997. *The Essential Gay Mystics.* HarperSanFrancisco.

Helminiak, Daniel A. 1996. *The Human Core of Spirituality.* Albany: SUNY.

Herek, Gregory. 1999. "Psychological Heterosexism in the United States." *Lesbian, Gay, and Bisexual Identified over the Lifespan: Psychological Perspectives.* Ed. Anthony R. D'Augelli and Charlotte J. Patterson. New York: Oxford Univ. Press.

Heyward, Carter. 1989. *Touching Our Strength: The Erotic as Power and the Love of God.* San Francisco: Harper & Row.

Hopkins, Jeffrey. 1998. *Sex, Orgasm, and the Mind of Clear Light: The Sixty-four Acts of Gay Male Love.* Berkeley: North Atlantic.

Hunt, Mary. 1991. *Fierce Tenderness: Toward a Feminist Theology of Friendship.* New York: Crossroad.

Irwin, Alexander C. 1991. *Eros Toward the World: Paul Tillich and the Theology of the Erotic.* Minneapolis: Fortress Press.

Isay, Richard A. 1998. *Becoming Gay: The Journey to Self-Acceptance.* New York: Henry Holt and Co.

James, William. 1959. *The Varieties of Religious Experience.* New York: Mentor.

Kelly, Michael. 1995. *The Erotic Contemplative, I-VI.* Oakland: EroSpirit Research Institute. Videocassettes.

LaHuerta, Christian. 1999. *Coming Out Spiritually: The Next Step.* New York: J. P. Tarcher.

Lebacqz, Karen. 1994. "Appropriate Vulnerability." *Sexuality and the Sacred: Sources for a Theological Reflection.* Ed. James B. Nelson and Sandra P. Longfellow. Louisville: Westminster John Knox. 256–61.

MacKnee, Chuck M. September 1996. "Peak Sexual and Spiritual Experience: Exploring the Mystical Relationship." *Theology & Sexuality* 5, 97–115.

Martin, James. 2000. "'and then he kissed me': An Easter Love Story." *Take Back the Word: A Queer Reading of the Bible*. Ed. Robert E. Goss and Mona West. Cleveland: Pilgrim.

Milhaven, Giles. 1993. *Hadewijch and Her Sisters: Others Ways of Loving and Knowing*. Albany: SUNY.

Nicolosi, Joseph. 1997. *Reparative Therapy of Male Homosexuality: A New Clinical Approach*. Northvale, N.J.: Jason Aronson.

Origen. 1957. *The Song of Songs: Commentary and Homilies*. Trans. R. P. Lawson. London: Green and Co.

People for the American Way. 1999 [1997]. *Hostile Climate*. Washington, D.C.: People for the American Way.

Perry, Troy D., and Thomas L. P. Swicegood. 1992. *Don't Be Afraid Anymore: The Story of Reverend Troy Perry and the Metropolitan Community Churches*. New York: St. Martin's.

Political Research Association, with the Policy Institute of the National Gay and Lesbian Task Force, and Equal Partners in Faith. December 1998. *Challenging the Ex-Gay Movement: An Information Packet.*

———. October 1998. *Calculated Compassion: How the Ex-Gay Movement Serves the Right's Attack on Democracy.*

Rambuss, Richard. 1998. *Closet Devotions*. Durham: Duke Univ. Press.

Ratzinger, Cardinal Joseph. 1986. "Letter on the Pastoral Care of Homosexual Persons." *The Vatican and Homosexuality*. Ed. Jeannine Grammick and Pat Furey. New York: Crossroad.

Stuart, Elizabeth. 1997. *Sex These Days: Essays on Theology, Sexuality and Society*. Sheffield: Sheffield Academic Press.

Thomas, Judy L. 2000. "AIDS in the Priesthood." *The Kansas City Star*, January 29, 30, and 31, 2000. <http://www.kcstar.com/projects/priests/>.

Thompson, Mark, ed. 1998. *Gay Soul: Finding the Heart of Gay Spirit and Nature with Sixteen Writers, Healers, Teachers, and Visionaries*. San Francisco: Calif.: HarperSanFrancisco.

Uhrig, Larry J. 1986. *Sex Positive: A Gay Contribution to Sexual and Spiritual Union*. Boston: Allyson.

Weston, Kath. 1991. *Families We Choose: Lesbians, Gays, Kinship*. New York: Columbia Univ. Press.

Williams, Robert. 1992. *Just As I Am*. New York: Crown.

Notes

1. Sexual theology examines our sexual experiences to understand God and to learn about the ways that we understand the gospels, how we read the scriptures, how we live sacramentally and ecclesially, and how we integrate our sexualities and our spiritualities.

2. *Queer* has been revived as a favorite postmodern term used by gay, lesbian, bisexual, and transgendered academics. I use it as a term of postmodern dissidence and political transgression, inclusive of the gendered and sexual transgressions of the above groups as well as queer-identified heterosexuals. In addition, I use queer as a theological principle. *To queer* is "to spoil the effect, to interfere with or disrupt." Queering exclusive theological doctrines or ecclesial practices is to make them more inclusive. See Goss 1996.

3. All future MCC clergy or transfer clergy into MCC are required to pass a thirty-hour proficiency course in Sexual Theology. This intensive course focuses on doing theology from translesbigay sexualities, the integration of sexuality and spirituality, and the connection of sexuality to justice. I have taught this class for the last five years. It has a profound impact on MCC clergy, on their pastoral practices, and on their development of grassroots sexual theologies that can address the queer community.

4. *Translesbigays* is coined from transgendered, lesbian, bisexual, and gay. It denotes a coalition of groups who find themselves outside of dominant gender and heteronormative patterns. MCC includes predominantly translesbigay Christians, but with its commitment to inclusive practice, there is a growing heterosexual population.

5. James's description of a divided self and the sick soul clearly describes the debilitating experience of the closet. Conversion represents a good description of coming out from such a state and coming into a more integrated self. See James 1959, 140–206.

6. In 1998 the American Psychoanalytic Association (APA) held a conference in New York. It published some of its conclusions online: In childhood, all children feel a great pressure to be like other children. Gay children feel different. Their difference is stigmatized (with epithets that wound), and the insults come from those to whom the young boy is attracted. The refuge is toward an internal world of longing for acceptance. In our gender-polarized world; they are beset by crises of identity: am I a boy or a girl? Some adopt the mannerism of girls and others may overcompensate by donning the mantle of hypermasculinity. "He both longs for boys and men and yet associates them with pain and rejection". This pattern may be unconsciously repeated in later life. Sex, which is forbidden, may become separated from friendship and companionship.

7. Exodus International has become an umbrella group for the development of a number of ex-gay ministries claiming to change people from a gay lifestyle to a heterosexual lifestyle. For a proponent of reparative therapy, see Nicolosi 1997. For a good critique of the ex-gay movement and reparative therapies, see the publications of the Political Research Association listed in the bibliography.

8. Many gay men have been forced to break ties with blood relatives, or if they maintained these ties with their biological families, they have also created "families of choice." Establishing kinship on the bonds of love creates a new paradigm for family. See Goss 1997a, 3–20; Weston 1991.

9. "Stonewall," named after a gay bar that police raided, was a rebellion in Greenwich Village from June 27 to July 2, 1969. It was a seminal event, catalyzing gay and lesbian activism not only in New York but around the United States. The event is commemorated in the United States as well as in Europe, Asia, Australia, and South America. Robert Williams has likened Stonewall to "the Queer Exodus" (Williams 1992, 85–90). For a more complete historical account, see Duberman 1994.

10. In 1999, I facilitated a five-week group "Men Talking Sexuality and Spirituality" within my own church in St. Louis. I repeated it as a workshop at UFMCC's 1999 General Conference for some sixty men.

11. Panelists on the video included Drs. Dale Martin, Saul Olyan, Deirdre Good, Ken Stone, and myself. For a basic overview of my position on the texts from the Bible often applied to homosexuality, see Goss, "The Practice of Safe Texts."

12. In an e-mail polling of a sample of MCC clergy for this essay, I promised to keep all identities confidential.

13. For some readers, gay promiscuity presents a problem when we work out of a model of pair-bonded, monogamous relations. While I celebrate and bless those relations within MCC, I am pastorally aware that not all people choose to live in a closed, pair-bonded relation. Some are polyamourous, some configure relations in threes or within communities. See the essays by Eric Rofes, Kathy Rudy, and Joe Kramer in Goss and Strongheart 1997. I also believe that the churches have not really developed an adequate sexual ethics for singles. Some maintain abstinence until marriage, while more liberal denominations allow for couples to live together for a period to see whether it works out. MCC is silent on single sexuality, thus allowing flexibility and promoting nonjudgmentalism on single members. I would refer the reader to Karen Lebacqz's (1994) essay "Appropriate Vulnerability." Her notion of appropriate vulnerability lends itself to the development of an ethic for single sexuality.

14. The only extant version of Origen's Commentary on the Song of Songs is a Latin translation. The Latin text translates the Greek *eros* with the Latin *amor*. In

his Prologue (Origen 1957, 35), Origen calls God *amor* or *passionate love*. The Song of Songs served as a meditative template for the relationship of the soul to Christ. The erotic relationship in the Song became a metaphor for depicting the rapture of mystical union. For contemporary theology, the recovery of the erotic in God and our eros towards God have become important to combat an erotophobic Christianity. For examples, see Avis 1989; Irwin 1991; and Heyward 1989.

15. For two examples of MCC clergy using Jesus as an erotic template, see Goss, "The Beloved Disciple," and Martin, both in Goss 2000.

Part Five

Community

14

"The Things We Do!" Nurturing the Authority of Men in Ministry

Philip L. Culbertson

> *Dysphoria:* " *An emotional state characterized by anxiety, depression, and restlessness." From the Latin, "hard to bear." Antonym: euphoria.*
>
> *Hegemony: "The predominant influence of one state over another." From the Greek, [to presume] "to lead." Antonym: [to presume that the assumed power structures are desirable.]*
> —American Heritage Dictionary

I do not wish to say anymore things that are critical of men. The beginning of this new millennium finds many men in the church too often confused, in emotional pain, insecure in their gendered identity, and shame-filled. This is what we mean when we say that men are suffering "gender dysphoria." It is my intention to speak frankly and without guile about men in the church, as I perceive them from my own personal experience, from my involvement in the men's movement, and from my thirty years of experience as a pastoral counselor. In particular, I want to speak of and to men who exercise the most fundamental and important ministry of the whole church: the ministry of the laity, however each man defines it.

Nor is it my intention to promote further gender dysphoria by denying that men are inherently good persons. On the contrary, I believe firmly that everyone, men, women, and even the patriarchs—the Biblical ones, as well as the contemporary powerbrokers, misogynists, and those who refuse to see the havoc they leave in their wake—are originally created in the image of God. Since God is good, God's image reflected in humanity is therefore inherently good. It is what happens after creation that should worry us all, men and women alike.

Men (and women) learn a great deal from their fathers that is good. In fact, we men have all learned a great number of good things from the men in our lives: our brothers, fathers, stepfathers, grandfathers, godfathers, mentors. They teach us to throw a ball around, to respect the dignity of others by watching our language, to drive carefully so that we will be safe, to volunteer to help, to be brave, at certain times to seek advice and support, the value of healthy competition, and how important little details are in showing others that one cares about them. I believe that men are good people, and that males are a wonderful part of God's creation. At the same time, I believe that the feminist critique of men also has a great deal to teach us about how we could be even better, if we will swallow our pride, defensiveness, and sense of masculine entitlement, long enough to listen.

It is also true that a few women, even in the church, have so little good to say about men and speak in such strident language that we men cannot listen to them effectively. As I discussed in my book *New Adam* (Culbertson 1992), most men whom I have encountered do not respond well to an aggressive confrontation with women about all the things wrong with being male. Aggressive confrontations easily tap into the deep shame that men carry woven through their sense of masculinity. Deborah Tannen, a writer and linguist whose research has made an important contribution to the continued sophistication of feminism, argues that instead of telling each other how wrong we are, we should accept the fact that men and women are very different from each other, even so far as speaking a different language. No doubt many people can be helped by learning to be both more sensitive and more assertive. "But few people are helped by being told they are doing everything all wrong. And there may be little wrong with what people are doing, even if they are winding up in arguments. The problem may be that each partner is operating within a different system, speaking a different genderlect" (Tannen 1990, 297).

Constructing Masculinity

Genderlect, as Tannen understands it, is part of the social construction of gender. When I first arrived in New Zealand to teach at university level, I included in my syllabus two books I had written in America on some psychological and spiritual issues for men (Culbertson 1992, 1994). A number of male students responded that while they had learned a great deal from reading the books, the fit between my theories and their experience of being men in New Zealand was not always a successful one. The problem was that the white American definition of masculinity and its resultant issues were not identical with the white New Zealand definition of masculinity and its resultant issues.

To begin to explain, a distinction must be made between *sex* and *gender*. According to sociologists Candace West and Don Zimmerman: "Sex is a determination made through the application of socially agreed upon biological criteria for classifying persons as females or males" (West and Zimmerman 1991, 14). Ordinarily such classification is assigned to babies immediately at birth ("It's a boy!"), based on whether the baby has a vagina or a penis. Gender has been more difficult to define, but is generally agreed to be primarily a socially or culturally determined artifice, or as West and Zimmerman define it, "a socially scripted dramatization of the cultural idealization of feminine and masculine natures" (1991, 17; see also Novitz 1990). James K. Baxter uses the term "civil fiction" to define the same artifice (Jensen 1996, 114). In addition to social and cultural determinations, I believe we need also to recognize historical determinations—definitions of gender based on the cumulative heritage of how men and women who preceded us had to learn to behave in order to cope with a variety of sequential historical conditions. Whether gender is defined socially, culturally, or historically, its definitions are systemically inherited from one generation to the next, and each generation must decide whether to adopt or adapt the gender roles and expectations it has received.

One may be born a male, but manliness and masculinity have to be achieved, or even earned (Mailer 1968, 25). Whether or not one has achieved masculinity is based on a set of standards and definitions that are quite culture-specific, though not usually spelled out systematically. The standards of definition are for the most part unique to the culture in which the male is living. The lack of congruence between one's assigned biological sex (male) and one's nature, characteristics, and behaviors (manliness, masculinity) usually results in a significant degree of interpersonal and internalized shaming. For example, most boys have memories of being verbally bullied on the playground if they somehow failed to "measure up." Other boys, and sometimes the girls, called them "pansies," "sissies," "fags," or "poofters"—traditional expressions of the feared incongruity between a person's biological maleness and his success at achieving masculinity (Phillips 1996, 262).

Some anthropologists claim that there is an essentialist definition of masculinity that is pan-cultural. For example, David Gilmore claims that in every culture, men are expected to carry out the roles of Protector, Provider, and Procreator (Gilmore 1990). Such a pan-cultural definition might be termed "the mythic masculine" and functions in the same manner as a Jungian archetype. But archetypes also have culture-specific incarnations—for example, the Trickster archetype is incarnate in classical Greek culture as Pan and in traditional Polynesian culture as Maui. Pan and Maui are not identical, yet both are cultural embodiments of the Trickster. Similarly, in one culture Man as Protector might be defined as going off to fight faraway wars, while in another culture it might be defined as protecting the immediate boundaries of the home. In one culture, Man as Provider might be defined as a nomadic hunter, in another culture as a settled gatherer of grain, and in a third culture as the man who works in an office and brings home a paycheck. Each specific incarnation is a product of the history and cultural heritage of the particular location and period in which it is acted out (Culbertson 1993).

If masculinity and femininity are merely historical and cultural constructs, however powerful—or, as Judith Butler (1990) would have it, ways in which we "perform" our gender—then masculinity and femininity are not character essentials, but character overlays. Men, then, are not categorically evil and abusive, nor, as I have observed elsewhere, are men categorically powerful (Culbertson 1994). The vast majority of the powerful patriarchs may be male, but the vast majority of males feel powerless, even in the face of their confreres in the patriarchy. Genderlect aside, when it comes to issues of power and powerlessness, men have more in common with women than not: both know something of the experience of powerlessness and oppression. They articulate it differently, they express themselves in different ways, and they choose extremely different ways to process their powerlessness. But men and women hold in common that both are victims of powerful others whose vested interests are in protecting their own power at all costs.

However, because men, even the powerless, live a one-up/one-down life, they too easily succumb to the temptation to behave like the patriarchs. At this point men need to listen more carefully to the feminist critique and to the growing volume of psychological and sociological literature on how men and women differ from and abuse each other. Fifty years ago, Paul Tillich, one of the great minds in modern Protestant theology, was urging the church to pay greater attention to modern psychological and sociological insights. He wrote, "The criticism by psychology and sociology of personalistic symbols for man's relation to God must be taken seriously by theologians. . . . " The symbols and language so uncritically accepted in the church's traditional Godspeak in fact have "shocking psychological consequences" (Tillich 1963, I.228). For Tillich, it was a tragic thing for the church to live in isolation from the research and conclusions of modern science. He understood that none of us can afford to ignore our critics or assume that we have a corner on the truth. For the church to turn its back on the "wisdom of the world" could only result in the increasing irrelevance of the church, perhaps with fatal consequences.

Engaging the Feminist Critique

I want to state quite boldly that I do not presently deem the middle-aged or older men that I meet to be at fault in continuing to carry an abusive, insensitive, or disempowering form of masculinity. If, that is, they have *never* encountered feminism, or even the social ills that hegemonic masculinity so complacently creates. I honestly think they do not understand. I am also convinced that it is the responsibility of us men who *have* encountered the deceits and detritus of patriarchy and the mythic-masculine to educate our brothers.

Just so, with Tillich as our mentor, men in the church cannot afford to ignore the feminist critique, either from within the church or without. We do not advance our own best spiritual selves by denying or minimizing what is legitimate and necessary in the feminist critique. The value of the critique is that it provides us with a background against which to measure where we are, the damage that continues to be caused by the traditionally inherited stereotypes and constructions of masculinity, and where we might begin anew with a more collegial, more community-oriented way of expressing our dignity as the male versions of God's human children. Deborah Tannen insists that when we can find patterns that allow us to evaluate and accept differences, we have found the starting point for both self-understanding and flexibility, "the freedom to try doing things differently if automatic ways of doing them aren't having entirely successful results" (Tannen 1990, 294).

If I have spoken bluntly of men, I have done so because I see the problems, the struggles within myself and of my male peers in the church, and believe not only that men can change, but *must* change. Change remains imperative for men if we are to:

- put an end to the violence we do to other men, to women and children, and to the environment

- unite with other groups of people who are as oppressed as are the powerless men, in order to challenge the exploitation by hegemonic masculinity
- encourage all men, whether they are ready to engage feminism and their own exploitation or not, to be healthier by being more whole
- help God build a kingdom here in this temporal realm

Each of these four tasks needs to be undertaken intentionally, both as acts of contrition and as Christian examples for those around us who are lost and seek answers. But as we who are ready for change continue to struggle through our new identities, we ask: "Who will teach us?" We know so few examples of men who have reached their goal of a healthy, reformed masculinity, either inside the church or outside, that at first it seems we may be lost before we even begin. Fortunately, the Gospel accounts of Jesus and his disciples remind us that our primary model as men seeking new identities must begin with Christ as he is found already waiting for us in the midst of the struggling community of feminist-sensitive men. We can thank God for this prevenient grace.[1] In community, we are both challenged and supported, if we can remember to look to the community as a whole rather than to individualistic models.

The men's movement outside the church is already thirty years old, but its full impact has yet to be felt by the institution. For thirty years the spirit of God has been at work among men seeking community and liberation outside the church. The time has come for us to recognize the spirit of God among men *within* the church who believe that God's kingdom-promises begin with things new, with liberation from the known, with the feminist struggle for new identity, and now with our own struggle for a new masculine identity as we men find ourselves empowered because we have first empowered women.

Nurturing the Authority of Men in Ministry

It is difficult for us as men to hang on to confidence in ministry when our sense of ministerial authority is undermined by gender dysphoria. But perhaps "authority in ministry" is more accessible to us if we look again at the origins of the word *authority* itself.

Authority is derived from the Latin word *auctor*: "he that brings about the existence of any object; or promotes the increase or prosperity of it—

whether he first originates it, or by his efforts gives greater permanence or continuance of it" (Lewis and Short 1879, 198). *Auctor* is, in turn, the past participle of the verb *augere*, meaning "to 'augment,' make grow, originate, promote, increase," though its most ancient meaning was even more pregnant: "to produce, bring forth that which is not already in existence" (Oxford English Dictionary [OED], 571; Lewis and Short 1879, 203–4). According to Pokorny's etymology (1959, I.84), the sense of the root *aueg-* is "to propagate, increase," or "to take on larger size or shape, to rise and swell." In these senses of propagation and swelling, *author* conveys much of the same sense as the Hebrew word "Torah"—something that causes something else to grow by inseminating it and thus imparting new power to it.

The two primary senses of authority in the New Testament parallel standard English definitions given by the OED: jurisdictional authority vested or exercised from above, or consensual authorization granted from below. But in either case, the meaning of "authority" is context-specific, that is, its meaning changes according to who is using it to express what sort of idea. For example, the Roman government, with all its power, certainly did not exercise authority over those outside its political jurisdiction (authority vested from above being refused), nor did the followers of the powerful Sadducees choose to recognize the authority of the Pharisees (authority delegated from below being refused). We recognize that the Russian government may exercise power over the Russian people, but it does not bear authority over the American people. Evangelists Jim Bakker and Jimmy Swaggert touted their spiritual authority via the mass media, yet once they had fallen prey to the temptations of the flesh, the public refused to continue to grant them authority at all, indicating that from the beginning, whatever authority Bakker and Swaggert presumed was only consensual from below. In spite of its claims to absolute authority, the Vatican has been unable to enforce its perceived dogmatic position concerning birth control upon the American faithful. The American public was quick to deny the authority of the presidential office at the end of the Nixon era. The point is that the power of extant authority is only consensual. Those who grant others authority can also "un-grant" authority to others!

Scripture itself seems to recognize no such concept as "absolute authority," even when connected to divine revelation. At Sinai, the Torah became authoritative only following the response of the people: "'All that the Lord has spoken we will do, and we will be obedient.'" (Exodus 24:7).

Gender dysphoria makes it clear that the authority that many men have assumed, by virtue of their biological sex and presumed privilege, is no longer granted to them automatically and consensually—not by most women, nor by many men. If men are to proceed with any authority at all in the church, it must now be redefined and reclaimed by those men who wish to construct a shared authority, based on the giving away of competition-based power rather than its accumulation. This sort of nurturing authority or nurturing power—authority that is recognizable only by the fruits of its capacity to nurture others—is the only form of authority that can be claimed to be truly inclusive and nonabusive.

Hegemony is the word often used to articulate competition-based power, the self-assigned "authority-over," assumed by the meta-masculine, or at least some of the traditional masculinities. Hegemonic masculinity signals that we live in a world in which males have primacy over females, or power, or a place of privilege, or at very least an entitlement to preference. But what if we returned to Exodus 24:7, "'All that the Lord has spoken we will do, and we will be obedient'"? What would it mean, for example, if we men were to imitate Exodus 24 in saying, "We will do something new, and we will obey our critics"?

Can I Stop "That" and Still Be a Man?

In an earlier collection of essays on men's identity (Boyd, Longwood, and Muesse 1996), feminist theologian Carter Heyward lists some of the things that Christian women need from Christian men, if we are to more faithfully live out our own call to New Being and Eternal Life. Here are a few of her suggestions about new ways for men to be:

> We want you to get to know us on our terms—as your sisters, lovers, spouses, mothers, daughters, colleagues, friends and political comrades. Listen to us. You don't have to "agree" with us. Just be quiet sometimes and listen.
>
> Set yourselves a project: learn about women's lives—the lives of women very different from the ones you know (or think you know) best as well as the lives of the women closest to you in life. Study women's history, novels, poetry, art, films, and music—and not just any women's work but the labor of women with a passion for justice for women. Let this work touch you, push and change you.
>
> Study feminist and womanist theory. Get to know why sex, gender, class, race, religion and culture can't be understood—or addressed—separately. Learn what the connections have to do

with your life and work, your love and commitments, your values and investments. . . .

Get together with a group of men—preferably gay, straight, and bisexual men of different colors—and study your own lives. Explore your internalized homophobia with these men. Learn to love one another as men and brothers. Learn to recognize and value the differences you find among yourselves.

If you haven't been active on behalf of either women's lives or men's consciousness, it's time to start, now. And it's not too late, not as long as girl and boy children are being born on the earth.

Dare to imagine your institutions and this society being reconstructed on the basis of visions that you and your feminist colleagues and friends can shape together. Dare to imagine that you can do it, with other folks. Do not fool yourselves into imagining that your "realism" or "pragmatism" has deeper roots or more staying power than your sisters' commitments to what can be—with your help.

Get out of the middle. Take sides. Stand with your sisters. Be yourselves, fully human brothers, having neither answers nor control, but hearts and minds, stretching beyond patriarchal logic in the ongoing creation of something new and wonderful and radical.

Dare to make mistakes, back down, and make amends.

Have compassion, always, for all people and creatures, including your enemies, but do not be fooled by the constancy of premature "calls" for peace, harmony, stability, and reconciliation. Always ask, at what cost, and to whom?

Be gentle with children, animals, and all living beings. And, if ever you are not, be aware that your behavior is violent and potentially deadly—and stop it. Dare to ask for help if your behavior is violent.

Don't worry too much about getting it right all the time, even feminism. Live a day at a time.

Keep things in perspective. Smile and laugh and cry and wail and sing and grieve and dance and make love, in your heart and with all your body if you can. (Heyward 1996, 268–70)

These are but a few of the suggestions that Carter offers as a challenge to male "being" in the church to come. These seem to carve out, at least in part, a beginning to the challenge: "We will do something new, and we will obey our critics." But interestingly, they also ring as potentially true answers to the question, "What must I do to inherit eternal life?" (Mark 10:17). The hard answer to the challenge and question—an answer that so often we have been conditioned not to hear—is that we need to be different than we are right now, whether through voluntary impoverishment, engaging the challenge of Christian feminism, or shifting from doing to being. Pray that we will not be like the inquiring man in Mark 10:22, who "when he heard this, he was shocked and went away grieving, for he had many possessions," and a great investment in the hegemonic status quo.

Even to engage Carter's list will demand some painful work for men, especially those who have not realized how abusive hegemonic masculinity feels to women, other men, and anyone powerless. How do we men begin? What "that" can we stop doing, and yet hang on to a masculine sense of identity? And what can we do instead?

Taking a "Fearless Inventory" of Our Masculinity

The first step is to get a realistic picture of how we men affect those around us. An ancient Jewish midrash reminds us that we do not know a person unless we know what he or she needs, including what is needed from us:

> The Rabbi sat among peasants in a village inn and listened to their conversation. Then he heard how one asked the other, "Do you love me then?" And the latter answered, "Now, of course, I love you very much." But the first regarded him sadly and reproached him for such words: "How can you say you love me? Do you know, then, my needs?" And the other fell silent, and silent they sat facing each other, for there was nothing more to say. He who truly loves, knows from the depths of his identity with the other, from the root ground of the other's being, he knows where his friend is in need. This alone is love. (Katz 1985, 50–51)

Need is a rich word in this story. It could mean the things that so many people feel individually:

- the strength I can't find in myself
- the unconditional love that I never found in my childhood
- the holes in my sense of self
- the hope for tomorrow that I can't muster

Or it could mean the things that we men don't always realize we do to those around us, or the way our behaviors and attitudes affect others:

- the chance to share the power, authority, and entitlement that men presume to have
- the opportunity to take risks at work and in relationships, presuming that everyone has the same safety-net that male privilege guarantees
- the knowledge that I am safe from male aggression, in my body and my sense of self
- the assurance that I will be heard, understood, taken seriously as an equal
- the trust that I will never be the subject of a joke, a sexist/ageist/racist/classist/homophobic remark, or a sarcastic and dismissive tone
- the security of knowing that I will be respected as a human being and as a child equal to you in God's eyes

Sometimes we men don't even know that we intimidate people by our physical size, the loudness of our laughter, or our assumption that conversations are competitive. And so we must take the first step, of asking those around us—our wives and partners, other men we know, our children—how they see us. And when they answer, we must take them seriously.

Among those we ask, it is important to include *profeminist* men—that is, men who are a step or two ahead of many other men, in that they have listened with their hearts to the critique of masculinity. Profeminist men are those who realize that non-abusive forms of masculinity can be structured only after men have taken feminism and feminist thought seriously. In itself, this is a lifelong commitment, for as James Nelson (1988) has pointed out, even profeminist men will always be "recovering sexists." We—at least we white men—will always have to struggle with the six "sins" of hegemonic masculinity that Steven Boyd (1997) identifies: femiphobia, sexism, homophobia, racism, anti-Semitism, and classism. We all have a long way to go in our recovery from patriarchy's damage.

The Church's Response to Men Who Are Changing

The church does not always know what to do with profeminist and other men who are changing. Men who have engaged the sorts of issues that Carter identifies will become different than they have been before, and different from the traditional construction of masculinity upon which the church has always relied for the assigning and brokering of power.

Profeminist men may become prophetic and challenging. They may ask hard "why" questions or promote traditionally unpopular options. They may call for affirmative action, nonsexist language, and the shattering of traditional vessels. Since the church as we presently know it assumes traditional gender-role behavior, it may in turn react badly, suggesting that profeminist men go sit on the bench on the sidelines.

When the church attempts to sideline profeminist men and others who are changing, men need to learn how to share authority differently with each other. We need to opt for nurturing authority as I described it above: "authority which is dedicated to helping others grow and thrive." Theologian Letty Russell develops a whole theology of consensual ecclesial community. She writes, "I understand authority as legitimated power. It accomplishes its ends by evoking the assent of the respondent" (Russell 1987, 21). Top-down authority rarely does this; consensual authority can more easily see who in our midst is suffering, because we stand on the same level with them. Consensual authority in an intentional community attempts to know what each person needs, thereby showing forth its love.

One of my mentors, Paul van Buren, spoke of Christian exclusivism as "the theology of scarcity": God, like a dysfunctional parent, seems to have only limited love, and so we have to compete for that love by making sure that we alone are conveyors of "the truth." Similarly, top-down authority is scarce authority, setting up forms of power that must be competed for. From-below authority, on the other hand, contains no competition or scarcity, for there is always plenty to share around with women and children, the elderly, the disabled, and the marginalized. Profeminist nurturing authority can look very frightening to those who have known only top-down, competitive authority premised on the disempowerment of others. Only with new models of authority in ministry will we recapture Christ's vision of healing works dedicated to justice, equality, mutuality, collegiality, and community.

Surely this is part of what Carter means when she encourages men to take risks and not fear mistakes. The riskiness of the first step—learning about ourselves from others—is that we have thus far too few role models to emulate as we change. Indeed, several of the essays in this volume have a tone of loneliness about them, as though these men in the church are not yet surrounded by a fulsome community of like-minded others.

Michael Kimmel (1995) and others suggest that we must completely deconstruct masculinity as we know it. Kimmel argues that masculinity is so infused with other-abusiveness that it cannot be reconstructed or reframed or remodeled; it deserves only to be deconstructed. I understand *kenosis* to be the Christian parallel to Kimmel's suggestion, as referred to in Philippians 2:6-7: "[one who] did not regard equality with God as something to be exploited, but emptied himself" of all that he had known, taking the risk to become something wholly other. If we must stop doing "that," and deconstruct the very masculinity upon whose traditional form the church relies so heavily, and if there are few obvious role models that provide us a goal to work toward, then the risk feels great indeed. We may once again find ourselves feeling like the comfortable middle-class man in Mark 10:22, who had a great investment in the status quo, and so ran away from change.

The Search for Security

One of the most powerful stories in the Bible tells of a man whom God uproots from all security and sends out on a journey, but God refuses to tell him where he will wind up (Genesis 12:1). The story mesmerizes me with fear, even though I've written about it several times previously. God said to this man: quit your job, pack up your family, dispose of your possessions, jettison your security and all else that you know, and above all, don't be afraid.

I'm tempted to tame that story. I want to say, "God didn't know what he was doing either; he was just making it up as he went along." I want to dismiss it as a cosmic joke. I want to pathologize the protagonist: "Surely he was a psychotic; it wasn't God's voice; he was having a nervous breakdown; he had collapsed into occupational burnout." And I don't want to engage the fact that, in order to be true to God, and in order to stop the church from being so abusive, *any* man would have to surrender the secure trappings of a hard-earned masculinity, instead learning to become something for which there is no model, no stated destination, no definable goal.

My academic fields—pastoral care and psychotherapy—are presently replete with literature encouraging everyone to find a systematically narrated identity, or a secure sense of self, or a proud ethnic identity, or a "home," a geography, a place and sense of belonging. Indeed, a basic presumption of psychology is that human beings desire continuity of identity and predictability from day-to-day. The technical term is "narrative conservatism," and in the classroom I illustrate its importance by talking about the protagonist in Kafka's "Metamorphosis," who goes to bed as a man and wakes up as a cockroach. Masculinity can seem like that: we work so hard to earn it, are barely secure in it, so we work hard to defend it in the face of shame, and are scared to death to imagine who we might be if we have to deconstruct it, to let it all go.

However much the church is premised on the traditional gender constructions of masculinity and femininity (for example, the entrenched assumption that men do public ministries and women do domestic ministries, or that if the gender balance in a congregation tips toward "too many" women, the men will feel threatened and leave[2])—the Bible is *not* about narrative conservatism. Difference, disruption, and counterculturalism are all that are predicted. It is *just* these that demand the three cardinal Christian virtues of faith, hope, and love. Without the three, we would find it intolerable to live in the midst of difference, disruption, and counterculturalism.

The New Creation of 2 Corinthians 5:17 is not defined. The New Heavens and New Earth of Isaiah 65:17 and Revelation 21:1 are not defined. The New Heart of Ezekiel 36:26 is not defined. The Coming Age of Ephesians 1:21 is not defined. The location, nature, and timing of the kingdom of God are not defined. The Bible is not a blueprint for how things will be and who we will be tomorrow, but rather an assurance: if you can find God with you today, then you should hope that God will be with you in whatever bizarre and confusing circumstances you find yourself in tomorrow. So perhaps this all we can hope for in the Christian understanding of gender construction: if we can find God in our sense of masculinity now, then we should hope that God will be with us in whatever emergent but totally different masculinity lies over the horizon of the future.

A New Vision of Men in Ministry

If men in ministry seek to engage Carter's suggestions, and thereby become profeminist men, we must undertake a journey of trust in the face of frightening uncertainty. At the risk of turning the journey to profeminist masculinity into yet another achievement-oriented program, I offer the following seven programmatic suggestions toward a new vision of how men in ministry can begin.

One: Learn to listen actively
The first thing Carter asks of men is "Listen to us." Listening is a gift that a few people have naturally, but a skill that eludes the majority. If listening were so simple, the Bible would not need to remind us repeatedly, "Let those

who have ears, hear!" In fact, the phrase in Exodus 24, "'All that the Lord has spoken we will do, and we will be obedient,'" uses a Hebrew word that means *listen* and *obey* simultaneously, for the assumption in the Hebrew language is that one *will* obey what one has genuinely heard. *To listen* means to hear without competition or defense, to hear with one's heart and not simply with one's ears, to "own" what is being said. *To listen* means to assume the presence of God in what is being said. And as I have already remarked, this is where we begin the journey to a profeminist masculine consciousness: by listening to others tell us how we have hurt them, and what they need.

Two: Read books by and about women

When my cousin Barbara turned fifty, she announced at a family reunion that she had spent the first half of her life reading books by men because she had to. She was now going to spend the second half of her life reading only books by women—because she wanted to. We cannot address Carter's challenge to "learn about women's lives" unless we read what women are writing about Scripture, theology, and their own lives.[3] Like all change, the decision to read books by and about women must be an intentional one. Learning about women's lives could also mean learning about the women in our own family tree.

Three: Covenant with a men's group

Across the church, closed-boundary men's groups are springing up in local parishes, with the support of pastors and other caregivers. It is within these new communities of men seeking a more supportive and sensitive identity that mutuality and love are being worked through in new ways. Love must be nurtured by a community of people who love (Vigna and Edwards 1992, 130), so it is to community that men seeking how to love again are turning. It is in relationship to others that we love, gaining a more acute self-awareness, and taking the risks necessary to create a newly centered profeminist and liberated masculinity.

To be involved in this sort of community demands of many men that they be brave enough to break their old masculine conditioning, shaped by men's abuse of other men. Collegiality and community are the opposite of competition, so to become involved in a community of men means that men's sense of competition must begin to change. Many men carry such strong memories of their fear of other men that to make themselves vulnerable in such groups raises extreme anxieties. Terrance O'Connor writes of his own first experiences in attending a men's retreat:

> Now I must admit that I am just plain scared. But what am I afraid
> of? Forced intimacy, competition, being judged and found want-
> ing, being dominated by a group? All of the above. I like to have
> control of my little world. I know that I will not be in control
> there. Can I trust a group of strange men? (1990, 37–38)

What O'Connor witnessed there was not just a community of men
enjoying each other's company, but men who were making major break-
throughs in their ability to feel and to express themselves:

> One construction worker, a man in his fifties, stands up and tells
> us that in all his life he had never let another man get physically
> close to him. This morning in mask-making his partner had
> touched his face with gentle fingers, and here he chokes up, "and I
> liked it." He bursts into tears. He is immediately surrounded by
> comforting men. (1990, 38)

This is a very different experience of men and vulnerability than most
men gain in the workplace, for example. It is an experience that may be
frightening at first, but if men are supported within the community and by
conscientious caregivers, they can break through their fear into new ways
of being.

Men in groups may also experience true friendship with other men for
the first time. These days, friendship is an endangered species. It does not
thrive in a social ecology that stresses speed, constant preoccupation, and
competition between men. The first requirement of friendship is slow
time. Like great whiskey, it must be seasoned. It must also be steeped with
patience and long-simmered.

Many types of men are benefiting from involvement in men's groups.
Some groups have a very homogeneous makeup, and others a heteroge-
neous. Carter Heyward challenges men to forms groups of "gay, straight,
and bisexual men of different colors—and study your own lives." Closed-
boundary groups, small groups with a static membership, offer men a
chance to learn to trust other men, and offer the experience of encountering
the "otherness" of Christian masculinities in their various forms.[4]

Four: Seek ministry supervision
with a peer group of profeminist men

Another type of group—peer supervision groups—can be particularly
supportive for lay and ordained men in ministry. Here men can share their

hopes, frustrations, doubts, fears, and experience in doing ministry, and can support and encourage each other in the process of theological reflection. Everyone who does ministry, no matter how it is described, should be in some form of regular supervision (Culbertson 2000, chap. 10). Peer supervision is a standardized form of ministry supervision. Men working together in groups can raise issues with each other, then, about how the ways in which they are performing ministry are working to support the creation of profeminist male identities within the church. The focused agenda and level of supportive critique must remain high in such groups, and the purpose should be sharply distinguished from that of men's "identity formation" groups as I have described them above. The task of peer ministry supervision groups is to help profeminist men carve out new ministry identities as healers, companions, colleagues, and nurturers.

Five: Spend time in the world of those who aren't like you

The true encounter with "otherness"—whether divine or human—is one of the most difficult challenges of being human. Here the question, "Do you know, then, my needs?" reaches the epitome of poignancy. Brett Webb-Mitchell's essay in this volume illustrates how much we who are "temporarily able" have to learn from the differently-abled. Engaging the essays by Robert E. Goss and Marvin Ellison will remind us of ways in which gay masculinities differ from straight masculinities. Engaging the essays of Michael Battle and Lee Butler will sensitize us again to African American masculinities. There are many masculinities, and it is ever presumptuous to assume that the particular masculinity *we* perform is therefore normative. This is a critical part of Carter's challenge to be "active on behalf of either women's lives or men's consciousness" (Heyward 1996, 269).

Six: Divorce the Lone Ranger!

A foundational tenet of ecumenism, known in the World Council of Churches as "The Lund Principle," pledges that "We will not do anything alone that could be done as well or better working cooperatively." Men in groups, men and women in groups, fathers and sons in groups, fathers and daughters in groups, and elder mentors and young learners in groups are some of the urgent models for the support and advancement of profeminist and liberating masculinity. For men to work in groups and teams is already countercultural, in societies that presume the rugged individualism (read: lonely isolation) of adult males. And with almost every group, profeminist Christian men must ask both, "How would this group be improved through the participation and voice of women and of men who are not like me?"; and "How will the work of this group stretch beyond patriarchal logic in the ongoing creation of something new and wonderful and radical?"

Seven: Connect your body and nature, your spirituality and sexuality
Atlanta-based theologian Michael Clark writes:

> Men, whether straight or gay, must reconceptualize their sexuality as something that is not external, alienated, and merely functional. They must learn that the erotic—or, more concretely, our sexuality—becomes a meaningless, genitally reduced notion unless we come to understand the erotic as part and parcel of our urges toward mutuality and human(e)ness. (Clark 1996, 350)

I find myself weary with spiritualities that divorce themselves from the human body. We need to incarnate, not transcend. The human body is a tool, a friend, and a home, not a limitation to be overcome, and we need to concentrate harder, therefore, on the integration of our sexuality and our spirituality, both as invaluable parts of the cosmos. St. Teresa of Avila reminds us, "We aren't angels; we've got bodies."

We men are interconnected spirits and bodies, at home in the world of nature. As Carter reminds us, we are called to "be gentle with children, animals, and all living things." We are to be gentle with our own spirits and with our bodies. Our spirits are not prayer machines, any more than our bodies are sex machines. In either case, as James Nelson reminds us (1988), we must learn to befriend our spirit when it is at rest and not pumped up, just as we must learn to befriend our penises when they are at rest. In the end, we can be neither Christian nor masculine without body awareness and body care.

Liberating Men's Ministries from the Patriarchal Church

Current liberation theologies pay close attention to the experience of those who are de- or under-empowered, regarding such experience as a source for theologizing. Feminist theologians regard the experience of women as having a corrective function, exposing the androcentric or patriarchal biases and preferences of traditional theology, which has always excluded women (Kuikman 1992). Anti-patriarchal, profeminist men, seeking a nonviolent and nonabusive new identity, are discovering that they too need the message of hope that liberation theology brings. This message is available to men only through reflection upon their experiences of oppression by inherited gender roles, victimization by other men, and the loneliness that comes from being without community.

Women are learning, as are other oppressed groups, that liberation happens, not overnight, but over a long and often painful process. There are many temptations along the way. One danger is that those who have gained a measure of freedom become the new oppressors. It is tempting for the oppressed to want to exercise power in the way it has been exercised over them. Much time and collaborative effort has been required for women to shed the internalized images of oppression and victimization they have accumulated over time and to find ways of being human first of all, in the image and likeness of God (Kuikman 1992). These lessons have much to teach men who are struggling toward a new identity as profeminist Christians, secure in a nonabusive and nonoppressive masculinity.

Patriarchy and the liberation of sidelined men are mutually exclusive. Patriarchs retain their power through manipulation, domination, and authoritarianism. Yet liberation theologian Paulo Friere reminds us that "Any situation in which 'A' objectively exploits 'B' or hinders [the] pursuit of self-affirmation as a responsible person is one of oppression. Such a situation in itself constitutes violence, even when sweetened by false generosity, because it interferes with [a person's] ontological and historical vocation to be more fully human" (1970, 40). The model of God that Christian men seeking liberation from patriarchy are called to emulate is the image of God in Philippians 2:5-8, the *kenotic* God, the God who empties self of power and privilege, seeking to know others by dwelling among them in solidarity with them. Patriarchy is by definition incapable of *kenosis*, or self-emptying, and thus is irreconcilable with men who are seeking a liberated self. Patriarchal power represents a misguided turning of one's back on the values of God that have been acted out in the life and self-sacrificial model of Christ.

Author John Sanford has called Jacob/Israel "the man who wrestled with God" (Genesis 32). But the original Hebrew of the biblical text is not clear with whom Jacob wrestled; only late in the text is the opponent identified as God, but prior to that he is called "a man." A masculine liberation interpretation of Jacob's wrestling reveals a struggle toward a new identity that is a model for Christian men who are changing. The meaning of the name *Jacob* is not clear, but some understand it as no name, but rather only a descriptor, "the deceiver." The firstborn, Esau, was given a real name; the secondborn, Jacob, was only given an adjective. In this interpretation then, Jacob has no name, and his struggle with the mysterious stranger is a struggle with patriarchy for the right of every human being: a name of his own, an identity of his own choosing. When Jacob wrestled, he thought he was fighting with patriarchy for a name. He won against patriarchy, for by the end of the struggle, he had a name, an identity of his own: Israel. He discovered that patriarchy was not invincible, and that its blessing bestowed upon Esau was a hollow blessing. Patriarchy's permission to be who Jacob/Israel needed to be no longer mattered; he had won the right to become his own man. Jacob's wrestling is the story of one man's efforts to individuate from patriarchal abuse and from inherited gender-stereotyped definitions of appropriate masculinity. The story goes on to tell us that Jacob also won against God. He won the right to be an individual differentiated from God, yet in committed relationship with God, other to Other. But he won liberation from a too-symbiotic relationship with God only through a great deal of pain.

Meeting the Challenge Ahead

The Christian community cannot be healthy until both women and men are liberated from the gender-role expectations that disempower and imprison them. Christ the Liberator has called the church to be a faithful community in service to the oppressed, affirming equality and justice for all people as mature beings in God's image, and modeling God's all-encompassing love for the human community.

Liberating men into a healthier ministry, undergirded by a profeminist masculinity, is the challenge that lies ahead of the nurturing church. The journey from where we are now, to where we know we need to be, will involve both pain and laughter for Christian men and women. The road ahead promises neither guide nor a clear destination. All the more reason that men who take feminism seriously must make that journey into the unknown surrounded by a company of others who are also committed to justice, equality, mutuality, collegiality, and community.

Bibliography

Astrachan, Anthony. 1986. *How Men Feel: Their Responses to Women's Demands for Equality and Power.* Garden City: Doubleday.

Boyd, Stephen. 1997. *The Men We Long to Be: Beyond Desperate Lovers and Lonely Warriors.* Cleveland: Pilgrim.

Boyd, Stephen, Merle Longwood, and Mark Muesse, eds. 1996. *Redeeming Men: Religion and Masculinities.* Louisville: Westminster John Knox.

Butler, Judith. 1990. *Gender Trouble: Feminism and the Subversion of Identity*. New York: Routledge.

Clark, Michael. 1996. "Gay Spirituality." *Spirituality and the Secular Quest*. Ed. Peter Van Ness. New York: Crossroad. 335–55.

Culbertson, Philip. 2000. *Caring for God's People: Counseling and Christian Wholeness*. Minneapolis: Fortress Press.

————. 1996. "Men and Christian Friendship." *Men's Bodies, Men's Gods: Male Identities in a (Post-)Christian Culture*. Ed. Björn Krondorfer. New York: New York Univ. Press. 149–80.

————. 1994. *Counseling Men*. Minneapolis: Fortress Press.

————. 1993. "Men Dreaming of Men: Using Mitch Walker's 'Double Animus' in Pastoral Care." *Harvard Theological Review* 86:2., 219–32.

————. 1992. *New Adam: The Future of Male Spirituality*. Minneapolis: Fortress Press.

Friere, Paulo. 1970. *Pedagogy of the Oppressed*. Trans. Myra Bergman Ramis. New York: Herder and Herder.

Gilmore, David. 1990. *Manhood in the Making: Cultural Concepts of Masculinity*. New Haven: Yale Univ. Press.

Heyward, Carter. 1996. "Men Whose Lives I Trust, Almost." *Redeeming Men: Religion and Masculinities*. Ed. Stephen Boyd, Merle Longwood, and Mark Muesse. Louisville: Westminster John Knox. 263–72.

Jensen, Kai. 1996. *Whole Men: The Masculine Tradition in New Zealand Literature*. Auckland: Auckland Univ. Press.

Katz, Robert. 1985. *Pastoral Care in the Jewish Tradition*. Philadelphia: Fortress Press.

Kauth, Bill. 1992. *A Circle of Men: The Original Manual for Men's Support Groups*. New York: St. Martin's.

Kimmel, Michael. 1995. *The Politics of Manhood: Profeminist Men Respond to the Mythopoetic Men's Movement (And the Mythopoetic Leaders' Answer)*. Philadelphia: Temple Univ. Press.

Kirkley, Evelyn. 1996. "Is It Manly to be Christian? The Debate in Victorian and Modern America." *Redeeming Men: Religion and Masculinities*. Ed. Stephen Boyd, Merle Longwood, and Mark Muesse. Louisville: Westminster John Knox. 80–8.

Kuikman, Jackie. Spring 1992. "Sexism and the Christian Tradition." *Holy Cross Newsletter*, n.p.

Lewis, Charleton and Charles Short. 1879. *A Latin Dictionary*. Oxford: Clarendon.

Lippy, Charles. Summer/Fall 1997. "Miles to Go: Promise Keepers in Historical and Cultural Context." *Soundings: An Interdisciplinary Journal* 80:2-3, 289–304.

Mailer, Norman. 1968. *The Armies of the Night: History as a Novel, the Novel as History*. New York: New American Library.

Nelson, James. 1988. *The Intimate Connection: Male Sexuality, Masculine Spirituality*. Philadelphia: Westminster.

Newsom, Carol, and Sharon H. Ringe, eds. 1992. *Women's Bible Commentary*. Louisville: Westminster John Knox.

Novitz, Rosemary. 1990. "Gender." *New Zealand Society*. Ed. Paul Spoonley, David Pearson, and Ian Shirley. Palmerston North: Dunmore. 98–113.

O'Connor, Terrance. May/June 1990. "A Day for Men." *The Family Therapy Networker*, 36–39.

Phillips, Jock. 1996, revised. *A Man's Country? The Image of the Pakeha Male—A History*. Auckland: Penguin.

Pokorny, Julius. 1959. *Indogermanisches Etymologisches Woerterbuch*. Bern and Munich: Francke Verlag.

Russell, Letty. 1987. *The Household of Freedom: Authority in Feminist Theology*. Philadelphia: Westminster.

Sanford, John. 1981. *The Man Who Wrestled with God: Light from the Old Testament on the Psychology of Individuation*. New York: Paulist.

Schilpp, Paul, and Maurice Friedman, eds. 1967. *The Philosophy of Martin Buber*. LaSalle, Ill.: Open Court.

Tannen, Deborah. 1990. *You Just Don't Understand: Women and Men in Conversation*. New York: Ballentine.

Tillich, Paul. 1963. *Systematic Theology*. 2 Vols. Chicago: Univ. of Chicago Press.

Vigna, Jerry, and Susan Edwards. May/June 1992. "Men Who Believe in Love." *The Catholic World*, 129–30.

Webb-Mitchell, Brett. Summer/Fall 1997. "And a Football Coach Shall Lead Them: A Theological Critique of 'Seven Promises of a Promise Keeper.'" *Soundings: An Interdisciplinary Journal* 80:2-3, 305–26.

West, Candace, and Don Zimmerman. 1991. "Doing Gender." *The Social Construction of Gender*. Ed. Judith Lorber and Susan Farrell. Newbury Park, Calif.: Sage. 13–37.

Notes

1. *Prevenient grace* might be defined as "the grace that arrived before we got there." It posits that God is already present in every situation. We can hardly "bring" God into a situation if God is already there! At best, we can hope to point out to those in need of God that God has been there all along. I am reminded of the words of Martin Buber: "I have no teaching. I only point to something. I point to reality. I point to something in reality that had not or had too little been seen. I take him who listens to me by the hand and lead him to the window. I open the window and point to what is outside" (Schilpp and Friedman 1967, 693).

2. The international evangelical Christian men's movement known as Promise Keepers is simply the fifth movement in the last two-hundred-or-so years that has arisen out of the panic that women were "taking over the church." The first such incarnation is known as "Muscular Christianity," in the first half of the nineteenth century. The second was the Freethought Movement, from 1880–1920, which characterized the church as feminized, numerically dominated by women, and therefore weak, sentimental, and irrational. The third was the Men and Religion Forward movement, from about World War I through to the 1950s; its slogan was "More Men for Religion, More Religion for Men." The fourth was the movement spearheaded by evangelist Billy Sunday, who uttered the famous statement: "Lord save us from off-handed, flabby-cheeked, brittle-boned, weak-kneed, thin-skinned, pliable, plastic, spineless, effeminate, ossified three-karat Christianity." See Kirkley 1996; Lippy 1997; and Webb-Mitchell 1997.

3. An enjoyable aspect of preparing this essay was making a list of women whose books stand out as particularly shaping my theology and my understanding of human psychology: Michele Bograd, Mary Boys, Rita Nakashima Brock, Esther Broner, Judith Butler, Betty Carter, Rebecca Chopp, Carol Christ, Nancy Eiesland, Susan Faludi, Elisabeth Schüssler Fiorenza, Carol Gilligan, Patricia Grace, Beverly Wildung Harrison, Susannah Heschel, Carter Heyward, bell hooks, Mary Hunt, Luce Irigaray, Elizabeth Johnson, Julia Kristeva, Karen Lebacqz, Audre Lorde, Monica McGoldrick, Alice Miller, Bonnie Miller-McLemore, Carol Newsom (particularly her 1992 *Women's Bible Commentary*), Judith Plaskow, Letty Pogrebin, Ana-Maria Rizzuto, Rosemary Radford Ruether, Letty Russell, Maggie Scarf, Eve Kosofsky Sedgwick, Elizabeth Stone, Deborah Tannen, Susan Brooks Thistlethwaite, Judith Viorst, Elaine Wainwright, Alice Walker, and Gail Yee.

4. An issue that men's groups have only begun to struggle with is that of the role of gay men in the men's movement. Some gay men who have attempted to participate in men's groups have felt a sense of tokenism about their presence: "every men's group needs one gay man, but not more." Lesbianism was less an issue in the early days of the women's movement, for women were already more accustomed to physical intimacy. The men's movement at this point remains divided not so much on whether gay men are welcome, for they generally are, but rather on how much of the platform of gay liberation will be incorporated into the emerging agenda of the men's movement. It appears to be most men's experiences in groups that there is much for heterosexual men to learn about identity struggles, oppression by other men, and friendship through conversations and committed interaction with gay men. Documentation of the men's movement's struggle with gay issues can be found in chap. 12 of Astrachan's *How Men Feel* (1986).

15

Men's Faith:
The Effects of Pre- and
Post-Retirement Masculinities

Ed Thompson

> *'Tis not too late to seek a newer world.*
> —Alfred Lord Tennyson in his ode to aging men, *Ulysses*

> *The way of faith is necessarily obscure. We drive by night.*
> —Thomas Merton, *The Ascent to Truth*

The province of religion is often said to be a more vital part of older men's lives, compared to younger men. Soon, baby-boom men who live for fifteen or twenty years beyond the traditional retirement age will be the powerhouse new group trying to figure out how to live, part of a secret society of spiritual adventurers. The projections are mind-boggling. Between 2010 and 2030, when the boom generation enters "the third age," the Census Bureau expects this later-life crowd to swell to one in five Americans. Jones and Gallup (2000) in *The Next American Spirituality* already forecast that the boom generation will be on journeys of the soul, a demanding group for ministers, pastors, and clergy.[1]

Age and Religion

Approximately three in five adults (56%) are considered to be "churched" in America today, a percentage that has changed little over the last two decades. The number of Americans who are without a church membership and/or did not attend regular services within the last six months—44%, according to a 1998 Gallup poll—is the same percentage recorded a decade earlier and is only slightly higher than that found in 1978 (Gallup and Lindsay 2000). The unchurched are more likely to be less than thirty years

244

of age (49%) and to be men (50%, compared with 39% of women). Young men, particularly the unmarried, epitomize the unchurched.

Evidence of the bearing of age on religious involvement is plentiful. A special analysis of Gallup Poll data collected from 1992 to 1999 highlights the finding that religious involvement increases in the later stages of life (Gallup and Lindsay 2000). One question asked Americans to rate the importance of religion in their daily lives. Of the 18- to 29-year-olds polled, 45% report that religion is "very important." This percentage increases steadily with age to 55% for those 30–49 years old, 70% for those 50 and older, and 77% among those 75 and older.

There are similar patterns for other measures of religious involvement. Membership in a church, synagogue, or mosque, attending a religious service, and intensity of belief all increase with age. Sixty-one percent of 18- to 29-year-olds say they are members of a church or synagogue, a figure that increases in all subsequent age brackets, with 66% of 30- to 49-year-olds reporting membership, 76% of those 50 and older, 79% of those 65 and older, and a high of 81% for those 75 and older. Attending a religious service within the past seven days increases with age, although these levels are lower than church or synagogue membership. Twenty-three percent of 18- to 29-year-olds polled attended at least once within the last week, a number that doubles to nearly half (46%) who attended among those 75 and older (Gallup and Lindsay 2000). This age difference is particularly noteworthy when it is recognized that some of the very old are no longer physically capable of attending public religious services (Ainlay, Singleton, and Swigert 1992).

Men and Religion

Just what is the relationship between religion and gender across the life course? Nearly every study that has examined the religiosity of adult men concludes that men are less religious than women. Regardless of how religiosity was conceived or measured, it has been found that for men, religion appears less salient to everyday activities, personal faith is weaker at all ages, commitment to orthodox belief is weaker, and involvement in religious ritual and worship is less common than for women.

It is a fair question to ask: why the consistent relationship between gender and religious involvement? The question is not a new one. Conspicuous are "difference explanations" that emphasize how "being a man" (whatever one's age, race, or class) and being religious are fundamentally incompatible. Religion, it is argued, is a woman's calling. Social-psychological explanations of this type, for example, presume that socialization configures men's *internal* lives to be at odds with the communal orientation and deep commitment characteristic of faith communities and being religious (see Argyle and Beit-Hallahmi 1975; Batson and Ventis 1982). The adult man is the grown boy whose childhood experiences directed him to be self-reliant and independent—characteristics in harmony with the culture of American manhood (Gilmore 1990), yet incongruent with the other-directedness associated with being involved in a faith community. Viewed from this perspective, gender is envisioned as two mutually exclusive categories, and all the diversity among men of different ages, denominations, and geographic locations is homogenized into one category.

Another oversocialized view of men's (and women's) lives is found in some sociological explanations (de Vaus & McAllister 1987; Lenski 1953). The premise is that men and women are supposed to live in separate spheres. It is their calling. Men's assignment as head of the family household and their ghettoization in the paid work force restricts their opportunities and defines their interests. Their "ultimate concern"—the basic value around which all other values are focused, the central philosophy of life (Moberg 1990, 6)—is with being a good provider, with success, and with social standing and economic power, and they have little time for much else. Their everyday relations are grounded on power politics and contracts, and consequently their religious involvement is skin-deep compared to women's faith.

These accounts of men's religious involvement are derived from a "sex roles" perspective that exaggerates the degree to which men's inner lives are directed by a common, well-defined script. The accounts accent a common denominator among men absent in most women's lives (for example, *to be* is *to conquer*). The differences between men and women are magnified, whether the comparison is the so-called instrumental-rational sphere to which men are assigned, versus women's integrative-expressive sphere. This comparative sex-role framework also assumes that just one masculinity script directs men's social lives across the life course, and the variation in men's religious involvement is assumed to be minimal.

Masculinities

Different masculinities coexist. People are accustomed to talking about boys and about men in midlife, older men, and elder men. We are used to calling attention to age-specific masculinities by singling out men who represent different generations and who are at different life stages. So, too, are geographical or regional masculinities commonly acknowledged. Growing up as a young man in the Bible Belt South versus the unchurched West should evoke images of different masculinities. The gender script that directed men's lives throughout the twentieth century in the South has been one that emphasized men's patriarchal responsibilities. Families' church attendance and nightly prayer were integrated parts of the masculinity script and reinforced men's social standing as family overseers as much as their participation in the labor force (Griswold 1994). In congregational New England or the unchurched West, by comparison, the dominant masculinity script did not prescribe religious involvement as part of being the family man. Especially in the second half of the twentieth century, work, sport, the military, and fraternal associations were the authoritative social forces associated with masculinity (Griswold 1994; Kimmel 1997).

As much as it is essential to recognize that distinct masculinities coexist in our society, it is also necessary to systematically restrict this analysis to just age-based masculinities. Temporarily closing one's eyes to the social norms that can differentially define later-life masculinity by geographic region and racial/ethnic background, for example, is advantageous to this inquiry. Later-life masculinities as distinct from earlier life stages must be sketched.

Later-life masculinities began to be systematically studied for the first time in the 1990s (Kosberg and Kaye 1997; Thompson 1994). However, the blueprints of older men's masculinities still need to be better outlined. Neither the general social norms scripting later life masculinity nor the behavioral customs older men establish have been systematically charted. Piecing together available information, later-life masculinity is defined more by norms of sociability and reveals more vividly men's seeking connections with others, instead of the acts of individuation. Older men's experiences become centered on the *emotion work* of relational concerns (Bleiszner 1989; Kahn and Antonucci 1981), and reflection (Ryff 1991; Thomas and Chambers 1989), and less by the yardstick of "accomplishments" and success that helped define them as younger men. A "busy ethic" (Ekerdt 1986) replaces the performance-oriented work ethic, and a search for coherence replaces the self-reliant, "give 'em hell" values of earlier masculinities (Erikson, Kivnick, and Erikson 1994).

Later-life masculinities also deemphasize men's segmentation of everyday life and unveil greater support to integrate life experiences. Subordinated are the younger man's norms for deep involvement in self-definition and the phallic, youthful machismo self-presentation. Side-by-side relations with friends, siblings, and others (Adams 1994; Matthews 1994), the generative opportunities of mentoring, grandparenting, and volunteering (Antonovsky and Sagy 1990; Erikson, Kivnick, and Erikson 1994), the sometimes primary and more commonly secondary caregiving responsibilities (Harris and Bichler 1997; Motenko 1988), the face-to-face socializing, life review, reminiscing, and the reconstruction of self though narrative (David 1990; Ryff 1991)—collectively, these social experiences have more priority and appear to replace the earlier acts of affirming one's sovereignty.

These patterns strongly suggest that older men remained involved in activities that define them as men, and their "gendered" activities distinguish them from younger and middle-aged men. Especially for the older men who retire and separate themselves from the ideological orientation of work, their lives are apt to be more deeply engaged in a sociability that acknowledges closeness and vulnerability. In retirement, men experience a new calculus for feeling good. Competition, accomplishment, one-upmanship, and the narcissistic spirit of individualism are no longer the "right stuff"; rather, self-in-association-with-others, cooperation, and deeper involvements come to redefine manhood for the older man.

One line of psychological research has put forth an explanation for why a man's network structure gets smaller and reflects a higher proportion of very close ties as he ages (Carstensen 1992). In later life, it is thought that men seek smaller networks consisting primarily of their closest ties because older men become less interested in novel experiences and prefer established relationships that yield enjoyment and satisfaction. This "downsizing" of social contacts is guided by a desire to maximize time spent in emotionally rewarding interaction.

Theorizing Older Men's Spirituality

Yet there is another explanation for why older men seek social contacts to meet emotional goals, and it does not equate aging with a dwindling interest in novel experiences. To the contrary, later life is an adventure. It is a third age. It is, for men, a time to pursue intimacy and meaning-filled relationships. Older men do not "retire" and retreat from seeking novelty; rather they initiate a number of spiritual journeys and redirect the growing of the self. They replace power struggles with conversations, engage solitude, and abandon loneliness. They turn toward the world, birthing themselves in the new journeys. Far from disengaging and becoming less interested in seeking novel experiences, the third age *is* a novel experience. And it is necessarily obscure, because it is uncharted. It requires faith.

To James Birren, "there appears to be a psychological dynamism in later life toward interpretation of life, the attainment of some grasp of the essential meaning" (1990, 50). At the same time, the infrastructure of men's later life seems more consonant with being religious and/or engaging in spiritual journeys. In comparison to earlier masculinities, the social and behavioral norms of late-life manhood do not dissuade men's religious questing and other efforts to locate the self in affiliations. A caveat: This premise that later-life masculinities prescribe new journeys should not be interpreted as wholly reconfiguring older men's lives, for as Atchley (1989) has persuasively argued, there is an underlying continuity of experience. The self-of-the-past that transcends midlife is the underpinning of the self-of-the-present that enters "retirement."

Prior to midlife, Barbara Payne has observed that men's faith experiences largely entail prochurch involvement. They translate their religiousness outward into acts of justice—such as building Habitat for Humanity homes (Payne 1994). Her observation is that men's religiousness shifts from ritualistic participation and a rational/logical orientation to spiritual journeys and an introspective orientation (cf. Fowler 1981; Stokes 1982, 1989). Biographical "turning points" help regulate the pace of faith development among men—that is, a marked change in health status or retirement can redirect a man's ultimate concern.

With retirement, where, when, and how individual men spend their day is no longer dictated by the absolute authority of work or the ideology of the work ethic. What then does "retirement" mean to older men themselves? As it is experienced, retirement is not strictly an event, rather it is a social-psychological process. It involves separating self from the work ethic and eventually leaving the work force. It is an extended process of retiring *from*, and men imaginatively rehearse what retirement will be for ten to fifteen years before the event (Ekerdt, Kosloski, and DeViney 2000). It is also a life stage, extending from the person's decision to exit the labor force to his death. And it is thus a movement *toward*. It is the process of questing and reconstructing one's ultimate concern, seeking spiritual wellness.

With "retirement," self-redefinition is situated in the new infrastructure of later-life manhood. Before this biographical turning point, matters of ultimate concern are located in the workplace and sustained by the work ethic (cf. Gilligan 1986; Tillich 1957). Fowler (1981) defined faith as a way of knowing. His premise is that in faith, our lives are shaped in relation to our beliefs and assumptions about reality. For Fowler, faith provides a sense of the world. Younger men's faith communities are typically secular—for example, the entrepreneurial culture and the highly symbolized art of bread-*winning*. Spiritual questing, journeys of the soul, reconstructions of the self—these are the midlife crises. They challenge social conventions and the underlying social order. In later life, men's spiritual development no longer affirms the values of traditional masculinities; rather, matters of ultimate concern become personal, spiritual, and by definition, more fuzzy (Zinnbauer et al. 1997). No longer directed by only the rational/logical ways of "knowing," middle-aged and older men begin to keep faith with new ways of knowing that have the power to unify existential life-issues and experiences. Spirituality increases because the social forces constraining men's (and working women's) journeys and questing ebb.

Studying Older Men's Religiousness

There is very little evidence to affirm that religious questing and spiritual development occurs in men's lives. Longitudinal studies of men's religiousness and/or their faith development over the life course have rarely been undertaken. Cornwall (1989) was able to reveal that because of changes in labor-force participation, as people move through the life cycle, men's religiousness begins to approximate women's. This finding suggests that men do become more religious with age. Payne's work (1994) offers case illustrations for men's level of faith development. Otherwise there has been no study to demonstrate that older men's religiousness is greater when they retire and leave behind the ultimate concern that is jointly defined by the work ethic and traditional masculinity. The present study was designed to provide an initial empirical evaluation of the *likelihood* of a developmental transition in men's faith.

If the idea is tenable that later-life masculinities support spiritual development, then a comparison of retired elder men to similarly aged men still active in the labor force should reveal evidence of greater religiousness among the retired. This hypothesis emphasizes that men (and women) who are engaged in the labor force will show less evidence of religious spirituality, presumably because their concerns and identities remain more involved in the conventional morality of the workplace. Restating this, labor-force participation is theorized to compete with journeys of the soul and religiousness by constructing employed men's conceptions of ultimate meaning to a work ethic, whereas older men in retirement should reveal greater faith.

Methods. Ainlay, Singleton, and Swigert's (1992) survey of community-based elders in Worcester, Massachusetts, provides data for the study. Interviewed face-to-face in early 1990 were 97 men and 132 women age 65 and older. The sample was stratified for three elder age groups (65–74, 75–84, and 85-and-older) and based on the 1989 city census. The completed sample of 229 (a 29% refusal rate) contains 60% Catholics, 27% Protestants, and 8% Jewish respondents. Both the state of Massachusetts and the city of Worcester are religiously diverse, with the Catholic (50%) and Jewish (5%) populations in the city sizably above the national averages.

The city of Worcester also has a larger elder population (19%) than the national average (12–13%). In the completed sample, ages range from 65 to 100, with a mean age of 76.3; 105 people are age 65–74, 80 are age 75–84, and 44 are 85-and-older. Forty percent of the sample is widowed, 4% remarried, and 46% continuously married. At some point, 89% had participated in the paid labor force, and 18% had been in the paid labor force within three months of the interview. Just shy of two-thirds of the sample completed high school or acquired a GED certificate, and almost one-quarter completed a year or more of college.

Measures. The measures of religiousness emphasize the subjective experience. The involvement dimension indexes the nonorganizational, more solitary forms of religious involvement. This *religious involvement* index consists of five items documenting how frequently each older person reported she or he prayed privately, read the Bible or other religious material, listened to religious programs on the radio, watched religious programs on television, and sought guidance from statements and publications provided by one's faith. The index is constructed by algebraically averaging five items that range from 0 (never) to 5 (every day).

An *intrinsic religious orientation* index was constructed to measure "faith." It consists of nine items selected a priori by three independent judges. Each item is scored on a 5-point Likert scale ranging from *strongly disagree* to *strongly agree*. The items indicate whether someone feels close to God, feels private prayer is one of the most satisfying aspects of being religious, feels religion answers many questions about the meaning of life, feels the need for God's continual care, feels religion keeps her/his life balanced, believes God answers her/his prayers, feels religious beliefs are what lie behind one's whole approach to life, recognizes she/he tries to carry faith into all other dealings in life, and feels religion offers comfort when sorrow and misfortune arise. This scale showed very strong internal consistency (alpha = .92), and after algebraically summing the items, the scale ranges from 1 (strongly disagree) to 5 (strongly agree).

Labor-force participation was measured using a single item that determined whether in the three months before the interview the older person was still employed full- or part-time. The item was coded to represent not-working/retired versus employed.

Findings. As would be anticipated by the traditional "gender difference" perspective, when the aggregate of men is compared to women, men were less religious than women on both the "religious involvement" scale

($t = 2.87, p < .005$) and the "religious orientation" scale ($t = 3.22, p < .001$). More important is the pattern of scores summarized in Figure 1 for the religiousness measures when analyzed for both gender and employment status. In analysis that controlled for people's religious denomination, the analysis of variance statistics that examined the separate effects of gender and employment status, and the two-way interaction (gender x employment status), variation in the religious involvement scale demonstrated that there is strong support for the hypothesis ($F = 9.65; df = 5,228; p < .001$). First, there was no main effect for gender ($F = 0.04; df = 1,228$). This outcome strongly suggests that it is because of men's participation in the labor force that we recurringly find men showing less evidence of religious involvement than women. Second, the main effect of employment status ($F = 5.17, df = 1,228; p < .005$) revealed that all elders who continued to participate in the labor force showed less evidence of religious involvement. Last, the observed significant gender x employment status interaction effect ($F = 5.17; df = 1,228; p < .05$) directly supports the hypothesis that men's continued participation in the labor force serves as a counterweight to their personal involvement in religious activity.

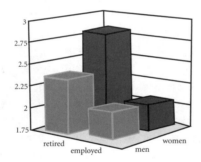

Fig. 1. Nonorganizational religious involvement by gender and employment status

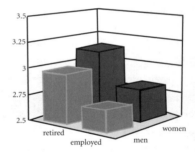

Fig. 2. Intrinsic religious orientation by gender and employment status

The second analysis examined men's intrinsic religious orientation (see Fig. 2). It, too, assessed the effects of gender, employment status, and the two-way interaction (gender x employment status) on variation in the salience of faith. Again, with religious denomination controlled, the general hypothesis was supported, albeit not as strongly ($F = 9.88; df = 9,228; p < .001$). There was no main effect for gender ($F = 0.21; df = 1,228$), but employment status ($F = 8.12; df = 1,228; p < .005$) did have a strong effect, demonstrating that people outside the labor force are more engaged in faithing. This pattern again is remarkable, because it questions prior studies that routinely show a gender difference. We see, instead, a difference only between those elders who remain in the labor force or not. The gender x employment status interaction further suggests that men's continued labor-force participation thwarts their faithing ($F = 2.78$; $df = 1,228$; $p < .10$). As we can see, the effect of continued labor force participation on faith development is important to understanding men's religiousness.

Conclusions

In the gerontological literature and in pastoral counseling, the relationship between masculinities and being religious has hardly been studied. This book is an exception. Most prior attempts to understand men's religiousness also are not sociologically grounded or empirically substantiated. This study is an exception. Theorized and found was that older men's religiousness is intimately tied to their retirement versus their engagement in the workplace. Despite the common sense perspective that aging yields spiritual development, we must become more sensitive to the conditions under which aging and spirituality are possible. Elder men who remained active in the labor force are not as likely to be oriented to spiritual journeys. Their experiences in the traditional world of breadwinning remain uninterrupted, and consequently they have not yet begun a search for new meaning.

What still needs to be traced is the different way older men experience their journeys of the soul. The place of religious involvement among men may very well shift over the life course from ritualistic involvement to faithing. In later life *and after retirement*, spiritual life was more evident. Men's spirituality and spiritual development thus may be truly supported in later life, when the infrastructure of later-life masculinities and retirement *define men's lives*. Their quest for a new ultimate concern is not contradicted by their ongoing involvement with the workplace and its values.

According to Geertz (1970), religion, like work, is a system of meanings embodied in social structure. For Berger and Luckmann (1966; Berger 1967), religion is a "sacred canopy" that envelopes the culture and provides roots for social arrangements and self-redefinition. It is certainly an underpinning of the work ethic (Weber 1958). From the perspective of what Weber called "the Protestant ethic," paid work was men's calling. This was especially true for the current generation of older men Brokaw (1997) has called "the greatest generation." When older men's work lives end and retirement is the defining status, the spirituality that envelopes the culture can (and does seem to) become more directive. Retired elder men were observed to be religiously involved, and their religious orientation is more salient.

Religion and participation in the labor force are thus two interdepend-ent social forces directing older men's experiences as men (cf. Thomas and Chambers 1989). The message is that working continues to impinge on older men's spirituality and expressions of religiousness, as noted for those men who remain employed. The same holds true for women. Ministers, pastors, rabbi, and other clergy need to be sensitive to this reason for the diversity among older men's and women's religious appetites.

With retirement, this present study affirms that elder men become much more personally *involved* in religion. The information provided by this sample of elder men and women supports the idea that men's spiritu-ality and ultimate concern are to be conceptualized as jointly changing. The pace of these changes appears to be very strongly related to their employment status, because "in retirement" seems to involve leaving behind some of the anchors of the traditional masculinity found in the work culture. Unknown is whether these ideas are generalizable to the boomer generation and its spiritual quests. Will the status and meaning of employment among boomer men (and women) constrain journeys of the soul? Or have these journeys begun, perhaps as a result of this generation's more personal involvement in parenting and fatherhood?

Bibliography

Adams, R. G. 1994. "Older Men's Friendship Patterns." *Older Men's Lives*. Ed. Edward H. Thompson, Jr. Thousand Oaks: Sage. 159–77.

Ainlay, S., R. Singleton, and V. L. Swigert. 1992. "Aging and Religious Participation: Reconsidering the Effects of Health." *Journal for the Scientific Study of Religion* 31, 175–88.

Antonovsky, A., and S. Sagy. 1990. "Confronting Developmental Tasks in the Retirement Transition." *The Gerontologist* 30, 362–68.

Argyle, Michael, and Benjamin Beit-Hallahmi. 1975. *The Social Psychology of Religion*. London: Routledge and Kegan Paul.

Atchley, R. C. 1989. "A Continuity Theory of Normal Aging." *The Gerontologist* 29, 183–90.

Batson, C. D., and W. L. Ventis. 1982. *The Religious Experience: A Social-Psychological Perspective*. New York: Oxford Univ. Press.

Berger, Peter. 1967. *The Sacred Canopy: Elements of a Sociological Theory of Religion*. New York: Anchor.

Berger, Peter L., and Thomas Luckmann. 1966. *The Social Construction of Reality*. Garden City: Anchor.

Birren, J. E. 1990. "Spiritual Maturity in Psychological Development." *Journal of Religious Gerontology* 7, 41–53.

Bleiszner, R. 1989. "Developmental Processes of Friendship." *Older Adult Friendship: Structure and Process*. Ed. R. G. Adams and R. Bleiszner. Newbury Park: Sage. 108–26.

Brokaw, Tom. 1998. *The Greatest Generation*. New York: Random House.

Carstensen, L. L. 1992. "Social and Emotional Patterns in Adulthood: Support for Socioemotional Selectivity Theory." *Psychology and Aging* 7, 331–38.

Cornwall, M. 1989. "Faith Development of Men and Women Over the Life Span." *Aging and the Family*. Ed. S. Bahr and E. Peterson. Lexington: Lexington. 115–39.

Culbertson, Philip. 1994. *Counseling Men*. Minneapolis: Fortress Press.

David, D. 1990. "Reminiscence, Adaptation, and Social Context in Old Age." *International Aging and Human Development* 30, 175–88.

de Vaus, D., and I. McAllister. 1987. "Gender Differences in Religion: A Test of the Structural Location Theory." *American Sociological Review* 51, 472–81.

Ekerdt, D. J. 1986. "The Busy Ethic: Moral Continuity between Work and Retirement." *The Gerontologist* 26, 239–44.

Ekerdt, D. J., K. Kosloski, and S. DeViney. 2000. "The Normative Anticipation of Retirement by Older Workers." *Research on Aging* 22, 3–22.

Erikson, E., H. Q. Kivnick, and J. M. Erikson. 1994. *Vital Involvement in Old Age: The Experience of Old Age in Our Time*. New York: Norton.

Fowler, James. 1981. *Stages of Faith: The Psychology of Human Development and the Quest for Meaning*. New York: HarperCollins.

Friedan, Betty. 1994. *The Fountain of Age*. New York: Simon and Schuster.

Gallup, G., and D. M. Lindsay. 2000. *Surveying the Religious Landscape: Trends in U.S. Beliefs*. New York: Morehouse Publishing.

Geertz, Clifford. 1973. *The Interpretation of Cultures*. New York: Basic.

Gilligan, Carol. 1986. "In a Different Voice: Visions of Maturity." *Women's Spirituality: Resources for Christian Development*. Ed. J. W. Conn. New York: Paulist Press. 63–87.

Gilmore, David. 1990. *Manhood in the Making: Cultural Concepts of Masculinity*. New Haven: Yale Univ. Press.

Griswold, R. L. 1994. *Fatherhood in America: A History*. New York: Basic.

Harris, P. B., and J. Bicher. 1997. *Men Giving Care: Reflections of Husbands and Sons*. New York: Garland.

Jones, T. and G. Gallup. 2000. *The Next American Spirituality: Finding God in the Twenty-first Century*. New York: Chariot Victor.

Kahn, R. T., and T. C. Antonucci. 1981. "Conveyors of Social Support: A Life-Course Perspective." *Aging: Social Change*. Ed. S. B. Kiesler et al. New York: Academic. 383–405.

Kimmel, Michael. 1997. *Manhood in America: A Cultural History*. New York: Simon & Schuster.

Kosberg, J. I., and L. W. Kaye. 1997. *Elderly Men: Special Problems and Professional Challenges.* New York: Springer.

Laslett, Peter. 1991. *A Fresh Map of Life: The Emergence of the Third Age.* Cambridge: Harvard Univ. Press.

Lenski, G. 1953. "Social Correlates of Religious Interest." *American Sociological Review* 18, 533–44.

Matthews, S. H. 1994. "Men's Ties to Siblings in Old Age: Contributing Factors to Availability and Quality." *Older Men's Lives.* Vol. 6 of Research on Men and Masculinities. Ed. Edward H. Thompson, Jr. Thousand Oaks: Sage.

Moberg, D. O. 1990. "Spiritual Maturity and Wholeness in the Later Years." *Journal of Religious Gerontology* 7, 5–24.

Motenko, A. K. 1988. "Respite Care and Pride in Caregiving: The Experience of Six Older Men Caring for Their Disabled Wives." *Qualitative Gerontology.* Ed. S. Reinharz and G. D. Rowles. New York: Springer-Verlag. 104–27.

Payne, B. P. 1994. "Faith Development in Older Men." *Older Men's Lives.* Vol. 6 of Research on Men and Masculinities. Ed. Edward H. Thompson, Jr. Thousand Oaks: Sage. 85–103.

Ryff, C. D. 1991. "Possible Selves in Adulthood and Old Age: A Tale of Shifting Horizons." *Psychology and Aging* 6, 286–95.

Stokes, K. 1989. *Faith is a Verb: Dynamics of Adult Faith Development.* Mystic, Conn.: Twenty-Third.

———. 1982. *Faith Development in the Adult Life Cycle.* New York: W. H. Sadlier.

Thomas, L. E. and K. O. Chambers. 1989. "Phenomenology of Life Satisfaction among Elderly Men: Quantitative and Qualitative Views." *Psychology and Aging* 4, 284–89.

Thompson, Edward H., Jr., ed. 1994. *Older Men's Lives.* Vol. 6 of Research on Men and Masculinities. Thousand Oaks: Sage.

Tillich, Paul. 1957. *Dynamics of Faith.* New York: Harper.

Weber, M. 1958. *The Protestant Ethic and the Spirit of Capitalism.* New York: Charles Scribner's.

Zinnbauer, B. J., K. I. Pargament, B. Cole, M. S. Rye, E. M. Butter, T. G. Belavich, K. M. Hipp, A. B. Scott, and J. L. Kadar. 1997. "Religion and Spirituality: Unfuzzying the Fuzzy." *Journal for the Scientific Study of Religion* 36, 549–64.

Note

1. The "third age" refers to a distinct new part of the life course that has often been called "later life" or "old age." Distinguished from childhood and adulthood, this third age is defined by new opportunities and relationships that were never present several generations ago, such as the expectation to be a grandparent and to experience retirement. This "third age" was first discussed by Laslett (1991), and subsequently by Friedan (1994).

16

Xodus to the Promised Man: Revising our Anthropodicy

Lee H. Butler Jr.

"Who knows what evil lurks in the hearts of men?" To this old radio theater question, many women reply, "We know!" Who knows what evil lurks in the hearts of men of African descent? To this question, many people the world over reply, "We know!" Satan, as the personification of evil, has often been described as the "dark one." Because the "dark one" is thought to be the bringer of destruction, people become extremely anxious in the presence of an African American man. If one pays attention to most any evening news broadcast, the heinous crimes committed by European Americans are rarely reported with an accompanying photograph. Crimes committed by African Americans, on the other hand, are always reported with an accompanying photograph, whether the crime is heinous or not. The planet is encouraged to fear black men, and black men live with the constant pressure of being regarded as less than human. Men of African descent are thought the world over to be the beastly embodiment of evil. As a result, many African American men have come to believe that we do embody the evil that others have said we possess. The most important question to be asked, therefore, is: How will African American men be able to exorcize the internalized evil that has been projected upon us?

Defining XodusCare

Although the African American church stands as a stronghold against racism, it continues to struggle with racialized sexism. The black male body has been identified as the most violent on the planet and the locus of sexual offending. This view inhibits our full participation in relationships, leaving us to die in isolation. How can we transform the pain that black men feel from being forced to live outside intimate relations, always being seen as less than we are? We know from Marsha Foster Boyd's (1997) "WomanistCare" that African American women confront their tridimensional oppressions—of race, sex, and class—through narrative systems of support for the purpose of healing. While African American men do not experience the tridimensional oppressions in the same way as do African American women, the influence of those forces are no less destructive of our being. While narrative is an integral part of African American culture, the healing of African American men will require narratives that encourage the restoration of relationships and of our dignity as black men created in the image of God.

Xodus, a term developed by Garth Kasimu Baker-Fletcher, identifies the journey toward socio-psycho-spiritual liberation for African American men. Xodus is the vision and hope of a sacred space where our noble African past is perfectly blended with our struggle for freedom and justice in America. The content of Xodus space is the fruit of the Spirit made known through our life in family, community, church, and communion with God, self, and others. The Xodus witness is not individual or monoperspectival, but it is communal and comprehensive. Xodus is the journey of experiencing the fullness of our black humanity in all of its radiance and splendor (Baker-Fletcher 1995, 1997).

Pastoral care is the ministry of sharing responsibility for the well-being of another. Much of pastoral care is structured around the issues of crisis. Therefore, the caregiver offers support and stability to another in times when life seems to be shaken and without a stable foundation. During those crisis moments, the pastoral caregiver symbolizes the presence of God and declares the assurance that the person in crisis has not been abandoned by God in their time of uncertainty and need. When sufferers ask the questions "why" and "how long," the pastoral caregiver must nurture the sufferer to speak the answer using the resources of faith and spirituality. There is also a social-justice dimension to the practice of pastoral care that attends to suffering resulting from societal oppressions. This dimension of pastoral care exercises the liberating aspects of the gospel and seeks to restore people to human life.

Synthesizing the two perspectives, XodusCare[1] should address the African American crisis of manhood and seek to restore us to full humanity and relationship. As a liberation approach to African American suffering, XodusCare should seek to launch a counterattack against the reductionist, dehumanizing, malevolent forces that promote our death. XodusCare should be the creative efforts of caregivers to insure that

Xodus space nurtures pride, provides defenseless comfort, and reveals the everpresent benevolence of God, who is always with us and within us. XodusCare should declare that the journey is a salvific inward journey that results in the outward expression of peace, love, joy, faithfulness, hope, and healing. XodusCare should lift the veils of our false selves and restore us to relationship and life.

Defining Anthropodicy

One of the critical questions I raise with new students is, "What do you believe about humanity?" This theological anthropology question is intended to probe what people believe about the divine-human relationship and human nature. Not only does this question probe assessments of the human condition, it also explores people's beliefs about the condition of creation and God's location in the world. Furthermore, the first question provokes additional questions about the presence and activity of evil in the face of a good God. When the evil in the world is located within human nature, however, the divine-human relationship is a never-ending war between a good God and an evil humanity. Identifying evil as the essence of humanity is the meaning of *anthropodicy*.

When we consider the origins of humanity, we see that human beings were created good, with evil as a separate force outside of human nature. We bear the divine image and contain God's own breath that gives us life. Onlookers, however, have distorted our created goodness and declared us less than human. They have developed an understanding in their minds that Africans are less human and have an origin other than divine. Such misguided thinking has resulted in ideas that portray Africans as beasts and three-fifths human. Regarding Africans, and subsequently African Americans, as subhuman has resulted in the idea that we have no souls and therefore have no part with God. As a result, numerous stereotypes have developed that have us seeking pleasure and evil before seeking God. Our dark skin has come to represent all the evils of the body. Unfortunately, in many instances we have succumbed to the pressure and believed ourselves to be less than human.

Revising our anthropodicy must be a critical component of XodusCare. Whatever a person believes about humanity and human nature will direct his or her approach as a pastoral caregiver. If one believes that humanity is good and that everyone bears the image of God, then the caring relationship will be guided by acts that support that divine goodness. If, on the other hand, one believes that humanity is bad or evil and that the fallen state is the essence of humanity, then the caring relationship will be guided by acts that reflect disapproval and a disdain for others. XodusCare must take into account that our human condition has been distorted by the oppressive, misguided thoughts of others. God did not make us less than human. We were not placed on a "dark continent," void of light and history. If a caregiver believes that men of African descent are inferior, then the care ministries will treat us as sick, inferior men. Our care must look beyond the false descriptions and false understandings of African manhood to see the man that God made. Although there tends to be a range of beliefs related to anthropodicy, recognizing those beliefs is critical before engaging in any ministry of care with African American men.

Projected Evil

Our primary way of interpreting life is through establishing polar opposites. Most people conduct themselves with the belief that if there is a good, there must also be an evil. Distinguishing the two is often a matter of first declaring what is good. The extreme opposite of that declared good is identified as evil. This interpretation of how good and evil are determined as polar opposites in our daily living points to a very subjective human process. Contrary to what may seem to be the case, I do believe that evil is a real and active force in the world. Evil is not simply the opposite of good. I understand evil to be a harmful spiritual force that can lead to human destruction. Of course, not everything that we identify as evil is necessarily evil. Nevertheless, people have had a strong desire to separate themselves from evil and to be counted on the side of good.

Projection is one of the relational processes used to separate good and evil. Although an unconscious process, projection actively seeks to eliminate any internal and personal characteristics that an individual or group experiences as negative or evil. The process occurs in relation to an established external value. Within American culture, European culture is regarded as more valuable than African culture. A friend, for instance, when talking about the music he listened to as a child, stated that he was not permitted to listen to popular music because the drumming was close to African, which was heathen. When one experiences the unacceptable within one's self, which in this case is African, those feelings must be eliminated. Projection is the act of seeing and identifying only good characteristics in one's self. Rather than recognizing the undesirable characteristics within one's self and simply acknowledging the feeling as a part of life, the

presence of those characteristics is denied. Human beings convince themselves that the undesired feelings are the result of seduction, being close to
the one whose being is evil by nature.

To describe projection in another way, people are movie projectors and
we use other people as screens. We project our unacceptable negative images
onto others so we can feel good about ourselves. Frequently, the behaviors
we find most annoying in another are the very behaviors we deny as parts of
ourselves. This is how many persons go about maintaining a self-image of
being good.

The oppositional characteristics of good and evil are regularly colorized.
In other words, we tend to talk about good versus evil as white over black.
White represents purity and goodness, and black represents contamination
and evil. Under this design, white is always superior to black. Consequently,
the eternal struggles of life—that is, the goodness of God against the evils of
humanity and the world—are regularly cast in "white and black." The colorization of our understanding of good versus evil has easily been applied to
white and black people. Our color-consciousness has prompted the racial-
ization of our lives. Our American categories of good and evil people are
frequently reduced to race. Europe and white bodies have been equated
with good, and Africa and black bodies have been equated with evil. This is
further reduced to classify the black male body as representing one kind of
evil, and the black female body as representing another kind of evil.

The perception of black embodiment is of the oversexed, brutal beast
with no mechanisms of self-control. Socially, I am considered a dangerous
"thing." I am the dark-skinned, violent criminal who raises anxiety wherever
I go. No matter how I cover this dark skin, in casual, business, or formal
wear, the anxious response is the same because my dark skin tends to be all
that is seen. A white guy can walk past a white woman on the street, and
there will be no reaction; but if I walk past that same woman a few steps after
that white guy, she gets nervous and clutches her purse. The perception is
that I am walking through a community because I am on the prowl, waiting
for the right moment to strike. I am not seen as a shopper but as a shoplifter.
I am not seen as mature but as a child with poor control management skills.
My dark skin makes me the rapist, the robber, the murderer. A white woman
murders her children, accuses a black man of her wrongdoing, and immediately gains the attention and sympathy of the nation.[2] Had she accused a
European-American male of the crime, this case would likely not have
received national coverage. The black body is regularly represented in the
media as "the thing" to fear.

No one appreciates being identified with evil. In fact, most people do all they can to eliminate the perception of evil from their lives. This is where the process of projection is activated. People project their perceptions of evil onto other people as a way of preserving the good of humanity. Furthermore, because good is associated with God and humanity, projecting evil is an act of self-preservation. What is rarely recognized, however, is the destructive nature of the projection process. When God, good, white, and humanity are considered the same, all those who serve as screens for the projection are considered less than human and associated with the "dark one." As good and evil are always at odds, God is always working to vanquish evil. The human act of projecting evil, therefore, gives us the opportunity to be like God, not just knowing good and evil, but working to destroy evil in the world. Once perceptions of evil have been projected, evil can be avoided, controlled, or destroyed. As a result, African American men have a long history of being regarded as evil beings, worthy only of enslavement, incarceration, or genocide.

There is another process that works in tandem with projection. The related process is introjection. Also an unconscious process, introjection accepts the images that are being projected on the self. Rather than just reflecting the undesirable negative images like a screen, the person receives the projection as a descriptive internal truth. When evil is colorized and attributed to an entire people through projection, life becomes a house of bondage. Under this structure, we build monuments to others and long for a freedom that represents the projector's way of life. When we look ourselves in the face with introjective eyes, what we see is death as the essence of our being. What we engage in is fratricide to eliminate the evil that we see and feel. So, how can African American men escape the evil in the world if we introject the evil? What are we to do with our black selves if we perceive our skin to bear the mark of death?

Revising Our Anthropodicy

The Cain and Abel narrative is illustrative for helping us to revise our anthropodicy. After Adam and Eve were expelled from the Garden of Eden, Eve gave birth to two sons (Genesis 4:1-16). The first born was Cain and the second was Abel. Cain became a farmer, and Abel became a shepherd. Both sons presented an offering to the Lord from their labor. Here is where their troubles began.

For an unspecified reason, Abel's offering was appreciated by God and Cain's was not. However, if we consider God's follow-up questions to Cain, we could very easily conclude that God was not dissatisfied with Cain, but simply more appreciative of Abel. The questions are: "Why are you angry? and "Why has your countenance fallen?" These questions suggest that God saw no reason for Cain to experience anger or a fallen countenance. A more accurate interpretation might be that Cain felt as though Abel had been given some advantage over him. Unable to control his feelings, Cain killed his brother in what was probably a fit of rage.

When Cain was questioned by God as to the whereabouts of his brother Abel, Cain lied about his actions. And to add insult to injury, he asked the question, "Am I my brother's keeper?" This resulted in Cain being "cursed from the ground" due to the blood of his slain brother. The soil would no longer yield bounty from his labors, meaning he was forced to give up his farming life, and he was forced to become a wanderer. Cain, fearful for his life, declared to God that his punishment was too great and his wanderings would result in his death at the hands of another. Consequently, God placed a mark on Cain so that no one would kill him. Cain went out, settled, and became a family man.

In many ways, Cain is seen as the prototypical African American man. Like Cain, we are seen as those who refuse to give our best. We are thought to be rage-filled, violent, and marked killers. There hardly seems to be a space in the world where we are seen as having an identity other than fratricidal or genocidal. Even when we are being invited to church membership, the invitation describes our reality in socially negative terms. Our present condition, as it tends to be defined, seems to suggest that our being has been consumed by evil, our destiny determined by its power, and our end being to die at our own hands. When we consider discussions of black-on-black crime, the rationales seem to emphasize the self-hatred brought on by an evil within. Thinking this way, however, distorts the essence of our being, presenting our nature as domineering and destructive.

Cain has been interpreted as a murderer resulting from a sense of inadequacy and inferiority, and, subsequently, this is the way African American men have been understood. As Cain was marked by God, the color of our skin has been identified as a curse marking us for suffering and death. Yet, a closer look at the text reveals that Cain's mark was a mark of mercy. Cain's mark, whatever it might have been, set him apart but was not a condemning mark. Cain was not marked for death. In fact, God's sevenfold vengeance would fall upon the one who would kill Cain. The one who was fated for ultimate punishment was the one who harmed Cain. Consequently, if African American men are Cain, anyone who harms us will experience God's sevenfold vengeance.

There are a variety of explanations for the plight of the African American man. These range from individual fratricide due to self-hatred, to absentee fathers, to the disintegration of the black family. But brother killing brother is not the act of one race alone. This narrative lets us know that the fratricide so exclusively associated with African Americans is actually a human problem. Adam was at home with his sons, but Cain was still unwilling to support the success and blessing experienced by his brother Abel. This story illustrates that our tendency not to support one another in brotherly love is not a "black thing," it is a "man thing." Our fraternal estrangement is a male socialization problem. Even the best of family systems experiences heartache and problems. A child of the "first family" caused great grief by murder and deceit.

Viewing the murder of Abel by his brother Cain in our contemporary context lets us know that we still have not learned that we have a responsibility to and for one another. Changing the black family system to match another's system will not end our suffering.

The Cain in each of us is constantly rising up against the Abel in another. There seems to always be something about someone else that we do not like, something that we perceive gives them more benefits or advantages. We are color-struck, class-struck, hair-struck, and genital-struck. We have yet to learn the African lesson, that if one is going to make it, we all must make it. The estrangement we feel has brought separation, which in turn promotes isolation. Furthermore, to be isolated from the community is a punishment worse than death. Isolation is a tormented existence. Cain, however, was not marked by death. He was not condemned by "an eye for an eye." He was shown mercy and given a second chance to live and love.

The Ministry of XodusCare

Bridging the distance between what we are as African American men and what we are to become as Xodus men is the task of XodusCare. As a ministry of care for the distorted African American male soul, XodusCare should inspire the spiritual journey, which is a liberating quest, to become God's promised man. In order to not be seduced by several contemporary ideas of spirituality, XodusCare should introduce God and the Church. Common today is a notion of spirituality that operates independent of God and community. These ideas foster individualistic, independent journeys and have the potential to isolate. Remembering that isolation is death for a communal being, XodusCare must be directed toward the restoration of relationships and community.

XodusCare is an extremely difficult ministry. To effectively minister to the lives of African American men requires the caregiver to face America's history of anti-African and anti-blackness activities. American culture has projected many of its social maladies onto African American men. Ignoring this fact means ignoring the conditions under which African American men have had to live. Noting the force of anthropodicy, the central tasks of XodusCare should be to eliminate the process of projecting evil, to end the practice of introjecting evil, and to heal our broken and distorted hearts, souls, and bodies. The ancient Egyptian edict becomes an essential guiding principle for XodusCare to combat projection/introjection and to promote healing: Know Thyself!

If one is to be an effective caregiver with African American men, then one must become familiar with the dimensions of American life that have influenced the identity formation of African American men. Recognizing these dynamics reveals the appropriateness of XodusCare for ministry with African American men. The dynamics are:

- The history of cultural diffusion
- The "philosophy" of Manifest Destiny and social supremacy
- The impact of racism and sexism
- Individualism as the mode for survival

The XodusCaregiver must also be equally familiar with the dynamics that constitute the African American response to these influences. The response requires knowledge of:

- The intrapsychic life of African Americans
- The establishment of sacred space

The History of Cultural Diffusion. Although America's national identity no longer emphasizes the "melting pot" as the process for becoming an American, the process of denying significant features of one's cultural heritage when they are in opposition to American culture still exists. Historically, American culture has meant white English culture. Even today, when we speak of the dominant culture of America, it is understood that we are referring to white (English) American culture. Yes, there are environments that emphasize cultural diversity, yet there remains a tendency to select those features of a culture that are valued as "normative." Unfortunately, normative usually means the dominant cultural values. People are still encouraged to give up cultural distinctions in order to fit (melt) in. Just as high society continues to honor European arts exclusively, American culture seeks to preserve its English heritage.

The cultural diffusion of the nation has racial overtones. Because culture tends to be described according to one's racial-ethnic heritage, the value of a culture is attributed according to racial categories. Usually described as subcultures of American life, a cultural distinction like "African American" is not considered an *ethnic* heritage like "Irish American," but is a *racial-*cultural category. Race continues to determine the value and prominence of an expression within American culture. Consequently, African Americans continue to be encouraged to value Western European (white) culture above African (black) culture.

Manifest Destiny and Social Supremacy. America has been built upon the ideology: Fulfill your destiny of reigning supreme. Americans live each day through the ideal of entitlement. The things we have believed ourselves entitled to we have taken without thought of the entitlement of others. The destruction of lives and the control of land have been the result of feeling entitled to be the superior presence. The American history of the enslavement of Africans and the genocide of natives are two examples of America's conduct being determined by entitlement.

The feelings of supremacy can be an insatiable desire. For America, this has resulted in the creation of enemies where there were none, and the dehumanization of those perceived as different. There can be no equality where ideals of superiority dominate the context. And any efforts to transform a system based upon hierarchy will be met with severe consequences. African Americans continue to be seen as the "enemy" of social stability as well as the inhuman element within America that must be tolerated or eliminated. There are some folks that like to joke: "What's mine is mine and what's yours is mine." For those governed by manifest destiny and social supremacy, it is no joke.

Impact of Racism and Sexism on the Family. The family is another place where we continue to experience the negative effects of race and sex attitudes. Our family structure has frequently been described as matriarchal and extended. Neither system should be a problem, except that America values the patriarchal and nuclear systems. These values have been used to illustrate a belief that Africans are inferior and incapable of social responsibility. The racism and sexism of the society have limited our opportunities, requiring us to redefine our role responsibilities for the sake of survival. African American men have been relegated to menial, incredibly low-paying jobs that are insufficient for maintaining a family. Why should we model our homes after a patriarchal system when we are constantly being denied patriarchal privilege?

Our survival has required African American women and children to work, making it impossible for our families to look like the "ideal" American family. Whenever we strive to prove that we are patriarchal Americans and not matriarchal, we unwittingly accept the perception that our families are inferior and thereby devalue our family heritage. Our motivation for replicating the ideal is that if we look the same, we will receive the same. Devaluing our African American family heritage is no different than Cain killing Abel because of a perception that another is receiving more benefits. Ultimately, our devaluing tendencies are the introjected ideas of another's projected negativity. To introject negativity means that we are participating in our own demise. We are Cain killing Cain; and therefore, we are inviting the sevenfold vengeance of the Lord upon ourselves.

Individualism. Americans have taken a great deal of pride in the ideal of individual achievement. Our individualistic belief system states that, with hard work, a person can achieve anything that is desired. This has been epitomized by the idea, "pull yourself up by your own bootstraps." We live by a founding belief that every person is an autonomous being who is entitled to "life, liberty, and the pursuit of happiness." Because American individualism is not a supportive paradigm, it instinctively seeks to limit the freedom and possibilities of another for personal gain.

In America, individualism developed in concert with our rebellion from British authority. As the American sense of autonomy grew, so grew our sense of the importance of the individual whose humanity was based upon a sense of independence. This new sense of autonomy marked a shift in our self-understanding as human beings, in the presence of and in relation to God, from dependent to independent. Desiring to end its dependence on England, the colonial pursuit for freedom produced a Declaration of Independence. Unfortunately, the document was limited in its application to the disadvantage of the masses. While "all men" were considered to be created equal, all males were not considered men. Individualism not only declares God-human and human-human space relationships, it also declares who is human by virtue of one's independence and dependence. Those who were not considered men were regarded as dependent rather than independent beings.

African Americans have been regarded by America as dependent beings. Being forced to stand on the outside, denied equal participation, we have lived by a system that is the complete opposite of individualism. We have survived through a community socialization process rather than an individual socialization process. This means that we learn early that our space relationships are to be connectional and interdependent. Community socialization emphasizes "lift as we climb." Contrary to the individualism of America, African American humanity is declared by our responsibility to and for one another. An often unrecognized feature of American individualism is the way it declares who is human and who is not. To the extent that individualism means autonomy and defines humanity, African Americans have been declared nonhuman, because racism and sexism promote dependence upon the one declared as superior and normal.

The Intrapsychic Life of African Americans. Each of the above points is a part of the dynamic interplay of stressors that confront African American men. We, however, have not been without resources for confronting the oppressive forces. Our religion, spirituality, and faith have been the stabilizing forces of our experience. They have provided us with the necessary tools for redefining and transforming the assaults of racism and sexism. While the American context has frequently sought to distort our humanity, we have covenanted with God and one another to remain human. Our identity is linked with the image of God, declaring us holy beings. When we have failed to make this connection, fratricide has been the result. Because our future survival depends upon a reliance upon our African American religion, spirituality, and faith resources, XodusCare will have to know the depth and breadth of these resources. Our healing will require nurturing the roots of our rituals and traditions, as well as developing new rituals and traditions that will enrich us for our journey into the future.

The Establishment of Sacred Space. Healing is a spiritual process. Unlike many approaches to pastoral care, XodusCare must be directed specifically toward healing African American men. The establishment of a sacred healing space begins by recognizing that we are spiritual beings. The profoundness of that recognition is that it stands in direct opposition to the message of America that says that African American men are only physical beings. Once we see our internal space as spiritual and good, the expansion of that sacred space is only a matter of acknowledging the Holy in another. To cease from introjection by dismantling projections is a life choice, and life is stronger than death. Sacred space grows as we reorient different aspects of our being to spiritually and physically embrace fraternity, sorority, family, community, nationality, internationality, and Divinity.

Once we change our interpretation of the mark of God, recognizing it as the image of God and not the mark of death, our Xodus to the promised man will have begun.

Bibliography

American Justice: The Susan Smith Story: A Mother's Confession. Videocassette. <http://www.aetv.com>.

Baker-Fletcher, Garth Kasimu. 1997. *My Sister, My Brother.* Maryknoll: Orbis.

————. 1996. *Xodus: An African American Male Journey.* Minneapolis: Fortress Press.

Boyd, Marsha Foster. 1997. "WomanistCare." *Embracing the Spirit: Womanist Perspectives on Hope, Salvation and Transformation.* Ed. Emilie Townes. Maryknoll: Orbis. 197–202.

Butler, Lee H., Jr. 2000. *A Loving Home: Caring for African American Marriage and Families.* Cleveland, Pilgrim.

Notes

1. I am suggesting this new term to describe pastoral care with African American men. The term is a combination of "Xodus" (coined by Garth Kasimu Baker-Fletcher to describe African American male spirituality and ethics) and the pastoral care of men.

2. The "American Justice" video advertisement describes the case as follows: "At 9 P.M. on October 19, 1994, a frantic, crying woman showed up at a home in Union County, South Carolina, and said a black man had stolen her car at gunpoint with her two young boys asleep in the back. For the next nine days, Union County and the entire nation shared Susan Smith's anguish and prayed that her beloved babies would be returned unharmed. 'American Justice' revisits those nine days and the months that followed to tell the tragic story of a mother driven to murder her own children. The community whose hearts went out to the young mother in her tragic days of grief couldn't believe that she could perform such an act. When she confessed, sympathy turned to hate. The black community was outraged that she had fabricated a black perpetrator, and became even more incensed when police continued to search for a black man while they investigated the veracity of Smith's confession."

Afterword

Philip L. Culbertson

We have come to the end of the book, but we are still only at the beginning of the many issues raised here. We men who are changing need to remain in dialogue with the church about these critical issues of masculine identities. However much we need to withdraw to do our work with each other, we must also take care not to withdraw so far from the church as a whole that we lose touch with it, or it with us.

Few of the questions raised in this book have easy answers; few of the problems raised have simple solutions. Indeed, since men are only in the very beginning stages on the road to new nonvictimizing masculinities, we should be wary of premature closure. Harvard law professor Martha Minow (1998) writes about the danger of assuming that any dialogic process or restorative procedure can resolve all the human issues involved. No matter how anxious an institution, such as the church, is to lay issues to rest, including issues of gender and sexuality, there will never be a time when all voices critical to the dialogue have been heard and satisfied. Minow says:

> Saul Friedlander, a historian who attempts to address the Holocaust, argues that it is imperative for people to render as truthful an account as documents and testimonials will allow, *without giving in to the temptations of closure*, because that would avoid what remains inevitably indeterminate, elusive, and inexplicable about collective horrors. Crucial here, Friedlander reminds us, is an effort to introduce individual memories and individual voices in a field dominated by political decisions and administrative decrees (Minow 1998, 24; italics original).

Similarly, in her essay "Men Whose Lives I Trust, Almost," Carter Heyward (1996) reminds us not to be too quick to jump to conclusions, or to close off dialogue:

> Have compassion, always, for all people and creatures, including your enemies, but do not be fooled by the constancy of premature "calls" for peace, harmony, stability, and reconciliation. Always ask, at what cost, and to whom?

Dialogue is about process, not content, and so the dialogue between the church and men who are changing will not reach conclusions eagerly or quickly. Certainly, as I indicated in the preface, there are many men's voices yet to be heard—voices of those for whom we have not yet found the right medium or venue, voices for whom the church is not yet a safe place to speak out, voices of those who do not yet understand that the inclusive nature of the church-to-be means that Christians want to listen.

Another important principle in the psychodynamics of dialogue is that each party must be clear about its own identity. First, we must understand our own "performed" masculinity—how it is rooted in culture, mythology, and history; what we have adopted or adapted from our forefathers; and what those around us tell us about the fallout from individual ways of being a man. Then, in order to know who we are as men who are changing, to be secure in our masculine identities, we need to talk to each other. We need to talk about the obvious things that men talk about—sports, cars, work, and relationships—but we also need to talk about the things that men don't usually talk about, including the issues raised by these essays.

One of my great hopes for this book is that men in parishes and congregations across the English-speaking world will use the essays here as a place to begin to discuss hard issues in the construction of Christian masculinities. The strength of these essays, after all, is that they collect together in one place the cutting-edge issues for men who have chosen to stay in the church. The men who speak in these essays are representative of the men who are already among us, as deeply committed Christians struggling to find God's way and God's will. If their words, thoughts, and challenges have sounded unfamiliar, then we should be grateful that at last we have "ears to hear" (Matthew 5 and elsewhere). Through reading and discussing these essays together as men in the church, we can begin to learn to listen, and can ask the community to make room for the issues raised in these essays and to take them seriously.

What are some of the issues identified in these essays that commend themselves to us for discussion? Here I will name just a few; you in your reading will surely find many others.

Mark Muesse:

> What are the forms of meditation and prayer that you find most helpful in developing your spiritual life as a Christian man? Is there anything particularly "masculine" about these forms?

Michael Battle:

> How would you define the "community" from which you draw your identity as a man? Can you define its boundaries? If you could add a few people to your personal community, what sort of characteristics would you prefer?

Stephen Boyd:

> What sorts of people irritate you and why? How would you articulate the clash between their presumed values, and your values as a man? How could you practice "hospitality" toward the people who irritate you the most?

David J. Livingston:

> Name some instances in which you have forgiven someone. Then name some instances in which you were unable to forgive someone. Would your experience of forgiving have been different if you had been supported by a community in your efforts? And can you define "accountability" in a way that does not fall into the trap of gender-role expectations?

Donald Capps:

> In what ways have you, like Faust, sold your soul as a man? Can you find the Don Quixote–like nature of your present ministry? If so, how would you defend its "rightness"?

Mike Bathum:

> What is the "spiritual geography" in which you find God most present, and why? Do you feel "at home" there? In what forms of artistic expression do you find God most present, and how?

James N. Poling:

> Do you agree that the construction of masculinity includes competition and violence? Where do competition and violence figure in the ways you perform your own masculinity? How could you reconcile male competition and violence with the "masculine" characteristics usually attributed to God?

Merle Longwood:

> Can you describe ways in which the women in your life have been victimized by other men's needs for power and control? How have you been able to empathize with and support these women? How does "vulnerability" show up in your present relationships, and how do you respond to it?

Marvin Ellison:

> Has your church ever "caught hell" for its advocacy of justice issues for "unpopular" causes? Are there forms of abuse that you don't think should be the concern of the church? Do you believe that men who are the victims of domestic violence should respond differently than women who are?

Philip Culbertson:

> What is the relationship between a Christian man's body and his spirituality? What are the standards against which you judge the bodies of other men, or your own body? If you judge women's bodies by different standards, how do these differ? What does it mean "to objectify" another person's body?

Brett Webb-Mitchell:

> In what ways are you "temporarily abled"? In what ways are you "disabled"? How could you explain the relationship between your body and the Body of Christ? The corporate body of your congregation?

Jerrald Townsend and Robert Bennett:

> Recently the church has spent considerable effort discussing the sexual behavior of men. What are other health issues that should concern men of all ages in the church? What stands in the way of the church claiming a voice in men's health issues?

Robert E. Goss:

> To integrate sexuality and spirituality, we must be able to define the relationship between the erotic and the divine. How would you explain that relationship? Do you believe that God is present only in heterosexual relationships? If so, how, and why would God not be present in homosexual relationships?

Philip Culbertson:

> Where do you find a sense of "authority" in your ministry as a man? What men serve you as models of healthy masculinity, and how? What women or women writers have been most influential in the shaping of your faith? What are some things you would have to change about yourself to adopt a nonvictimizing masculinity?

Ed Thompson:

> How do the expectations of "being a man" and your involvement in the labor force stand in the way of your deepening your faith and religious practice? In what ways do you hope your spirituality will change over the next ten to twenty years?

Lee Butler:

> In what ways do racism and sexism continue to impede your development as a healthy Christian male? What resources do you need from others to begin the process of healing the brokenness in your masculinity? What resources can you find within yourself?

These questions, hard as they may seem, are only the beginning of our journey as men toward a new, nonvictimizing, profeminist, and Christian masculinity. A hard journey is always more tolerable in the company of others. Pray that we will be among the company of men who journey together, rather than the man who passed by on the other side. As Stephen Boyd wrote of his own journey in the company of others, "Because one good Samaritan, among others in the ensuing years, stopped on the road to attend to me lying bleeding and half-dead, I who was blind, mute, and lame can now see a little better, speak a little more audibly and truly, and walk a little more steadily as a partner in the cocreation of the world as God intends it."

Bibliography

Heyward, Carter. 1996. "Men Whose Lives I Trust, Almost." *Redeeming Men: Religion and Masculinities*. Ed. Stephen Boyd, Merle Longwood, and Mark Muesse. Louisville: Westminster John Knox. 263–72.

Minow, Martha. 1998. *Between Vengeance and Forgiveness: Facing History after Genocide and Mass Violence*. Boston: Beacon.

Author Index